Vision Quest

Vision Quest

Native Spirituality & the Church in Canada

Janet Hodgson
and
Jayant S. Kothare

Anglican Book Centre
Toronto, Canada

1990
Anglican Book Centre
600 Jarvis Street
Toronto, Ontario
Canada M4Y 2J6

Typesetting by Jay Tee Graphics Ltd.

Canadian Cataloguing in Publication Data

Hodgson, Janet
  Vision quest: native spirituality & the
Church in Canada

ISBN 0-921846-04-5

1. Indians of North America - Canada - Religion and mythology. 2. Spirituality - Anglican Church of Canada. 3. Anglican Church of Canada - Doctrines. 4. Anglican Communion - Doctrines. I. Kothare, Jayant S. II. Title.

E78.C2H6 1990   248′.089′97071   C90-094252-5

Note on Terms

(The Revd. Laverne Jacobs, Co-Ordinator of the Council of Native Ministries, Anglican Church of Canada) Technically speaking the word "Indian" refers only to those with Indian Status, i.e. are Treaty Indians or have Indian Status according to the Indian Act. Current practice is to use the word "Native" or "Aboriginal". Both terms include all native peoples: Indian, Non-Treaty, Metis and Inuit.

Contents

Acknowledgements

In the past several years we have met many native brothers and sisters of Canada, both professionally and in a personal way, and our lives have been greatly enriched by these encounters. Contrary to most people's way of looking at Canada, it is an ancient land with an ancient indigenous culture. Meeting these people has meant a quickening of our spiritual life. Our understanding of the church as the community of believers, healed and redeemed together through the working of the Holy Spirit in Christ, will never be the same again. We believe that these much-maligned sons and daughters of the north could play a major role in helping the church recover its prophetic vision.

We are grateful to the Council on Native Affairs of the Anglican Church of Canada for their motherly care, especially those who hosted Janet — the Reverend Laverne Jacobs of the Kettlepoint Reserve and Walpole Island, Ontario, who took over as co-ordinator of the Council in 1987; Nina Burnham of the Six Nations Iroquois Reserve at Ohsweken, Ontario; Willy Hodgson in Moose Jaw, Saskatchewan, and her extended family in Sandy Lake Reserve near Prince Albert; and the Reverend Percy and Doris Tait at New Aiyansh in the Nass River Valley, British Columbia.

We would also like to thank Bishop Fred Crabb and his wife Margery; Garth Walker, chairman of the General Synod Archives Committee, and his wife Florence; Liz Jackson, acting co-ordinator of the Council on Native Affairs; Terry Thompson, General Synod archivist in Church House, Toronto; Dr. Carl Starkloff SJ; Father Jacques Johnson OMI; the Very Reverend Dr. Lois Wilson, former moderator of the United Church of Canada; the Most Reverend Michael Peers, Anglican primate of Canada; the Reverend Clarke Raymond, executive director of program for the Anglican Church of Canada, the Calgary Institute for the Humanities, for their support and helpful suggestions in the preparation of this book.

Janet's fieldwork in Canada was made possible by the generous funding of the Fellowship of the Maple Leaf in Britain, the Council on Native Affairs in Canada, and the Human Sciences Research Council, the Institute for Catholic Education, and the Harry Oppenheimer Centre for African Studies at the University of Cape Town in South Africa. The Fellowship of the Maple Leaf has further funded the writing up of this report, while the University of Edinburgh has given her an honorary fellowship in the Department of Divinity, New College; and the United Society for the Propagation of the Gospel, a visiting fellowship at the College of the Ascension, Selly Oak, Birmingham. We would like to express our gratitude to all these bodies.

In particular Janet would like to acknowledge the financial assistance of the Institute for Research Development of the Human Sciences Research Council towards this research. Opinions expressed in this publication and conclusions arrived at are those of the author and do not necessarily represent the views of the Institute for Research Development of the Human Sciences Research Council.

Jay would like to thank all the native people he met on reserves, in parishes, and at Morley for their friendship and understanding. As a Canadian priest exploring the vision for the Canadian church, he cherishes the time he spent learning from elders and medicine men about the mysteries of native spirituality.

Finally, a special word of thanks to Canon Stephen Burnett, honorary secretary of the Fellowship of the Maple Leaf, who did so much to encourage us in our research and saw this work to fruition.

Dr. Janet Hodgson
The Reverend Jayant S. Kothare

Chapter 1

The Monochrome Church and the Quest of the Rainbow Covenant

The One Holy Catholic Church on the Air Canada Route

I, Jayant S. Kothare, am a black Canadian priest in Holy Orders in the Anglican Church of Canada. I spent the formative years of my life in an orthodox Hindu Brahmin milieu in Bombay, where, as a Hindu, I had my initial brush with the institutional Christian church. My first memories are of huge Victorian Gothic church buildings looming over poor housing areas. There, surrounded by the war memorials and monuments of imperial Britain, brown Anglicans worshipped with strict adherence to the 1662 version of the *Book of Common Prayer*, in blissful ignorance of the rich indigenous spirituality of India. Years later, when I moved to Canada and met native Americans worshipping in Christian churches, I had little difficulty in making a connection between what I had seen in native Bombay and the cultural and spiritual alienation of native Christians in Regina, Saskatchewan, or Kenora, Ontario.

All round the world the Caucasian tradition has invariably been regarded as the norm in the churches, and as a rule there has been little latitude for the incorporation of cultural diversity in the expression of Christian faith. For instance, outside England the Anglican church tended to begin life as an integral part of the colonial system. Chaplains were attached to the imperial forces, and churches were founded to minister to the needs of English settlers. The missionary enterprise served as handmaid to the imperial dream, opening up new areas for colonial conquest, with Christianity and "civilization" being presented as part of the same western cultural package, together with loyalty to the British Crown. Nationalism and political independence have since brought about significant changes, but the development of an indigenous Christian spirituality has lagged far behind.

What is true of the Anglican Communion may equally be predicated of all the other Christian denominations which took a hand in colonizing the minds and spirits of the indigenous peoples. To make matters worse, missionary societies exported their specifically European sectarian feuds and rivalries to Asia, Africa, the Pacific Zone, and the Americas, insisting that it was not good enough to be a Christian, but that one had to be an Anglican Christian, a Roman Catholic Christian, or a Methodist Christian, etc.

In most parts of the mainline churches in the world there seems to have been little concerted effort to encourage the growth of an indigenous Christianity which would allow its members to draw sustenance from their own spiritual roots. The church is the poorer because it not only drives away the very people it is supposed to serve, as witnessed by a continuing drop in membership in many parts, but it also misses the opportunity to be enriched by the theological, liturgical, and pastoral insights of the spiritual diversity of its world-wide constituency.

In the past, any attempt by converts to Christianity to draw on the spiritual riches of their native traditions was denigrated by the incoming culture as pagan, heathen, savage, and even demonic. Cultural imperialism reigned supreme. Today, evidence indicates that European paternalism in the churches dies hard, and that this is experienced by many indigenous people as spiritual colonialism.

As a convert from an ancient spiritual tradition, I have watched over the years the monochrome European church painting itself into a lonely corner, slowly but surely alienating itself from Christians hailing from different religious and different racial backgrounds. I was twice stripped of my ordinand status in two mainline churches of Canada because of my concern to incorporate my Hindu spiritual tradition into my Christian faith. Far from honouring my Indian Hindu black spirituality, the church made me feel guilty for being myself. I love to chant and meditate and read Hindu and Buddhist literature along with my daily regimen of Christian Scripture; but I was warned that it was not good for the integrity of my faith. ''Stop all association with your past, and be a good Christian,'' I was counselled. Of course, being a good Christian meant losing my identity as a black person, for-feiting my black spirituality, becoming thoroughly brainwashed into the western Caucasian mode of consciousness, and swallow-ing hook, line, and sinker the white version of Christianity as the only way to understand the gospel of Christ.

At the seminary, from the pulpit, in personal conversations, during interviews, and at social get-togethers, I was constantly confronted with the eleventh commandment: "Thou shalt not be a syncretist." By syncretism the church meant my integration of black, third-world spirituality with the Christian faith. Those in the church, who were so worried about my heresies, hardly paused to see that on a daily basis they themselves were injecting their own white, western, middle-class ideology into their under-standing of Christianity. It was quite acceptable to quote Plato or Hegel while discussing the Christian doctrine; but God help me if I ever mentioned Kabir, Rumi, or the Buddha. This is my experience in the Canadian church. Hence, I perfectly understand and empathize (not just sympathize) with native Americans in their legitimate struggle to preserve and affirm their own unique spiritual identity and still be accepted in the church family.

When I came to England for a three-year stint to work in a multi-faith, multi-race, inner-city parish in Handsworth, Birmingham, I realized that I was indeed part of the one holy catholic church! Even here, in all-black parishes, I found white priests, pastors, and bishops pulling the strings, foisting their white values on black Christians, equating Anglo-Saxon with Anglican. Hands-worth, with its diverse Asian and Afro-Caribbean population, is unbelievably rich spiritually. But even here, the monochrome white-led church refuses to take cognizance of the unique spiritual contribution of black minorities. For instance, in a local seminary a white person teaches black ordinands a course on black iden-tity and how to minister to black people! White priests continue to be in charge of predominantly black parishes and have total control of all decision-making processes. Everything, right from the sermon content, theology, understanding of mission, coun-selling, down to group dynamics is dyed with the Anglo-Saxon hue. Black Christians are not encouraged in any sort of dialogue with their black sisters and brothers practising non-Christian faiths and spiritualities.

There has been so little room for black people in Handsworth to live out their Christian faith using black symbols, liturgy, and theology that already a large percentage of them have left the Anglican and Methodist churches and started their own so-called black-led churches where you see a real flowering of their black identity. Alas, whether it is Bombay, Kenora, or Handsworth, the monochrome white church seems to be insensitive to the quest for the rainbow covenant, the covenant embracing Christians of all races, all colours, and all spiritualities.

The Monochrome Church in Black Southern Africa

Dr. Janet Hodgson, who has co-authored this book with me, comes from a high-church Anglican tradition in Cape Town, South Africa. The Anglican church has for long prided itself on following the middle way, giving it a flexibility which has not only allowed for extremes of churchmanship but also has included various forms of folk religion. The Church of the Province of Southern Africa, for example, has a membership which is more than eighty percent black. Over the years it has come to embrace a whole spectrum of African organizations and movements, structured and unstructured, within its fold. This development has sometimes gone unrecognized by the church hierarchy. Where it has surfaced, however, to threaten as an alternative power base, it has too often been confronted as a problem to be suppressed or else severely contained within church structures. On the other hand, where such spontaneous religious creativity has been welcomed as the working of the Holy Spirit, it has been a source of spiritual vitality in the life of the church.

Folk religion in Southern Africa challenges the Anglican church to become aware of its cultural blinkers and move away from the shadow of its Anglo-Saxon history. The traditional church has been concerned less with spirituality and more with maintenance: of buildings, administrative structures, episcopal authority, the status quo and, last but not least, the underpinning of white power in economic and political domains. Too often the church has become a service agency among African people for ''Sunday Christians'' — baptizing, marrying, and burying its members — while the black-led, independent churches, new religious movements, and non-Christian indigenous religions provide for the people's basic spiritual and physical needs, frequently in secret and with the threat of excommunication.

The church has failed to respect or encourage African forms of religious belief and practice within its liturgical life, labelling them un-Anglican or even unchristian. But this kind of indigenous worship has been going on within the Anglican fold for more than a hundred years, although one will not find it documented in church history books. Grassroots black Christianity is being practised in the bush, down by the river, in the backyard, in the garage, at cemeteries, in village huts, and in townships, while in the chancels robed black acolytes swing the thurible and black choirboys lead the singing of ''Onward Christian Soldiers'' and the Halleluia Chorus.

The church has generally frowned upon any spontaneous expression of African Christianity which nourishes the roots of local communities. Thousands more will go on a pilgrimage to a healer's service or a prophet's shrine than will support some official diocesan event, because the healer and the prophet relate to the urgency of their immediate black experience and provide the means of coming to terms with it. This is what feeds these people spiritually, not the church. Belonging to any of the non-Roman Catholic mainline churches, whether they be Methodist, Anglican, Presbyterian, or Congregational, is a sign of middle-class respectability, of upward social mobility and status in a community dehumanized by socio-economic and racial discrimination, beleaguered by structural violence sanctioned by the ideology of the state, and deprived of all freedom and political responsibility.

For the past eighteen years Janet has worked in the Department of Religious Studies in the University of Cape Town, teaching courses on African religion, African Christianity, new religious movements, and history of mission in Africa. Her academic experience has provided a framework of reference and a set of guidelines to fashion a viable methodology for field research in Southern Africa. Fieldwork has taken her to every corner of the country: to the bustling black townships of New Brighton in Port Elizabeth, Mdantsane in East London, Jabavu in Soweto, and Khayelitsha and Crossroads in Cape Town; to remote resettlement camps in Qwa Qwa and Ciskei; to isolated towns and villages in Swaziland and Lesotho; to African holy places in Sekhukhuneland, Bophuthatswana, and Transkei.

Fieldwork has meant bumping along for endless hours over tortuous gravel roads, choking in clouds of dust in the blistering heat of summer sun or the searing cold of winter nights. Janet has journeyed far to meet with African people in their homes, to visit them in their work-places, to attend their meetings and conferences, to worship with them in their churches, to witness their traditional ritual practices, to participate in their pilgrimages, to celebrate with them in their great festivals. Sadly, the entrenched white-led church has taken little cognizance of the rich spiritual tradition of its black majority. When Janet visited Canada to do research for our book, she was struck by the parallel between the spiritual alienation of the black and native peoples from their respective national churches.

The Challenge of the Rainbow Covenant

Our purpose in looking at the church operating in different cultures throughout the world is to become sensitive to the ubiquitous existence of the monochrome white church in the midst of the rainbow people of diverse races, cultures, and traditions. Where whites have left the scene of their former colonies, the myth of the supremacy of white spirituality and tradition dies hard, as in the church of India. So it could be said in fairness to the Canadian churches, that the failure to recognize the native contribution and their spirituality is not solely a Canadian problem. It is only a reflection of an endemic disease that besets the world-wide Christian church.

The domination of indigenous, black, non-white, non-European spirituality by the white, western, European ideology marks the sad story of the Christian church's mission everywhere. The struggle of the native people of Canada to preserve their spirituality is an integral part of the universal struggle of all non-Caucasian Christians throughout the world. The healing of the monochrome church is needed as much in Kenora or Regina as in Handsworth, Johannesburg, or Bombay. The Canadian churches should not be overly sensitive, nor the overseas churches too patronizing, when the fate of the native people's spirituality within the Canadian churches is discussed. Here we are dealing with a problem which looms larger than the Canadian or any other national church. We are faced with the heresy of the white monochrome church.

When God sealed his covenant with Noah he embraced the whole creation and sent down the rainbow as a sign of his concern. This excluded nothing (Genesis 9). For our purpose we may take up the symbol of the rainbow to signal God's impartial and unconditional love for his children of all races and colours. If the church is to live up to its promise of being catholic, it has to model itself after the promise contained in the rainbow covenant. Future mission work will have to deal with this task which concerns a renewed questioning of the identity of God's church and its role in the world.

The Hendry Report

A significant sign of this new missionary consciousness is evident in Charles Hendry. In 1969 he made a major contribution towards assessing the work of the Anglican Church of Canada with the native people in his report, *Beyond Traplines*. Hendry observes:

> Something patently is wrong. Despite years of Church ministry and despite a formidable expansion of health and welfare services by government agencies, the plight and blight that still haunt the lives of hundreds of thousands of Canada's native peoples speaks poignantly of tragic failure. Something sinister can be discerned arising from the cynicism that results from chronic frustration and failure. The time has surely come to take a new and a hard-headed look at this condition.[1]

Hendry challenged the church to a prophetic mission, with clear intentions and well-thought-out missionary goals. He saw the need for the church to redefine its role, redeploy its resources, vitalize its education for the ministry, and develop strategies looking towards basic innovation. His understanding of prophetic mission was based on a relationship of mutuality with the native people in the fullest sense of the word. He expands:

> This means developing a relationship of mutual respect, understanding, trust and helpfulness. It means plugging into the reality of their lives and their living . . . identifying with their needs in their environment . . . sharing their problems, discovering and drawing out their strengths, listening and learning and living in their daily midst.[2]

Hendry expected the Anglican church not only to "mobilize its membership," but also to "seek the cooperation of sister Churches in determined political action aimed to influence national, provincial and local government policy."[3]

Since the report the Anglican church has in fact done pioneering work in developing new modes of selection and training for ministry together with new pastoral models. It has also become increasingly active in its concern for aboriginal rights and ecological issues, particularly through the ecumenical involvement of the church in Project North. The establishment of the Council on Native Affairs (now Council for Native Ministries) was another significant development spawned by the Hendry Report, giving native Anglican people their own platform in the church.

Hendry's report is subtitled "Does the Church really care?" and many native Christians have taken up this cry with increasing bitterness. They feel that the church has not been able to recognize that they have a vision of their own. Hendry himself in his otherwise brilliant survey, executed with great integrity, did not devote much space to discussing how the church could be more supportive of traditional native spirituality. Ungrounded in the dynamics of the native people's Vision Quest, the church continued to seem as uncaring as before. If the church sought to implement Hendry's recommendations to the full, it would have to complement Hendry by taking native spirituality seriously.

The Native People's Vision Quest

Vision Quest is a term uniquely employed to refer to the revolutionary rite of passage celebrated among many native people. It is a young man's quest for a vision or an understanding of his own true self, in solitude away from the clan.

Embarking on the Vision Quest, the youth would first enter a sweat lodge and go through a bodily purification. Then, clutching sage grass in his hand, he would climb to an elevated site, either on a hill-top or a makeshift perch in a tree, high above the mundane world. There the youth would fast and pray, chant and dance, meditate and repent, waiting on the Great Spirit. Eventually, he would make contact and directly commune with his totem spirit, symbolic of his spiritual identity. Through this vision he would come to terms with the secret drives of his innermost self, and acknowledge and accept his strengths and weaknesses. Like Jesus in the wilderness, he would grapple alone with temptation and bait the luminously dark forces of his interior soul. He would submit himself to this ordeal and pass through countless courts of trial in the spirit-realm until he was ready to emerge as a spiritual warrior, crowned with self-affirmation. Now the young man would know who he was and where he belonged in the world, having become bonded with the whole of creation through the Great Spirit. This newly won self-awareness and self-transcendence signalled his entry into adulthood. He would become a whole new person.

The Indian youth would burn sweetgrass as an act of thanksgiving for the gift of the vision which he had received from the spirits. Then armed with the knowledge of self and attuned to all things, he would return to the plain where his waiting community would welcome him back and celebrate his new identity with feasting. Being restored to his people after this period of soul-searching and solitude was an integral part of his spiritual experience. This rite was by no means to encourage narcissistic navel-gazing. Rather, it was an exercise in communal solidarity.

The native Canadian would readily identify with Moses' encounter with God on Mt. Zion and Jesus' struggle with the Tempter in the wilderness as classic scriptural cases of a Vision Quest. Lame Deer, a Sioux medicine man, makes such a connection:

The Holy White Stone Man — that's what we call Moses. He appeals to us. He goes up alone to the top of his mountain like an Indian, to have his vision, be alone with God, who talks to him through fire, bushes and rocks. Moses, coming back from the hill carrying stone tablets with things scratched on them — he would have made a good Indian medicine man.[4]

Jacob wrestling through the night with the angel of God at Peniel, and finally winning out with a broken thigh but an ever unbroken spirit, typifies an early patriarch engaged in a Vision Quest. Another was Daniel, flung into the pit with a pride of lions; his quest later flowered into prophetic dreams and visions. In the New Testament we have John the Baptist traversing the wilderness on a Vision Quest and proclaiming the kingdom, while John, marooned on the island of Patmos, penned a whole book bursting with visions and revelations. The many patriarchs, judges, prophets, saints, martyrs, apostles, and desert fathers were each in turn anointed by the Holy Spirit and led on a Vision Quest, so exemplifying the ancient spiritual lineage that links the native tradition and the Judaeo-Christian religion.

The Vision Quest in the Judaeo-Christian Tradition

The term for *dream* in the Old Testament is *khalam*, which can also mean to make whole or healthy. Thus, almost anticipating Freud, the Old Testament canon recognized dreams as agents of emotional catharsis and spiritual healing. In the Old Testament the terms *dream* and *vision* are used interchangeably: ''If there is a prophet among you/ I reveal myself to him in a vision/ I speak to him in a dream'' (Numbers 12:6); ''It will be like a dream, like a vision at night'' (Isaiah 29:7); Daniel had a dream and visions that passed through his head as he lay in bed (Daniel 7:1). So too, in the native tradition, dreams and visions form part of the same indistinguishable reality.

Dreams are not mere sleeping patterns but an opening into the spiritual realms beyond the ken of normal consciousness. For example, Yahweh uses the medium of dreams to give assurrance of his blessings to Abraham (Genesis 15:1-6), Jacob (Genesis 28:11-16), and Gideon (Judges 7:13-15). Solomon is blessed with dreams in which he receives deeper teachings about the covenant (1 Kings 9:2–9). Again in dreams the magi are warned not to return to Herod; Joseph is forewarned about Mary's pregnancy and later counselled to take his family to safety in Egypt. In a dream Zachariah foresees the birth of the Baptist.

It is a Judaeo-Christian belief that God uses paranormal states like dreams and visions in order to communicate with human beings. Job has it:

> God speaks first in one way/ and then in another, although he [man] does not realize it/ in dreams and in night-visions/ when slumber has settled on humanity/, and people are asleep in bed/ he speaks in some one's ears/ frightens him with apparitions/ to turn him from what he is doing/ and to put an end to his pride/ And thus he preserves his soul from the abyss/ his life from passing down the canal.[5]

Dreams were thus spiritual visions, intimations from God, full of wisdom, giving insight into the past, present, and future course of history, piercing beyond the facade of the work-a-day world and reaching out to the hidden reality of God. Dreams were the portal through which the prophets and wise men of ancient Israel entered the tabernacle of God's truth. In fact, the Old Testament saw wisdom and the ability to interpret dreams as synonymous. After Yahweh reveals to Daniel, in a vision of the night, the key to interpret the king's mysterious dream, Daniel praises God:

> Blessed be the name of God for ever and ever/ to whom belong wisdom and might/ he gives wisdom to the wise/ and knowledge to those who have understanding/ he reveals deep and mysterious things/ he knows what is in the darkness/ and the light dwells with him/ To thee, O God of my fathers/ I give thanks and praise/ for thou hast given me wisdom and strength/ and hast now made known to me what we asked of thee/ for thou hast made known to us the king's matter.[6]

Those who received these dreams and visions became prophets. In Deuteronomy (13:1) a prophet is actually called a dreamer of dreams. These visions are the stuff authentic prophecy was made of. These were paranormal, mystical, numinous experiences in which these highly gifted men became sensitive to the callings of the spirit world. Thus Samuel engaged in converse with God (Samuel 3:1); Elisha clearly perceived Elijah taken up into heaven on a chariot of fire (2 Kings 2:12); Isaiah, praying in the temple, sees God's holy glory (Isaiah 6); Ezekiel, crouched amid the disconsolate exiles, is suddenly transported before the chariot-throne of God (Ezekiel 1:1); Jeremiah beholds an almond rod and a boiling cauldron (Jeremiah 1:11–13). These are all famous instances of Hebrew prophets making contact with the numinous world in visions brought on by a heightened sensitivity. The Oracle of Habakkuk, the dreams of Joseph decoding the pharaoh's dreams, the visions of the prophets Nahum and Obadiah, and the revelatory dream of Pilate's wife; are all in the historic tradition of the Hebrew Vision Quest, born out of prayer and crisis.

St. Paul himself was a great charismatic visionary, according to 2 Corinthians 12:1–5, where he refers to his paranormal visions. His encounter with Christ on the road to Damascus is a classic example of a Vision Quest in crisis. The New Testament does not cite visions with the same frequency as the Old Testament. However, we do have the glorious Book of Revelation, unrivalled as an exercise in Vision Quest. And Acts 11:28 tells the story of Agabus the prophet, who, when seized by the spirit, stood up and predicted an impending famine. All said, Jesus himself is the master of Vision Quest, epitomizing the finest of his Hebrew tradition.

For the Hebrews as well as for native peoples the Vision Quest was not the preserve of a select few, nor was it something that happened to people only sporadically. Dreaming was a spiritual vocation for an entire people, men and women, young and old (Acts 2:17–18; Joel 2:28–29), who were all called to pierce the veil of what the Lakota medicine man Lame Deer calls the "green frog-skin world," ("the green frog-skin" being Lame Deer's euphemism for the almighty dollar bill):

> The world in which you paint a picture in your mind, a picture which shows things different from what your eye sees, that is the world from which I get my visions. I tell you this is the real world, not the Green Frog-skin world.[7]

Joel opens the promise of visionary experience to the sons and daughters of Israel. There is an enduring thread of continuity between them and the children of native Canadians.

Will the Canadian Church Take up the Vision Quest?

Under the European system of education native people were denied the Vision Quest and their spiritual and political subjugation was thus assured. In some form or other this rite of passage was in fact always part of the diverse spiritual traditions of all the native people right across the Turtle Island (i.e., North America). The liberation of native peoples will come when they resume their Vision Quest. But this time they will be joined by the white man because all of God's children, white and native, need to engage in such a spiritual journey.

The church has lost its Hebrew spirit of Vision Quest and has become fossilized as a colonial institution. Now is the time to make amends and acquire a renewed understanding of the tradition which, as we have seen, is very much part of its Judaeo-Christian heritage. The monochrome church can reclaim its credibility by realizing the full potential of the rainbow covenant in calling the faithful, both native and others, to an ongoing nation-wide spiritual odyssey with a vision of God's kingdom in a just Canadian society, where the native people shall regain the long-lost dignity of their humanity shared by the Lord Jesus Christ. The only effective image we see for the Canadian church is that of a vision-questing church, living by the promise God spoke through his Hebrew prophets of old:

> I shall pour out my spirit on all humanity.
> Your sons and daughters shall prophesy,
> Your young people shall see visions,
> Your old people dream dreams.[8]

Chapter 2
Black on White about the Red People

This brief survey of historical and contemporary secondary sources aims at giving some idea of available resource material relating to the religious life of native American people, with special reference to Canada, and to establishing the type of work that still needs to be done in the field of native church history and theology. Our library research was fairly haphazard and is merely intended to open up the subject for discussion. The criteria for selecting books, journal articles, and unpublished essays for the bibliography are based on their relevance to the themes in this book, and should in no sense be regarded as exhaustive. The most glaring omission of course is the absence of information on academic dissertations.

Missionary Writings

There is a wealth of anthropological and historical material on the native people. Indeed some claim that they are the most studied ethnic group in the world. But much if not most of this material has a decidedly Eurocentric bias. The authors of the early descriptive works included explorers, traders, pioneer settlers, government officials, army officers, Indian agents, travellers, missionaries, and church leaders. Without exception this material was written from the vantage point of the incoming culture and the native peoples were invariably portrayed as less than human with lurid epithets being used to reinforce notions of their otherness as savages and barbarians. Their supposed lack of civilization thus provided the rationale for their subjugation and enslavement if not outright extermination. Even where the romantic idea of the noble savage surfaced, the native was still depicted in negative imagery, thus ensuring his childlike dependence on European protection. And, throughout, the Bible was constantly invoked to sanction every shameful aspect of domination and exploitation.

One wonders if this early stock of literature was not churned out to reinforce already existing European biases, and even to provide a philosophical and theological justification for the sordid political realities. One almost hears an undercurrent of parallels between the whites and the Hebrews as God's Chosen People, justified by divine sanction in their forcible taking of the land. The folklore of the white man fulfilling his manifest destiny to tame and pacify the west is a nineteenth-century rewriting of the Old Testament tradition.

Early Canadian mission histories abound, and their writers were as culpable as the rest. The one abiding theme was the need to civilize the heathen savages before they could be converted to Christianity. In a catechistic book written by the New England Protestant missionary, John Eliot, way back in 1671, the church's mission is said to be

> to instruct, exhort and persuade them [native people] to pray unto God, to turn from their lewd and lazy life to the living God, and to come forth from the dark dungeon of their lost and ruined condition, into the light of the Lord Jesus.[1]

The missionaries assumed that the native peoples had neither religion nor an acceptable way of life, whether this be seen in their mode of ornamentation and dress (or undress!), dwellings, food, languages, political organization, social life, ritual dances, drumming, or singing. Native religion was usually discussed in terms of superstitions and unsavoury practices. The breaking of the power of the shamans, "the spiritual centre of native culture," was regarded as an evangelistic victory.

Mission histories focus on the opening up of different fields of work by the various mission societies, religious orders, and churches, with often rivetting stories of heroic endeavour, triumphs, and disappointments. There is no doubting the sacrificial role of many of these pioneers, although recent historical analysis presents some of the more dramatic episodes in a new light. So, for example, the Jesuit martyrs in the seventeenth century are said to have sought their own deaths and the reports in the Jesuit *Relations* exaggerated "Iroquois ghoulishness in order to glorify the martyrs"[2]. The historical chronicles written by the early missionaries are mostly tendentious and one-sided, calculated to highlight the Christian saintliness of the martyrs by depicting their native executioners as unchristian, demonic savages. The native peoples, in all probability, were only protecting their lands, honour, and spirituality in the face of the colonial aggression of the church.

These early missionaries saw aboriginal people not only as lost infidels to be saved from hell, but at times even delinquents to be reformed. In one of the missionary dialogues in John Eliot's book, he has a native convert saying to his countryman: "Your prayers and powwowings are worshipping of the Devil, and not of God, and they are among the greatest of your sins. Your murders, lusts, stealing, lying, etc., they are great sins."[3].

The attitude of the white settlers, both in the government and the church, that prevailed during the Victorian era can be best illustrated by the following quotation from a volume signifying the tacit collaboration between the two wings of white power. The book is entitled *The Queen, the Empire, and the English-speaking World, a Diamond Jubilee Issue*, published in 1897 by the Society for the Propagation of Christian Knowledge.

> Placed under the charge of superintendence appointed by the authorities of the Dominion, and amply supplied with all the modern machinery of education, nothing but their inherent incapacity prevents their attaining complete equality with the white race. But this disability exists, and all that the most philanthropic can hope for the native races of America is their gentle dimunition, followed by their peaceful extinction. When they cease to be indolent of body and predatory of disposition, life loses its charm for them, and there is some little justification for the old frontierman's saying that "the only good Indian is a dead Indian."[4]

What can one say of a church that could wish the "native races" little more than "gentle dimunition and peaceful extinction"? Gentle and peaceful indeed!

Eliot's *Indian Dialogues* are a fascinating genre in the earliest literature on cultural interaction between whites and natives in Canada. In the preface to his work he admits that his dialogues are not in fact historical chronicles but are rather a series of imaginary debates between "praying" and non-believing natives. He thus follows in the tradition of Christian writers who have employed this literary device to expound their beliefs since Justin Martyr composed his "Dialogue with Trypho the Jew." Eliot's dialogues were meant to be used as a training manual for native missionaries and catechists. Mercifully, his example was not followed by other white missionaries, as his writing has a divisive, patronizing, and condemnatory quality about it. Eliot was a prime apologist of New England puritanism embattled with native spirituality and his writing bespeaks the early settlers' phobias about every aspect of native culture, which was to be damned in its entirety.

For Eliot, and those who came after him, pre-contact civilization was all "filth and folly," the ritual ceremonies and dances were just "noise" and "works of darkness," and the native peoples were merely part of the landscape infested by "wolves, bears and other wild beasts." What is frightening about Eliot's sort of writing is that natives are portrayed as having internalized these very same white attitudes. The bottom line of such missionary literature is that whites possess the unadulterated Christian truth in contrast to the pagan falsehood of the native peoples. Thus Eliot puts these words into the mouth of his native missionary speaking to a non-believing native: "I am a Praying Indian. I have left our old Indian customs, laws, fashions, lusts, powwowings, and whatever else is contradictory to the right knowledge of the true God."[5]

A case can be made for the fact that the missionaries of the Victorian era were typical products of their day and age, confident in the superiority of their western civilization and their calling to conquer new worlds for the white man, and that they should not be judged out of context. What is really saddening though is the persistence of such attitudes up to the present time, as shown in chapter three.

Church Histories

James Walker has charted the changes in Canadian historical writing about the native people in an incisive bibliographical essay. He notes that in earlier works "Indians were treated as part of the setting, the environment in which the history of the European newcomers could unfold." After 1885 they were largely ignored until "a burst of scholarly activity" in the 1970s brought them back on to the historical scene. Bibliographical guides have aided the recovery of research material but old attitudes die hard. Although the negative images of native peoples have basically disappeared, the European in Canada is still central in historical writing. The native presence is peripheral, and then only "in the role of client or problem."[6]

A look at some examples of Anglican church history in Canada since the turn of the century is a depressing exercise, mirroring the same trends in scholarship as in the wider historical field discussed by Walker. The focus generally remains firmly fixed on the white man and his concerns in the church. Church and state relations figure prominently as do ecclesiastical issues. T.R. Millman in *The Churches and the Canadian Experience*, edited by John Webster Grant, notes that the popular name of the Anglican Church of Canada has always been "the English Church." This is symbolic of the perpetuation of the traditions and attitudes of the Church of England, and has been reinforced by episcopal tradition, the *Book of Common Prayer*, and canon law.[7] Typical of the ethnocentric bias of church historians even in comparatively recent works is the following quotation from H.H. Walsh in *The Christian Church in Canada*:

> All our histories are in agreement that the most determining factor in Canadian development is the existence of the two major culture groups within one national framework. The clash of culture is the great Canadian theme.[8]

The two competing cultures are of course French and English. There is no mention of the invisible people of the First Nations. The *History of the Anglican Diocese of Qu'Appelle*, celebrating the seventy-fifth anniversary of its founding in 1884, is a classic case in point. "Our Indian Work" takes up precisely one page out of seventy-two in a recital of the good deeds of bishops and other white church leaders, and the good works of diocesan institutions, associations, missions, and the rest. The native people are the church as much as anyone else and yet so often they continue to be relegated to a mission context, marginalized as a group

apart. Inevitably this must reinforce paternalistic and racist attitudes. In this regard Hugo Muller has written a useful study, *Why
Don't You? A Look at Attitudes towards Indians*, based on his experience as an Anglican priest working among the Inland Cree people
in the diocese of Moosonee in northwestern Quebec.

Modern mission histories in Canada still tend to be written from
the perspective of those who brought the gospel, concentrating
on the usually heroic role of the white missionary pioneers and
their bishops, with minimal reference to the native response and
the native contribution to the church, although some recent excep-
tions give promise of better things to come. But we searched hard
to find information on the first Indian priests, and then the
presentation was outdated.[9] Katherine Pettipas has edited *The
Diary of the Rev. Henry Budd 1870–1875*, but the diary of James
Settee remains unpublished. The biography of Simon Gibbons,
"first Eskimo priest," by Leonard Hatfield (1987) is a move
towards recording the pioneering work of native church leaders
but much still needs to be done. Donald Smith's biography *Sacred
Feathers*, of Peter Jones (1987), the first Methodist native minister,
is a brilliant achievement in writing church history from the native
people's point of view. According to Smith, there is a dearth of
material on native church history and the early work has a
hagiographical bias. The biographies of the Blessed Kateri
Tekakwitha (Tegaquitha) within the Catholic tradition are a good
example.

What is needed now is a comprehensive history of the native
church in Canada which records the ministry of the many faithful
native catechists, trapper priests, church leaders, theologians,
holy men and women, and many loyal lay people, written by
native people themselves. Oral sources are central to such
research. In the past the history of the native people was a living
tradition handed down by the elders. With the increase in
urbanization, modernization, and literacy, this custom is fast
dying out. But the elders are still the repository of a living history,
as much in the church as in the wider society, and there is a sense
of urgency in recording their stories before they are lost to poster-
ity. The tape recorder is an invaluable tool in such research and
theological institutions could provide the motivation for an oral
history project as part of their training. This should be supported
by the collection of orations, oracles, poetry, sacred songs, stories,

myths, legends, sermons, prayers, and chants in order to obtain a complete record of oral native resources.

In recent years some church historians have taken a more critical view of mission history. The work of E. Palmer Patterson II on the Anglican evangelization of the Nisga in British Columbia, and that of John Webster Grant in a broader sweep, are notable examples. In his book, *Moon of Wintertime* (1985), Grant follows the encounter between white missionaries and native people in Canada since their first contact in 1534. He is sympathetic towards the need of native Christians to integrate faith with their own culture and maintains that the resurgence in interest in native spirituality should lead to a livelier native Christianity. But in the end the main concern of both Grant and Patterson is still with the missionaries' story and the native voice seldom speaks except as it affects mission interests. The problem here is the heavy reliance on European records and written sources, and the dearth of oral and written native material. The McCullums have overcome these problems in a well-balanced history of the Anglican church in Caledonia, written to mark the centenary of the diocese in 1979. This brings the everyday concerns of the people to life.

From an academic point of view, Bowden's study of *American Indians and Christian Missions* (1981) offers a model for analyzing the dynamics of religious change in an historical context. In addition to providing a short history of Christian missions among native people in North America, he gives a general description of precontact civilizations, charts the role of religion in subsequent cultural conflicts, and assesses the priority native people still give to their own diverse spiritualities.

Dee Brown's *Bury My Heart at Wounded Knee* is an adequately illustrated, blood-curdling account of the circumstances surrounding the massacre at Wounded Knee. Written with great passion, this work has, to our knowledge, shaken quite a few complacent hearts and converted them to a sense of solidarity with the native cause.

With regard to fictional history of mission, Margaret Craven's novel, *I Heard the Owl Call My Name* (1967), is based on the real-life experiences of a young white Anglican priest with a tribe in northern British Columbia. It is a sensitive story of the growth in consciousness of native spirituality as the priest participates in the hunting, fishing, festivals, and funerals of the local people. Problems relating to the conflicting claims of competing cultures and religious views are also realistically portrayed.

The native writer, W.P. Kinsella, uses humour to poke fun at the white man and his civilization without taking a sentimental view of contemporary native life. His short stories involve the doings of a colourful bunch of characters on an Alberta reserve who are all nominally Catholic. There are devastating comments on how "the white man's religion" comes across to native people especially as purveyed by the fundamentalist Pentecostal churches. Kinsella's fictional writings are couched in a native patois and succeed in evoking the sense of the native wasteland in the Canadian prairies.

Ethnographic Studies

This century has seen an outpouring of ethnographic studies on various nations across North America which show how native spirituality permeates every aspect of their life. But in line with new developments in anthropology, the closed "traditional" society, "tribe," or ethnic group, which has been the focus of functionalist methodology in the past, is no longer regarded as an appropriate unit of study. Diamond Jenness stands firmly in the functionalist school, but his book, *The Indians of Canada*, first published in 1932, remains a classic of its kind.

Scholars like Hultkrantz, Underhill, Epes Brown, and Gill, have analyzed Indian religions in North America as a whole using a variety of methodological approaches. In fact, as Hultkrantz shows, the very study of native American religion has an impressive history of its own, with different schools of religious history and ethnology in Europe staking their respective claims as to the merits of their academic interpretation. But here again there is the ever-present danger of spiritual colonialism. How willingly would the European submit to having his religious history written by North American native people and his religious beliefs and practices dissected as something exotic and strange?

At issue is the often myopic selection of biased sources and the processing of native spirituality into phenomenological pigeon-holes, the bland assumption being that the Judaeo-Christian tradition is at the top in an hierarchical pyramidal model of spirituality and the western analytical framework the norm. How would white people feel if a native holy man like Black Elk were to devise a methodology to look at Christian spirituality?

Even sympathetic studies by authors such as those cited above risk being patronizing by the very nature of their analytical approach. For the native people spirituality is not a neat metaphysical construct but a daily encounter with the reality of life. It is something experienced at the deepest emotional level, not abstracted and observed through the keyholes of anthropology and charted in academic theses. When a Sioux elder returned from a visit to "experts" on native religion in West Germany, he exclaimed, "They seemed to know more about us Indians than we Indians did ourselves." This is a sad but revealing commentary on the way in which native peoples have been relegated to objects in academic circles. There is a whole colonial gulf of difference between "knowing Indians and knowing about Indians."

Through Native Eyes

Any authentic sources on the native world-view should teach us to see it through native eyes, and there are indeed white as well as native authors who achieve this empathy. Such is *The Gospel of the Redman* by Ernest Thompson Seton (1937), which is not scholarly but a nonetheless useful representation of the heart of native spirituality. A very readable compendium on native tradition, it should be of interest to both young and old.

Vine Deloria Jr. is a prolific native writer who in his *God Is Red* (1973) maintains that Christianity has failed among his people and offers an alternative through a return to Indian beliefs and concepts. His works, *Custer Died for Your Sins* and *We Talk, You Listen*, written in a racy militant style, lead a scathing attack on the white, middle-class stereotypes about native people.

The autobiographies of native holy men with firsthand experience of Christianity, such as Black Elk and Lame Deer, give a penetrating critique of western values and attitudes. These are based on a profound understanding of their own time-honoured native spirituality. In the words of Lame Deer:

Indians chase the vision, white men chase the dollar. . . . So we have the green frog-skin world in which all things have a price tag. . . . You could almost say that a man with no vision can't be a real Indian. . . . Dreams are dangerous to the frog-skin world which tries to keep them away with cannons.[10]

Lame Deer, never bitter or even cynical, has a typical native sense of humour. That is why his trenchant indictment of white civilization is more telling than that provided by the militant native writers such as Vine Deloria Jr. Lame Deer is one of the most articulate spokesmen of his race. He writes:

Maka tanhan wicasa wan — I am a man of the Earth, as we say. Our people don't call themselves Sioux or Dakota. That's white man talk. We call ourselves *Ikse wicasa* — the natural humans, the free, wild, common people. . . . We aren't divided up into separate, neat little families — Pa, Ma, kids, and to hell with everybody else. The whole damn tribe is one big family; that's our kind of reality.[11]

Lame Deer has a disastrously funny way of expressing the most annoying and painful experiences. On leaving the army his nonchalant comment was: "I settled down to my only full-time job — being an Indian."[12] His incisive critique of the church, white civilization, and the American Dream, presented without a trace of resentment, testifies to his integrity as a holy medicine man. His raunchy sensuality only enhances the tone of his mystical insights.

The need is for white observers to move away from analyzing native spirituality through preconceived prisms which assume that western scholarship and theology are the norm. Why not acknowledge that Black Elk, Lame Deer, and Chief Seattle can and do offer an equally viable norm against which Euro-Caucasian spirituality can be tested and examined? It involves a major shift in consciousness to explore native spirituality with Lame Deer. One has to learn with him to see through "the eye of the heart." As he explains:

I had no need of their churches. I carried my own church within me. I went to peyote meetings and had visions. I wanted to feel, smell, hear and see, but not see with my eyes and my mind only. I wanted to see with *cante ista*, the eye of the heart. This eye had its own way of looking at things.[13]

The *Memoirs of Chief Red Fox* is another example of autobiographical writing celebrating the pride in himself and his native's culture which he continues to prefer to the tinsel of the materialistic western alternative. Red Fox writes:

Pride in them [scientists] and their achievements has not overawed me, for I am not convinced that the comforts and advancements which they brought into the world have made people more content and happy than the Indians were through the centuries on the mountains, prairies, and deserts of the primeval, virgin continent.[14]

The task then is to find authentic sources on native spirituality such as Lame Deer, Black Elk, and Red Fox.

When in the nineteenth century Tecumseh was asked by a missionary whether his people had a book to tell about their religion, the chief spread his arms out wide indicating that the whole earth is their book. Native peoples had a basically non-literary tradition. In recent times, however, a renaissance has inspired a move to publish native literature which should facilitate a dialogue with the western culture with its obsession with the printed word.

At the risk of oversimplification, one might say that while the European culture prefers visual images and symbols, native peoples, not unlike the Hebrews of old, favoured images which were auditory in content. They heard the voice of the Great Spirit. Hence, the importance of the sacred oral tradition being handed down from generation to generation and moulded according to the changing context and experience of the people. There was little urgency to fix the bounds of the canon, as in the literary traditions of other religions. But the head-on collision with western culture established new priorities. Medicine men, fearing the total extinction of their tradition, saw in the printed and recorded word a strategy to rescue native spirituality from oblivion. Another reason to capture the floating mass of oral traditions in the printed form was the growing need to provide an interpretation of native spirituality that would become universally acceptable. This would help close the ranks of the feuding native nations and confront the invading white Christian ideology with the united and disciplined alternative of native spirituality. An outstanding example is the Lakota medicine man Nicholas Black Elk, who found in Epes Brown and Neihardt able and sympathetic listeners. Their edited versions of Black Elk's teaching are recorded in *The Sacred Pipe* and *Black Elk Speaks* respectively. In his preface to *Black Elk Speaks*, Deloria rightly maintains that the medicine man's teaching is "the central core of the Native American theological tradition."

Pseudo-Autobiographies

Paul Radin is responsible for creating and popularizing a genre of native literature in the shape of autobiographies allegedly dictated by native subjects and supposedly presented by Radin without any attempt to edit or interpolate. These writings of the Winnebago people include Jasper Blowsnake's personal reminiscences, Sam Blowsnake's autobiography, the testimony and prayers of Thunder-Cloud, a Winnebago shaman, an expansion of Sam's autobiography, *Crashing Thunder*, and numerous fragments scattered in other scholarly and popular works.

Radin was trained in zoology and wrote a thesis on the embryology of the shark! Later he moved from zoology to anthropology and a study of native people. Radin proclaimed his mission was "to throw . . . light upon the workings of an Indian's brain" and to give an "inside view of the Indian's emotional life."[15] But as Nancy Lurie, a close associate, has shown, Radin's claims to allow the native person to tell the facts in his own way without editorial comment, and not to influence his subject in the selection of data, do not match the evidence and manifest a marked lack of integrity. In fact, Radin appears highly patronizing, pseudo-scientific, and manipulative. He himself admitted to giving chase in a horse-wagon to overcome Crashing Thunder's reluctance to talk about his life, and to tricking Jasper Blowsnake into revealing confidential details of the sacred Winnebago medicine rite and aspects of his personal life.[16] Paul Radin's genre of autobiography is thus yet another vehicle for the manipulation of the native spirit.

Natives Write about Natives

Various native groupings in Canada are in the process of compiling a whole range of publications by and about the indigenous peoples, spanning their past and their present. These include folklore, myths, legends, children's stories, colouring books, poetry, tribal history, dictionaries, grammars, and studies relating to language, culture, ecological issues, and aboriginal and human rights. Much of this material is being fed into the educational system and must foster a recovery and encouragement of native identity. For example the Nisga, who were the first to have a native-controlled school district in Canada, have a bilingual-bicultural program in their schools. They are also busy with an oral history and tradition project, while the Saskatchewan Indian Languages Institute is making a collection of Cree oral literature. Other bodies like the Saskatchewan Indian Cultural College and the Woodland Indian Cultural Education Centre in the Six Nations Iroquois Reserve have promoted native art. Native elders, including ministers of religion, have played an important part in these various projects. The Neewin Publishing Company was set up in Toronto in the late 1960s to fill the gap in publishing native material but sadly only survived a couple of years.

Fireweed, a Canadian feminist quarterly, devoted its winter 1986 issue to the writing of native women in North America. Marilou Awiakta's short essay on Cherokee myth is a good example of a woman's perspective on the dialogue between the old native beliefs and the new Christian ones. She makes the point that to understand myth fully (and one might include all aspects of native spirituality) "one must understand its resonance — the ways of the people who gave it voice."[17]

Chief John Snow did pioneering work in writing up the history of the Stoney Indians in Alberta, from before the coming of the white man to the present day, in *These Mountains Are Our Sacred Places* (1977). Wesleyan mission history is interwoven throughout the story, including the missionaries' rather dubious role in treaty-making. Through John Snow the Nakoda Institute at Morley has also recently published three volumes of occasional papers dealing with native political and justice issues and native education.

Anthologies such as Frederick W. Turner's *The Portable North American Reader* provide a feast of material ranging from Indian myths, tales, autobiography, poetry, and oratory, to accounts of cultural interpenetration and conflicting image-making from white and native sources. Much of this has a religious dimension. Turner argues that contemporary native writing "has forced white writers to re-evaluate the Indian and his part in the American experience."[18]

New Visions in Mission Writing

Significantly, it is Catholic religious like the Oblates — Johnson, Goulet, and Peelman — and the Jesuits — Starkloff, Steinmetz, and Steltenkamp — who have broken new ground in studies relating to dialogue with native religious traditions and the formation of the local church. The Kisemanito Centre at Grouard, Alberta, and the Tekakwitha Conference National Center just south of the Canadian/U.S. border at Great Falls, Montana, both publish newsletters aimed at a native Catholic audience. Through a variety of educational methods they are searching in their different ways to find theological answers to being native and Christian today, and to building up and supporting their following.

The Roman Catholic church must be congratulated for its sustained effort to create a body of literature in the shape of newsletters, pamphlets, and essays on the complex theological problems of developing a native Christian spirituality. It has engendered a climate of dialogue, and taken the native symbols seriously, thanks to its sacramental vision. However, even when Catholic writers like Steinmetz have earnestly entered into the sacramental character of native spirituality, they never really seem to allow for an open-ended dialogue in the spirit of freedom and parity. There is always the danger of a hidden agenda which may imprison the native spirit within the ecclesiastical bounds of the institutional Catholic church.

In 1985 the United Church of Canada committed itself to a two-year dialogue with native peoples — A Time to Weep and a Time to Laugh (Ecclesiastes 3:4). As Stan McKay, the native ministry co-ordinator, said in the editorial of a special edition of *Mandate*,[19] native Canadians did not wish to continue being examined as objects. The process had to change from a "mission study" to a "dialogue about mission," so that the church community could move from ''an objective perception to a subjective involvement,'' which would allow ''for commitment and solidarity with Native people.'' This volume of *Mandate* was devoted to listening to the native church, as was the July 1985 edition of *World View* for young people. The Consensus Native News has, under the editorship of Stan McKay, continued to publish a newsletter through which native people in the United church can voice their concerns and maintain contact with one another. Articles are widely ranging and include news items relating to native issues, poetry, stories, speeches, profiles, and reports on church meetings and political consultations. All are permeated with insights into native spirituality and provide an ongoing forum for developing a contextual theology done by native people for native people.

Ron Atkinson, a United church minister, has an unpublished book of meditations for each week of the year, *Full Circle*, based on his experiences with the Kwakiutl people of Cape Mudge on Quadra Island. His concern is with spirituality rather than with the purveying of doctrines and creeds. In his ministry with native people he found that he had to move from a theology of salvation to a theology of creation. The former is obsessed with sin and a low estimate of the human spirit and the consequent urgency to escape and transcend the created world. The latter, however, is characterized by a positive attitude towards man as made in the image of God, and the world as God's creation (and not a pit of temptation), and the goal of spirituality to be integrated with Mother Earth and God's children. For Ron, Christ is a symbol of God's incarnating energy in creation.[20]

The Anglican Church of Canada has no publication resources devoted to its native membership. The need to establish such a communication system would seem to be a priority. The need to encourage native writing in the church appears equally urgent. For us the search for a written indigenous theology among Anglican native people became a treasure hunt which has only just begun. The talent and the expertise are there, but they either remain untapped or else fail to find an outlet in print. Seminal essays by the Reverend Dr. Adam Cuthand are a case in point, as is the example of his brother, the Reverend Stan Cuthand, in the field of folklore, myth, and legend.

Canon Edward Ahenakew first set down material for his book,

Voices of the Plains Cree, in 1923. But it seems that the notes were not published during his lifetime for fear of ecclesiastical reprisal because of the criticism which he had levelled against the established order including the church. His writings only came to light after his death in 1961, and, fortunately, were expertly edited for publication by Ruth Buck in 1973. But the book is not widely known and deserves reprinting.

Ahenakew's stories of Chief Thunderchild in the first section are part of his collection of Cree stories and legends. But in ''Old Keyam,'' which follows, Ahenakew himself speaks out through the voice of an old man of the band. This allows us to enter into his experience, often autobiographical, and share in the pain and confusion of the Plains Cree in a situation of rapid social change. The integrity of his writing is in marked contrast to that of John Eliot, speaking through imaginary natives to present them in compromising theological postures. Canon Ahenakew employs the same genre to give the voiceless an authentic voice. He obviously used this ruse of speaking indirectly for fear that if he represented Old Keyam's feelings of hurt and pain as his own he would probably fall foul of the church.

Hendry's report, *Beyond Traplines* (1969), on the work of the Anglican church with Canada's native peoples, was a milestone in social analysis of the native situation and in the raising of consciousness of non-native Anglicans. But the information needs updating together with a stocktaking to assess how far the church has moved in implementing the recommendations twenty years later. This could be a sobering experience. It must be said to Hendry's credit that he rattled the conscience of many in regard to the plight of native people. His findings make bold reading for his day. But the time has come to be even bolder. Academic reports written in a cool, objective, scientific manner are not enough. The challenge now is to evolve a prophetic theology based on Hendry's vision. We need to hear from native people themselves as they are increasingly liberated to engage in a Canadian contextual theology that addresses their needs and expectations. This is the real hope for the church in Canada. This is the true genesis of the Vision Quest.

Chapter 3

The Unmaking of the Native Vision Quest

Did We or Did We Not Wrong the Native People

Innumerable books are filled with historical documentation and social commentary to chart the progressive decline of the native people following their contact with the white man and their subsequent subjugation. Our purpose is not to give a potted history of past events or a comprehensive social analysis of the present situation, but just to highlight some of the issues that provide a launching pad for our Vision Quest. Where possible the native voice will speak for itself.

Our fieldwork throughout Canada has shown an amazing lack of awareness on the part of many white people, within and without the church, of the past and present suffering of native people. Far from recognizing this suffering there is often a patronizing attitude which regards native people as getting a good deal. This lack of historical consciousness of white people is readily understood when one sees the bias of history books written by professionals who should have known better. But *being ignorant of native history means being ignorant of one's own Canadian history.* The reality of the native situation is seldom properly seen or experienced because native people are so often far removed and isolated on reserves or else separated in the cities by class and racial prejudice.

During our visit to Sandy Lake Reserve, west of Prince Albert in Saskatchewan, we were twice hosted by Dick and Grace Ahenakew in their spacious timber-frame home overlooking the lake. As we sat long hours on the porch, watching the water birds paddling in the reeds, and feasting on home-cooked delicacies such as wild duck soup, fish from the lake, bannock, and cranberries and cream, Dick would talk of his present work as consultant to various prairie bands and of his concern to educate them about their treaty rights and to develop a political strategy in seeking a fair deal for Treaty Indians. He draws on many years' experience as a former chief of the Federation of Saskatchewan Nations and chief of the Assembly of First Nations. He has also been awarded an honorary doctorate by the University of Regina and the Order of Canada. One evening he gave us a two-hour lecture on his consultancy work. The dining room and living room were appropriated for a display of the visual material which he uses in his presentations, the walls and chairs covered with posters listing the Treaty Indian brief.

Dick identifies four historical approaches in Canada's policy to native people: civilization, assimilation, termination, and integration. He maintains that this policy continues to this day. The ultimate goal of government legislation has always been to eliminate the Indians' special status and with it their treaty rights including land and identity rights. Beginning in 1876 the Indian Act, and its various amendments, has been used to assimilate Indians into Euro-Canadian society. The Act defined who was a "legal" Indian and what could be done on Indian reserves. The purpose of "civilization" was to inculcate western Europe values and attitudes, while school education has been a major factor in facilitating the integration of native people into the dominant culture as a minority ethnic group. The end product of this policy was to be the complete loss of Indian identity and culture and their disappearance as distinct peoples. And in many respects this policy has succeeded.

Initially there were more than fifty aboriginal nations in Canada. Over many thousands of years each nation evolved a way of life that was adapted to survival in a particular environment and included socio-economic and political systems of organization, distinct languages and customs, and a spirituality which embraced their whole world and infused it with sacred power. The circle symbolized the wholeness of creation, harmony between man and nature, and between the living and the dead. Rituals were designed to enter into that harmony and maintain the balance. Sacred power was made manifest in people, places, objects, and all living creatures. Above all there was a sacred relationship with the land, with certain places, including burial grounds and vision mounds, being designated as points of contact and communion with the Great Spirit, the ancestors, and the spirit world. Peter Nabokov shows how in these holy places "an entire environment [was] reconsecrated as a sacred geography forged from the holy elements: earth, air, fire and water."[1] With the coming of the white man to North America most aboriginal nations were displaced from their sacred spaces, the land despoiled, and the harmony of the holy elements destroyed. Black Elk's lament gives some insight into the spiritual rape experienced by his people.

> Everything an Indian does is in a circle, and that is because the Power of the World always works in circles, and every-thing tries to be round. In the old days when we were a strong and happy people, all our power came to us from the sacred hoop of the nation, and so long as the hoop was unbroken, the people flourished. . . . But the Wasichus [white men] have put us in these square boxes. Our power is gone and we are dying, for the power is not in us any more.[2]

Black Elk's sentiments have been voiced thousands of times over in a litany of laments as in the past two hundred years aboriginal people have expressed their grief and their pain for all that they have lost and for the consequent breakdown of their society. They mourn for a time past when the native nations were sovereign and the people had complete control of every facet of their lives, organizing their own polity and following their own laws; where economic survival depended on co-operation and the effective utilization of the environment; where food and belongings were shared for the good of all; where a strong kin-ship system and social structure gave a sense of belonging to a community; where everybody knew their place with their assigned roles and mutual responsibilities; and where values such as integrity, unselfishness, self-reliance, regard for the wisdom of the elders, respect for all living things, right conduct, and loyalty to the tribe were inculcated from childhood. Above all, they grieve for a spirituality which gave this culture sacred mean-ing, which allowed them to enter into the seasonal rhythm of nature and to mark the passages of life from birth to death and beyond with ritual and ceremony.

Writing in the 1920s, Edward Ahenakew graphically depicts the trauma of these changes for his people in his book *Voices of the*

Plains Cree. He himself was proud of his Cree ancestry, his grandfather's older brother being Ah-tah-ka-koop (Star Blanket), one of the most influential chiefs in Saskatchewan during the 1870s and 80s and a signatory of Treaty Six. Edward Ahenakew was born at Sandy Lake, Ah-tah-ka-koop's reserve, in June 1885. He first attended school on the reserve and then went as a boarder to Prince Albert. After a spell of teaching at mission schools, he trained for the ministry at Wycliffe College, Toronto, and Emmanuel College, Saskatoon, graduating as Licentiate in Theology in 1912. He was then ordained Anglican priest and began work assisting at Onion Lake mission. Deeply affected by the suffering of his people during the influenza epidemic of 1918–19, he attempted a study of medicine at the University of Edmonton. But he had little money and his health broke down forcing him to take a year off in 1923 to recover. During this time he lived at the mission on Chief Thunderchild's reserve near Turtle Lake, and as a means to his own healing persuaded the chief to allow him to record the Cree legends, history, and traditions.

Some of the chief's stories appear in the first half of Ahenakew's book and tell of the buffalo chase and battles between rival tribes, of horse-stealing and encounters with bears, of the mythic coming of the first man and of sacred dances. Ahenakew wanted to depict the vitality of the days when aboriginal peoples roamed freely on the plains, in order to contrast the soul-destroying effects of their removal to reserves. In the second half of the book he reflects on the present situation through the words of the fictitious figure, Old Keyam. The Cree word *keyam* means ''I do not care!''; but this name is seen to be a disguise, hiding the feelings of hurt and bewilderment experienced by so many native people who seemed not to care because they did not know what to do. And it was this sense of apathy and defeatism that Ahenakew sought to redress through his writing and his involvement in the first Pan-Indian movement in Canada.[3]

In his role as an elder who speaks at tribal gatherings, Old Keyam recalls how his people were hobbled like horses on their reserves; hemmed in by alien laws and totally unequipped to make their way in the wider western society. With the buffalo herds decimated and their land surrendered in treaties, they were forced to give up their nomadic life and become settled as farmers in fenced-off areas. The reserve system may well have ensured the native people's survival in the face of the white advance; but these drastic changes were a severe shock to the Plains Cree, and they had neither previous experience nor training to ease the transformation. Old Keyam agonizes over the disastrous consequences to his people's health that result from the change in their lifestyle: their poor housing in log shanties, overcrowding, ignorance of new rules of sanitation and cleanliness, unfamiliar clothing, and susceptibility to the white man's diseases. Added to which their first efforts at farming yielded poor crops, and they struggle to survive with hopelessly inadequate government assistance.[4]

As the norms and values of the incoming culture became ever more pervasive and oppressive, the growing anger of the Plains Cree finally found expression in armed resistance. They were routed at Frog Lake in 1885. Tracing the history of these events Old Keyam says:

> What people, unless totally devoid of spirit, unless slavish for a thousand years, would not have felt bitter resentment, would not have blamed the white man for it all, for all the misery, and all the degradation? Looking back now, we can recognize that the massacre at Frog Lake was the last effort of the Indian to register in letters of blood his opposition to the ever-increasing, and irresistible power of another race in the land that had been his.[5]

In his turn Chief Thunderchild stresses the emotional and spiritual suffering caused by the prohibition of the Sun Dance and other forms of Indian worship, ''the strength of our people for centuries.'' A move towards suppressing the ritual celebrations was begun in 1882 and led to an amendment of the Indian Act in 1895 forbidding all native dances, festivals, and ceremonies. The Sun Dance was continued surreptitiously in some places but always with the fear of imprisonment. Chief Thunderchild gives vent to the sorrow and indignation of his people at this gross interference in their tradition:

> Can things go well in a land where freedom of worship is a lie, a hollow boast? To each nation is given the light by which it knows God, and each finds its own way to express the long-

ing to serve Him. It is astounding to me that a man should be stopped from trying in his own way to express his need or his thankfulness to God. If a nation does not do what is right according to its own understanding, its power is worthless. I have listened to the talk of the white man's clergy, and it is the same in principle as the talk of our Old Men, whose wisdom came not from books but from life and from God's earth. Why has the white man no respect for the religion that was given to us, when we respect the faith of other nations?[6]

A similar scenario was played out in many other parts of Canada with similar feelings of alienation, powerlessness, suffering, and oppression, except that for each aboriginal nation the historical circumstances were somewhat different. On the west coast they lost their freedom to hunt and fish as they wished, while their potlatch ceremonies were forbidden and their totem poles destroyed. And whereas innumerable treaties were signed in Ontario and the Prairie provinces, large tracts of land were never negotiated in many areas including British Columbia, the Yukon, much of Quebec, and the Atlantic provinces. Here various groupings have had to rely on the Canadian legal and political systems over the years to negotiate and defend their aboriginal rights. The Nisga for example have long struggled to establish their claim that they have never forfeited the aboriginal title to their traditional tribal territories and have persistently affirmed that ''Nisga land is not for sale.''[7]

In times past many native people chose the path of passive resistance to the white encroachment rather than armed confrontation. In the nineteenth century this often took the form of religious movements which sought to draw on the sacred power of both the native tradition and Christianity so as to strengthen or revitalize native cultural identity in an attempt to cope with white domination.

Of those who led these movements some were for assimilation with the European way and others against. To the first category belong Handsome Lake of the Iroquois, and John Slocum of Puget Sound, who masterminded the founding of the Indian Shaker Church. They called on native peoples to give up their old ways and try Christianity as a new framework for native spirituality. Albert Hensley was one of those responsible for introducing the use of peyote on the Pine Ridge reserve in South Dakota among the Oglala Lakota Sioux people at the turn of the century. He advocated a blend of Christian dogmas and a ritual consumption of the peyote. This has blossomed into the Native American Church of North America embracing a number of branches distinguished by their relative emphasis on Christian dogma. Among the prophets of dissent were "the Delaware Prophet" of Lake Erie, who inspired the revolt of the Pontiac; Tenskwatawa, a Shawnee medicine man, who preached immunity from the white man's weapons through the power of his medicine; Smohalla of the Columbia River Plateau, who urged the performance of a traditional Indian dance which would automatically destroy the whites and renew the earth; and last but not least, Wowoka of Nevada, famous for his advocacy of the Ghost Dance.

In the end, however, the net result of the European influx into Canada was much the same for the different native peoples. There was wholesale displacement from their land and an all-enveloping disruption of their cultural, economic, and social bonds. The native vision of the community of man, beast, bird, plant, and stone, living in interdependence under the Great Spirit, was banned and criminalized. A materialistic culture lacking in vision took over, and the stage was set for a planned underdevelopment and impoverishment of the native people.

The Trapline of Native Poverty

Hendry's investigation of the native situation in Canada in the late 1960s, *Beyond Traplines*, showed that although some Indians and Metis seemed to have become completely assimilated into Euro-Canadian society with a measure of success, a large proportion of native peoples were "economically distressed and socially disorganized."[8] Hendry examined available statistics on poverty, unemployment, education, health, and mortality rates among native peoples to give some idea of the stress and suffering involved. But he points out that there are no means of measuring psychological and cultural factors and argues that "cultural deprivation is as self-perpetuating as the culture of poverty." Further, he warns against masking the reality of the situation by imposing false categories of statistical assessment:

The Indians and Eskimos face a total life situation created by two centuries of exploitation, discrimination, paternalism and neglect. . . . The white conqueror sought his own profit and his own power. The Indians were pushed out of the way, were excluded from the new streams of wealth and development. A legal frame was provided so that they could be kept in their place. . . . They were segregated in reserves, fed on charity and welfare and deprived of every possibility of sharing in Canada's progress. Instead of becoming the first subjects of a new country, they became unwelcome objects for private and government programs.[9]

More recent reports give little indication that the socio-economic situation has improved for native people in Canada. They are still trapped in poverty. The native population in prisons and correctional institutions is still abnormally high, while alcoholism and drug abuse continue to wreak havoc. The statistics on unemployment, housing, mortality rates, violence, and underachievement in education are equally depressing. The gravity of the situation was graphically brought home to us when the Reverend Laverne Jacobs, co-ordinator of the Council on Native Affairs, took us to his home at Walpole Island, on the St. Clair River boundary between Canada and the United States. As we drove round, he spoke of the excessive number of funerals he had taken when he was pastor there, the result of drowning, suicides, child-battering, and accidents.

A large majority of native people are said to be battling to survive on welfare in rural and urban ghettos and racism is rampant. With a native population of about thirty-five thousand, Regina is known as the Alabama of the North. The Reverend Dr. Adam Cuthand has for some years worked with the Ecumenical Native Ministry in Regina and has also been an adviser to the school board on race and ethnic relations. When we visited him in his home, he shared his sadness at the way violence in the native community is at present turned inwards on itself. ''Our people are hurting each other,'' he said. ''Every night there are shootings and stabbings. Indian pimps hold young girls almost like slaves. And then there are the drugs and alcoholism.'' But he foresaw a time when this violence could well turn outwards against white people and there could be rioting as in the United States.[10] Mrs. Bea Cuthand spoke out of her own experience too in an interview with a local Anglican church magazine:

> I have found Regina to be the worst place for discrimination against natives, in comparison with other places where I have lived. On top of that, the church is the worst of all social institutions for discrimination, not only the Anglican church, but other denominations as well. You feel when you walk in the door that you're not welcome.[11]

The Right Reverend William Wantland of the Seminole nation and bishop of Eau Claire, Wisconsin, believes that the root of racial conflict, in Canada as much as in the States, is cultural. Addressing the Anglican consultation on "Native Ministries and Our Future" at Edmonton in September 1985, he maintained that the cultural conflict between European and native American is compounded by the fact that although it began openly on both sides, it is continued today by the dominant society through its ignorance of the differences in culture and values. Worse still, he argues, "the non-Indian is ignorant of his ignorance."

Clearly socio-economic and political factors also feature prominently in the bitterness and resentment which native people feel towards the dominant society today. Furthermore, it would be naive to regard the cultural and socio-economic factors as being unrelated. Indeed, the traditional vision of the Indian was so all-encompassing and comprehensive that the cultural supra-structure of native society implied a specific economic infra-structure. The latter was based on the values of sharing, co-operation, and respect for man and the ecology, whereas the classical western economies have always been an exercise in competition, exploitation, and individual accumulation of wealth. Hence what Bishop Wantland would like to believe to be a war between two cultures is in reality a war between two economic philosophies, a sharing and a non-sharing one.

Hendry rightly argues that the legal and political systems in Canada have served to reinforce a situation of dependency among native peoples, the overall trend being from "partial guardianship to total tutelage." This left them unprepared to take responsibility for decision-making. According to Hendry "the last one hundred years appear as one single historical trend in which the role and the power of governments were maximized while the self-determination of the Indians and the Eskimos was minimized.'' He concludes by saying that ''dependence, as well as poverty, is self-perpetuating and its bitter harvest will be with us for a considerable time.''[12]

Alex Greyeyes, president of the Saskatchewan Indian Language Institute in Saskatoon, recalls that the early 1950s were a turning point for the worse for native people following government institution of the welfare system. Up until then the native family unit had remained reasonably intact, but after that time people could see no future on the reserves and there was a mass exodus to the cities with all of its attendant problems. For Alex the tragedy is that under the impact of the dominant culture native people not only lost their identity but became ashamed of being native. His college has been actively involved in the revitalization of native culture and they have set up a Pipe Centre where elders can lead ritual ceremonies. But this must not detract from the native people's main concern which is self-determination.[13] This issue was taken up time and time again by native people right across Canada.

The aboriginal rights which have been identified for constitutional recognition include the right to be distinct peoples, the right to an adequate land and economic base flowing from aboriginal title, aboriginal rights and treaty rights, and the inherent right to self-government. Research showed little enthusiasm for recent changes in government policy which allow a greater measure of independence for native people, while the political debate concerning the future of the native peoples grinds on without much prospect of a satisfactory solution. In 1987 the failure of the last in a series of four constitutional conferences between the prime minister, the provincial premiers, and the leaders of four of Canada's largest native groups, followed immediately by the Meech Lake Accord allowing for constitutional accommodation with Quebec, indicated the present government's priorities in the constitutional process.

However, if the white government in Ottawa failed the native peoples the work of recapturing the vision and regaining their dignity has been underway for some decades in native society. Since 1919 Indians have become organized to fight for their rights.

The League of Indians of Canada was the first Pan-Indian association to be formed. Its purpose was to unify the scattered tribes so as to secure ''a representative Indian opinion and some unity of action.'' Its principal aim was equality for the native person as a citizen in terms of both privilege and responsibility. Edward Ahenakew was a founding member and provincial president of the Saskatchewan branch.[14]

Subsequently, cultural nationalism inspired the formation of a succession of native brotherhoods, Indian associations and leagues across the country, but it is only since the 1960s that both provincial and national movements have really gained momentum on a broad front. The different native organizations incorporate a variety of interests and issues — educational, cultural, and political. Their aims include affirming native identity, preserving traditional customs and culture, campaigning for control of native education, rallying support for social justice issues, and working for the right to self-determination. And their functioning is not necessarily in watertight compartments. As Adam Cuthand observes, ''Even in political meetings a sense of native spirituality is creeping in.''

What about the Church?

Reams have been written about the coming of the gospel to Canada from the sixteenth century on and about the work of the missionaries among the native peoples. The earlier accounts are descriptive, the more recent ones analytical, but without exception the authors are white, and almost invariably the spotlight remains firmly fixed on the white missionary at the centre of the mission drama. This is only half the story, however, and until native Christians record their experiences and achievements Canadian church history will remain sadly incomplete. In Canada as elsewhere the establishment, consolidation, and extension of mission work has been dependent on a large body of committed native workers.

Interviews with native clergy and laity have shown that almost every person has a story to tell of suffering within the church's fold, of patronizing attitudes, racial arrogance, and paternalism, of frustration, and the rejection of indigenous church leaders. We were told of many incidents of the autocratic and insensitive behaviour of bishops, clergy, and teachers:

- of an Anglican bishop who was furious when a delegation of a priest, a chief, and elders dared approach him without making an appointment. He sent them away without even a prayer so that they never had the chance to discuss their vision of combining native spirituality with gospel teaching. The net result was that the chief opened his reserve to other churches and the Pentecostalists took over. . . .
- of another Anglican bishop who threatened disciplinary action when a native priest dared to ask searching questions in synod about the dearth of leadership opportunities for native people in their diocese. . . .
- of an Anglican priest who locked the church doors when people came late for services even though many had had to come by foot from afar. Again this drove people into the Pentecostal corral. . . .
- of humiliation and ill-treatment in residential schools, of a little boy beaten and dragged by his hair because he greeted a schoolmate in Cree, and of a girl who at eight years old was repeatedly spanked for speaking her native tongue. . . .
- of many priests and teachers who said that native customs were barbaric and of the devil, and who forced medicine men to burn their medicine bags so that the Indian's therapeutic knowledge is now lost to us. . . .
- of a Catholic missionary who rushed into Black Elk's tepee, called him names, and threw out his peace pipes and other sacred instruments of native spirituality. . . .
- of the great hurt experienced by Indian ordinands when their native customs and beliefs were denigrated as heathen during their theological training. . . .
- of a United church missionary who claimed to have brought a message of a loving God to a native community but only preached "hell and damnation to all sinners," terrifying the people. . . .
- of the Anglican church dignitaries who at a meeting discussed native religion among themselves without ever consulting the native people present. . . .
- of white parishioners moving away from native people who

had had the temerity to sit next to them in their pews and who studiously ignored native people at church functions. . . .

- of a native couple being welcomed by whites in church but being ignored in the stores next day. They stopped going to church. . . .
- of native people always having to go through the back door of a missionary's house, of being given tea in the kitchen, and never being asked into the living room or dining room. . . .
- of white Anglican priests who refused to walk alongside their native colleagues in church processions. . . .
- of a native priest who was pressured into withdrawing his name for election as a suffragan bishop. . . .

The list is endless but perhaps we can give the last words to Alice Ahenakew, widow of the late Archdeacon Andrew Ahenakew, and to the Reverend Smith Atimoyoo, a former Anglican priest who has been working with various native cultural organizations for the past twenty years. We spent a day with Auntie Alice at her home across from the church in Sandy Lake Reserve. Her vivid account of her childhood and upbringing by a saintly old foster couple, steeped in the native tradition, was deeply moving. Auntie Alice's family would spend three months of the year in the wild up north, hunting and trapping, and she learnt to live off the land with never a morsel of food being wasted. She still goes berry-picking in the woods each summer and treated us to her own fruit preserves and bannock, an unleavened bread introduced by Scottish fur traders which the Cree have made their own. As she reminisced, her kindly wrinkled face beamed with the joy of her memories:

> We never used to sell anything. Everybody shared. We shared the meat we had brought home with us with all the other people on the reserve. Not like now when you have to buy everything. The people who lived years ago were very good people. Lots of priests said Indian customs were all of the devil. They used to preach about it. It kind of hurt me when they said that because I knew that the way I had been brought up was not from the devil. The priests said that Indians were using idols like stones and sticks, and that was all working for the devil. They still say that. It is not true. It is because they don't know the background of the Indian way of religion. You know

when Indian people pray they always start with God, everybody's God. And then they do talk about the Mother Earth, the self, the four directions, and so on; but they are not worshipping them. My grandfather refused to be baptized. He did not want to promise God a bunch of things he could not keep. But he was a saint. He used to get up at 5 o'clock every morning, winter and summer, and pray. He would burn the sweetgrass and pray out loud to the Great Spirit. Then he would sing a sacred Indian song. He knew God.[15]

We met Smitty Atimoyoo at a Chinese restaurant in Saskatoon and were greatly honoured that he spoke so freely about his native spirituality. But we made the great mistake of not bringing a gift of tobacco, the traditional mark of respect for an elder in seeking his counsel, and this had to be speedily rectified the next day. Smitty is a Cree from Little Pine Reserve. Over the meal he talked about his father's upbringing as a member of the Braves' Society, and of how his parents would also greet each new day with prayer and the burning of sweetgrass. Both sang native songs in the home and taught their children the traditional values of respect, community obligations, and a strict moral code. Smitty grieves for the part the church has played in destroying native spirituality:

The church said that the Indian beliefs and practices were heathen and wrong but it was the western way of life that led to a total breakdown of Indian society and the destruction of their moral values. This is the hurt. How can the Indian people ever recover their spirituality? How can they ever recover their values?[16]

Until we hear this voice, and weep together over past hurts, there is little hope of finding that forgiveness which is the first step on the long, hard road to reconciliation. What has constantly amazed us is the fortitude of so many native Christians in living out a faithful witness despite the difficulties. At the same time, they are the first to acknowledge the support of empathetic bishops, priests, and laity in times of trouble, and encouragement by the church in developing their talents.

The Anglican church began work among native people in

Canada in 1727 when the Society for the Propagation of the Faith gave a small grant to an army chaplain in Annapolis, Nova Scotia "as an allowance for teaching the poor children there."[17] But this Society's main thrust was amongst white settlers and it was the Church Missionary Society who took major responsibility for opening up the native mission field across the country and for providing the necessary man power and money to keep this work going. Starting early in this century the C.M.S. began to withdraw its support and transfer the responsibility of work among native people to the newly formed dioceses, many of which it had been instrumental in establishing.

The Anglican tradition came with the fur traders and the military and was thus identified with colonialism from the start. For a long time all the bishops came from England too. In line with their mission policy elsewhere in the world, the Anglicans achieved their most lasting results in the nineteenth century through contacts with chiefs. Chiefs could identify with the hierarchical church structure as a way of enhancing their power, even if it had to be shared with the catechist. The Anglicans also had the advantage of looking more official because they worked closely with the civil authority, even though this was obviously a problem for many native people. In contrast, the revival camp meetings of the early Methodists were unstructured and evocative of overpowering emotion which bordered on the shamanistic. Incidentally, the Pentecostals are using very much the same evangelizing methods today with the same appeal.

In the early days native people assumed that Christianity was a much stronger medicine and that white success was attributed to being in tune with the spirit world as yet undisclosed to them. But, as Grant has shown, they had problems in trying to appropriate the supposed benefits of Christianity because the missionaries kept tight control of the new sources of power: "the Indians wished to add to their stock of religious power, whereas the missionaries insisted on replacing old sources of power with new." Early prophetic movements in the northwest are thus seen as "attempts to open Christianity to appropriation by Indians on Indian terms," more especially to be free from the missionaries' control. These indigenous movements have been categorized as syncretistic, but as Grant indicates "authentically Christian witness requires authentic rootage in one's own culture" and these movements "can be seen as contributing to a process of indigenization in ways of which the missionaries were not capable."[18]

Accounts of the planting of missions and the ongoing development of church work among native people testify to a deep devotion and commitment, courage and self-sacrifice of the missionaries even when one cannot agree with many of their methods or the outworking of their message. Hendry describes them as playing a Jekyll-and-Hyde role in their interaction with native peoples, of being "both a disruptive and an integrative force":

> On one hand they have smashed native culture and social organization. On the other hand they have picked up the pieces of an indigenous way of life which had been smashed by other Europeans — traders, soldiers, administrators — and have helped the people put the pieces together in a new shape.[19]

The largest number of conversions took place at a time when the impact of the incoming culture was at its most severe and native communities were either disintegrating or else undergoing critical change from white contact. The mission model of Christianity thus provided an alternative world-view and a new community to replace that which had been lost or else too radically disturbed to continue functioning as a viable whole. But in picking up the pieces the church followed the government policy of assimilation and forced native converts into a western mould. The residential schools were a cornerstone of this policy of imparting "civilization" together with Christianity. Although no one can deny that this education equipped native people with the means of making their way in the dominant white society and provided the church with native leadership, it alienated native people from their roots and was in itself a source of pain and grief which has left its mark on intercultural relations today. In addition, it inculcated middle-class values with middle-class church-centred religious beliefs and practices which are hardly conducive to the recapturing of a native vision.

The purpose of the residential schools was to remove native children from their home environment at an early age and immerse them in a totally western milieu for extended periods of time. For many years the schools provided only basic literacy education and the standard of teaching was often abysmal. This severely limited the possibilities of native people carrying on with higher education. Half the school day was spent in "industrial" pursuits, such as domestic work and farming. Many parents considered this to be exploitation for cheap labour. The institutions were run on British public school lines with a heavy emphasis on discipline enforced through a harsh system of corporal punishment. An excessive concern for cleanliness and tidiness was also open to abuse. Health facilities were poor, susceptibility to new diseases high, and the death rate alarming. But even when school amenities and the standard of education were improved, the rule against speaking native languages still prevailed.[20] French and English were the only languages allowed and this had a catastrophic effect on native cultural identity and spirituality. As Hendry says, "When a language dies, much of the vitality of a way of living and thinking dies with it."[21]

The ability to think in and speak native languages was an open-sesame door to the deep holistic spirituality of the native vision. If English is said to be the language of shopkeeping, French of love, and German of military orders, the native tongues are vehicles of communing with the Great Spirit and communicating in an interdependent and interconnected ecology. With the loss of their richly spiritual tongues the native people forfeited their vision.

Another problem was that the purpose of native education was not clearly defined apart from integration into the dominant white culture. The products of residential schooling thus found that they had lost their identity and were unfitted for life in the reserves while they were denied equal social, political, and economic opportunities in European society. In the words of John Tootoosis, a Cree leader, they were left "hanging between two cultures," neither white nor Indian.[22] Edward Ahenakew echoes these sentiments in his notes written in 1923. He criticizes the residential schools for imposing a relentlessly ordered system which resulted in native dependence on white authority and in a lack of motivation: "We have been brought up as children, treated as children, made to act according to rules and regulations that are not our own."[23] Further, the school graduates were left "to sit" on the fence between the whites and the Indians, belonging to neither, fitting into neither world:

> They never needed to use their own minds and wills. . . . They are like children, and when suddenly given their freedom they do not know how to use it. Their initiative is lost. . . . To make matters worse, they have just enough learning to think themselves a plane above the rest of the band. They are not ready to take any advice from the older members, and though at first they are received joyfully, this feeling of superiority becomes evident and arouses ever sharper criticism. The young person is in a totally false position. He does not fit into the Indian life, nor does he find that he can associate with the whites. He is forced to act a part. He is now one thing, now another, and that alone can brand him an erratic and unreliable fellow.[24]

Ahenakew ends by saying, "You cannot make a white man out of an Indian. It is much better to make our children into good Indians, for we *are* Indians in our person and in our thinking." He believed that "the very roots of nation-building" lay in the schools, and through the League of Indians of Canada sought to transfer responsibility for Indian schools from the voluntary efforts of the churches to the government. Ahenakew urged equal rights and privileges for native people with respect to school education as well as some measure of native control over education in the reserves. This was a long time in coming.[25]

Native informants maintain that the dependency syndrome and alienation of their identity was inadvertently perpetuated in the parish situation through the paternalism and authoritarianism of the missionary and his wife. Too often they took control of every aspect of church life and treated their flock like children. As a woman leader in the United church complained, "We were not considered capable of doing anything ourselves."

Priscilla Joseph is one who is highly critical of the Anglican church for not giving native people any leadership training and then expecting them to take charge of their parish overnight. She is the daughter of the late Allen Ahenakew, chief for forty years at Sandy Lake Reserve. She trained as a nurse and has taken successive leadership roles in the local community, now being executive director of a drug and alcohol treatment program and co-ordinator of a new Alcohol Dependency Centre at Sandy Lake. Our conversation took place in the front room of her home in Prince Albert and was punctuated with jolly greetings and asides to members of her extended family as they drifted in to share in a sumptuous tea laid out on the dining room table.

> The minister and his wife were responsible for organizing every aspect of church life on the reserve. The women would clean the church but were given no part in preparing for services, changing the vestments, and so forth. The priest's wife did all the sacristan's duties and was always head of the Anglican Church Women on the reserve. The meetings were held in her house and she ran them, the women doing what they were told. She also represented them at national conferences. The priest in turn dominated the vestry meetings, organizing everything, and all but appointing the people who were to serve. He played a very dominant part and had complete say in choosing his Indian assistants.[26]

The consequence was that native people were for ever relegated to honourable but subservient roles in the church, as catechists, lay readers, and the like, and were given no opportunity to develop an independent, indigenous leadership. Only comparatively recently has there been a concerted attempt in the Anglican church to train a native ministry adapted to the needs of local communities. However, lay leadership training still lags far behind. A native priest told us that native people do not want to get involved in parish life. They just want to come to church, hear a good sermon, and do what they are told by the priest. Not surprisingly, a move in some dioceses to hand over responsibility to native parishes with the expectation that they would immediately become self-supporting has encountered considerable difficulties. There was no bridging in transferring leadership roles and no training in stewardship. To make matters worse decisions are taken in synod offices without consulting the people concerned on the reserves. Adam Cuthand recalled the anger which the sudden levying of parish assessments had aroused in one diocese a few years back:

When the missionaries first came the Indians were told that they would be supplied with everything they needed, clothing, shoes, the lot: that they did not have to pay anything. Now these people say, ''Why didn't you tell us that we didn't have to depend on you? Why didn't you tell us about your steward-ship policy? Now here we are struggling. We could have been self-supporting twenty years ago if we had only known. We don't want to depend on you people all the time. We want to be on our own, and we want to be consulted about every-thing that has to do with our church.''[27]

Adam emphasizes that this is part of the overall move towards self-determination, which is as much religious as political. He speaks out of his own involvement and commitment. Some years ago he wrote a high-level report warning the church that native people were now saying: ''We want to run our own affairs and do certain things ourselves. We are tired of you people being paternalistic.''

Returning to the stewardship issue, the Reverend Jimmy Isbister, another member of the Anglican Council on Native Affairs, raised further important points. He had been newly ordained as a priest and was serving the church at Sandy Lake when we first met. He questioned the rationale of enforcing a system of tithing in a community like this where up to ninety per cent are unemployed. The majority are on welfare and there is little money to spare. In no way could they support their priest. At the same time, all the year round they are involved in sacrificial giving to each other. Such is their generosity that one risks being given as a present anything one happens to admire. We came away from our travels laden with gifts, and had to resist being given more because of the problems of air travel. No native ceremony takes place without a sharing of food and gifts. At a Nisga wedding we attended at New Aiyansh we experienced an elaborate system of giving of time and money by the different clans which ensured that even the poorest couple would be able to marry in style. Jimmy Isbister is young and enthusiastic. What he wants to do on his reserve is to get a support system going by which people can give of themselves:

In this way they would be able to see that they are the ones doing the work, not the minister, and so begin to identify their responsibility. Somehow it is not the money that is going to get the people going but their giving, and they like to give of themselves. It is meaningless for them to give of their welfare money which they have not earned.[28]

Most of the native priests we met are largely self-supporting. For many this has become a bone of contention with the Anglican church because they feel that they are over-utilized and under-paid. The non-stipendiary native ministry harks back to the days when the fur trade was at its peak and there was a desperate shortage of pastoral oversight in remote areas. Trapper priests could make a good living while carrying out their tent-making ministry and were only too willing to support themselves in secular work. Later on the perpetual lack of money in mission areas led to native priests having to make their living as teachers or in some other profession.

This system evolved without malicious intent and has been perpetuated by the inability of native parishes to support their priests. The assisted dioceses of the North have in fact agreed to a policy of equalizing stipends, but only the diocese of Caledonia has a common stipend for native and non-native priests. Elsewhere there is a minimum stipend which can be added to and so the intention is abused. For some the self-supporting ministry is a meaningful vocation. But this is not the case when it is imposed because you happen to be a native person and feel called to work among your own people in a situation of poverty and deprivation. Many native priests feel greatly aggrieved by such discrimination. They voice their intense frustration at being forced to generate a living while carrying out a part-time ministry. This severely limits their priestly role and is exhausting.

Another sad legacy of the missionary era are the denominational divisions in the church. Not only was the bitter opposition between rival missions sometimes carried through into the foster-ing of hatred of each others' doctrines and even of each others' personnel, but some tribes became identified with certain denominations and this has perpetuated tribal divisions.

Thorns in the Body of an Indigenous Church

According to the Anglican primate, the Most Reverend Michael Peers, a major difficulty in the Canadian church has been that the brand of Anglicanism brought by the pioneers was Victorian evangelical. The proclamation of the gospel message was triumphalistic, focussing on the saving grace of Jesus Christ and on conversion in an other-worldly context. This theology was not strong on affirming creation, nor consciously incarnational, and has therefore not inspired a native expression of Christianity.[29]

Furthermore, redemption in the missionaries' eyes was as much from the "evil" of the native past as from any personal sense of sin, and a high level of moralizing involved total rejection of native culture and values. In fact in British Columbia it was due to the sustained efforts of the first missionaries that the potlach was outlawed by the government, totem poles destroyed, and traditional regalia and ceremonials banned. "A Call to Repentance" printed by "The Missionary" at Aiyansh in November 1917 is typical of the hell-fire preaching of the time. He rails against "the idolatry in the potlach," "the worship of the old heathen gods," and "the turning of the city hall into a heathen temple."

One can understand why the C.M.S. policy to indigenize the native church in Canada failed. The intolerance of every aspect of the native tradition was too great and the pressure towards European conformity too overwhelming. There is wide recognition of the damage done by cultural imperialism, yet the church still seems to lag far behind in its effort towards encouraging the development of an indigenous Christianity.

Indigenization is the expression of the essence of the gospel in cultural forms and thought-patterns by native people in a specific historical context. Such a contextual theology must therefore take account of socio-economic and political realities. In some parts of Canada there has of late been a measure of adaptation to native culture in the Anglican church with the introduction of sweetgrass, the sacred pipe, native regalia, drums, liturgical decoration, and so forth. Over the years considerable work has also been done in translating scriptures, hymnals, and liturgies into native languages. But when one considers the riches of the native spiritual tradition it is evident that these resources have barely been tapped. At the same time it is not for white people to tell natives how they can bring their culture into the church. For Grant the supreme failure of mission has been not to enable the Christian message to be received by native people ''in a manner that would release creative energies.'' He elaborates further:

> There have been no significant Indian contributions to theology or liturgy, and until recently no development of an indigenous Christian art. There has been only a handful of leaders influential beyond their constituencies. . . . Instead, a lack of opportunities to defend Indian culture legitimately within the church has commonly given rise to silent resistance, and such creativity as has been stimulated by Christianity has often been put at the service of movements hostile to the missions. If the measure of success is that most Indians have become Christian, the measure of failure is that Christianity has not become Indian.[30]

Grant argues that ''the factor most seriously inhibiting the transmission of Christianity in the past was a disparity in power between the senders and the receivers of the message.'' He believes that the emergence of militant Indians, articulate in their criticism of missions, ''is precisely the catalyst needed to make possible the fruitful encounter between Christianity and Indian culture.''[31] This militancy is increasingly surfacing in the church and needs to find creative outlet.

We attended an ordination of native Anglican priests in the diocese of Saskatchewan with Willy Hodgson, a member of the Council on Native Affairs. We were seated at the back of St. Alban's cathedral in Prince Albert when she suddenly took off in extreme agitation. Right opposite us was a marble plaque commemorating the death of white soldiers in an armed confrontation with native people at Duck Lake in 1885. The insensitivity of the wording was the cause of the upset. Such memorabilia, including the colours of imperial regiments, festoon many ''settler'' churches and have become symbols of the triumphs of imperialist oppression. They are something of an embarassment in that they are woven into the very fabric of the Anglican colonial tradition.

The Voice of the Voiceless in the Church

There is much talk about native issues in the church, but sadly native people claim that they are still not being listened to. This is their frustration. We were told that they do have a voice in the church, but to speak out as an Indian person tends to be perceived as being radical and therefore a threat to the status quo.

The native population in Canada is between one and two percent of the total and is on the increase. About half belong to the Roman Catholic church, which has the strongest Christian presence in the country. The largest Protestant body is the United Church of Canada, formed in 1925 by Methodists, Congregationalists, and Presbyterians. It numbers over two million but its native church is comparatively small. The Anglican Church of Canada is just under one million strong and has thirty dioceses grouped in four ecclesiastical provinces. About one quarter of all Indians are Anglican together with about eighty-five percent of the Inuit. This means that more than ten percent of Anglicans are native people. In the Arctic diocese the A.C.C. is more than eighty percent native; in Keewatin, Moosenee, and Saskatchewan between forty and fifty percent; and in Brandon, Caledonia, and Yukon about twenty-five percent. Yet few native people are said to come to church on a regular basis and even fewer find their way into the corridors of power.

One of the main challenges then has been to make way for indigenous leadership. Up until 1988 there was not a single native bishop in the Anglican Church of Canada. The appointment of an extra-diocesan bishop, such as the Maori bishop in New Zealand, is one model that was considered. But the many different native language groups would pose a problem in reconciling tribal rivalries. Instead, the diocese of Saskatchewan has taken the lead in electing a Cree-speaking suffragan bishop. Undoubtedly this will put pressure on other largely native dioceses to follow suit.

There has been some attempt in the last decade to seek native people on decision-making bodies in the Anglican church but their representation is still minimal. In the mid-1980s the only native sent to the provincial synod of Rupert's Land was from the diocese of Saskatchewan and he was one of a delegation of six. For a native person to be nominated to General Synod he or she has to compete with those who are possibly more articulate in English and are confident in working within the western parliamentary system of synodical government. Only recently were the first two native people elected to the National Executive Council of the church and by chance they are both from the Nass which limits their representation, while the Inuit, who are mostly Anglican, have not yet had a Council member. But the Council is not only unrepresentative of ethnic groups. In 1987 about thirty of the forty-five members are male and clerical (bishops and priests). There were no clergy women although the majority of the laity are women.

In urban church constituencies, where native people are heavily outnumbered by whites, racism ensures that even outstanding native men and women are invisible as potential leaders. Another difficulty is that the western way of functioning is foreign to the majority of native people so that they do not easily get elected to synod. Besides, native people find that synods deal with so many issues which are irrelevant to them. However, we have heard of a number of instances where they have taken the floor and even the most hard-bitten delegates have been moved to tears by their eloquence in speaking from the heart.

In the largely native dioceses the concern is for native people to start feeling their strength. For this they need support groups which would assist them in developing their life skills. The support groups that are already available in the church are fragmented and need to be brought together. Meetings of purely native groups in dioceses are a move forward as they provide a platform for discussing particular concerns and a means of concentrating energy in taking matters further. Where native leaders do become involved in church councils, usually in purely native affairs, the same few people become hopelessly over-extended, their time and energy consumed in fuelling the structures.

Native people in the Anglican church frequently give vent to their anger and frustration against white clergy setting themselves up as experts on native people, being given posts in charge of Indian affairs, and having total control of the training of Indian leaders. No matter that such people might have outstanding qualifications and extensive experience, the fervent wish in many places is for native people to be given charge of native work, and for them to be free to make mistakes. At church meetings bishops and clergy are said to take over and do all the talking even when they have been brought together specifically to listen to native people. And native people will not challenge this. Part of their respect is not to confront those in authority.

White priests serving in native congregations have always been held in high esteem as holy men. They would not be challenged, at least in public, because of the native people's respect for the religious power of holy men whoever they might be. The problem is that white clergy do not recognize that the source of their power is rooted in the native people's belief in the power of the shaman.[32]

Strategies for Survival

Robert K. Thomas, a Cherokee anthropologist from the United States, has identified four major characteristics essential to the survival of minority peoples around the world. In an article entitled "The Tap Roots of Peoplehood" he gives these characteristics as their own language, a unified religious base, a tie to a particular piece of land, and a sacred history. For native people in Canada all these aspects of survival are seriously at risk.

Language is the most important symbol of native identity because it is at the heart of native culture and spirituality. It is in the area of language that cultural institutes, school education, and conferences are doing good work in trying to recover that which has been lost. The Saskatchewan Indian Languages Institute hosted the first meeting in Canada of the Native American Languages Issues Institute at Saskatoon in May 1987, while the World Conference on Indigenous People's Education was held in Vancouver in June 1987. Of note is the fact that the focus in both conferences was the survival of distinctive indigenous cultures. Delegates found that it did not matter what part of the world they came from, nor whether they were Christian or not, the survival of their aboriginal identity depended on their learning their language and cultural traditions. This in turn was integrally related to the recovery of their native spirituality. One delegate to the Vancouver conference reported that "our young people are hungry for their identity. They need to know who they are in order to use their education in the right way."

Undoubtedly education is a determining factor in the survival of a distinct people, and in recent years there have been exciting developments in Canada as a result of native people taking over control of school education. For native people education is seen as a total way of life and the cultural revitalization programs are aimed at developing the whole person: body, spirit, and mind. So for example, there are native cultural survival schools across Canada which in different ways try to promote and preserve native language, values, and history. The Sacred Circle Project in Edmonton is directed at urban native children while the bilingual-bicultural program in the Nass Valley is specific to the Nisga people.[33]

All these programs have a spiritual dimension and native elders are constantly called upon to contribute their knowledge and experience. Attention has also been given to the training of native teachers to fulfil new educational roles and native studies programs are provided at various institutes of higher education. At the same time, there is a strong move to upgrade native education so that native people can be suitably equipped for survival in the dominant society. Chief Dan George is frequently quoted in this context:

> Like the thunderbird of old, I shall rise again out of the sea, I shall grab the instruments of the white man's success — his education, his skills. With these new tools I shall build my race into the proudest segment of society.

One of the main difficulties in getting native parents to take control of education in the reserves is apathy. This is born from bitter memories of their own schooling in times past. Poor school attendance and a high incidence of early drop-outs reflect the gravity of the problem. Attempts have been made to make education more relevant to young native people through mother-tongue education, adaptation of the curriculum, and the provision of better school facilities on the reserves. But some children cannot see the point of learning native languages as this will not help them in the wider world, while for many others higher education still has negative associations with the white way of life. Educated native people continue to be confronted with community suspicion. As Sykes Powderface, an educated Stoney native, explains, "Anybody with education, anybody accustomed or oriented to the dominant society's customs, is looked on as an apple — red on the outside but white on the inside."[34]

The suspicion of reserve native people is well founded because missionaries robbed the converts of their corporate spirituality and replaced it with a privatized spirituality. This is well expressed by Bowden and Ronda in their introduction to Eliot's *Indian Dialogues*:

> Christianity threatened to destroy that aboriginal under-standing of community. It menaced tribal solidarity by declar-ing that only individuals could be saved. The new faith separated them from all the rest who did not share its privi-leged status. This palpable exclusivism was a logical extension of Puritan doctrine. Its disruption of corporate identity stemmed from the fundamental belief that Indians, like all human beings, were permanently separated into the elect and non-elect, destined by God never to see each other again after this lifetime.[35]

Not only did the western gospel of individualism destroy the native understanding of corporate identity and destiny, but it also introduced divisive notions of class status and upward mobility.

What must always be remembered is that native cultures have not remained "pure and undefiled" by culture contact. Rather, they have been caught up in the historical process of change, and political, economic, and social influences have all left their mark. There can thus be no return to some romanticized pre-contact religion, because religion like every other aspect of culture is linked with present experience and is constantly responding to change. What is possible, though, is to recover the fundamental insights of native spirituality. This has never been lost and can be reawakened: "And then our hearts will once again dance with the pride of long ago and the circle will be complete."

Strategies for the survival of native culture have included the continued practice of native customs and rituals on the reserves, often in secret, and the handing down of the oral tradition in the mother tongue. The isolation of reserves has been a contributory factor as has a persistent sense of "Indianness" even among the educated elite.

Native Christians are in the forefront of cultural revival movements as they try to recover their lost identity and fill the spiritual void of a western belief system. Edward Ahenakew was way ahead of his time when in the 1920s he wrote, ''It is through knowing our past that we can come to know ourselves; if a man understands himself his heart is strong to meet the difficulties of life.''[36] But this is not without its problems as was pointed out to us by Reg Henry, a speaker of the longhouse on the Six Nations Iroquois reserve at Ohsweken, whom we met at the Victoria Day celebrations in May.

On this day each year every member of the reserve gets a block of cheese and a thick slice of bread as a treasured legacy from Queen Victoria. Nine long trestle tables were set up in the sports arena and were laden with mounds of bright yellow cheese and trays of freshly baked warm bread. After doing our stint at cutting up cheese, we were thankful to relax on the raked seats of the stadium in conversation with Reg Henry. He first explained his role as a speaker of the longhouse as being nothing more than the representative of the people in making contact with the spirits. He then discussed the move among the young to try and recover their past traditions and of the difficulties involved:

> University people are coming back because they are beginning to realize what they have missed, what really makes us Indian. They sit down and want things explained and they are becoming involved with the traditional doings that go on in the longhouse. But it is really difficult to be Indian in a white community because you have to be two people, one person fitting in with the white way of life when you go up to town, and a different person at home. Even on the reserve you have to be two people as this is basically a Christian community. At one time there was a lot of discrimination against longhouse people. Yet what people don't realize is that it is the few traditional people that make the whole reserve Indian because by their traditional beliefs they maintain the old way of life and keep the language. When we lose our language we lose our longhouse tradition.[37]

Later, as the bread and cheese ceremony got underway and young and old filed into the arena to get their share, we spoke with Hubert Buck, another speaker of the longhouse. Our conversation was punctuated by the boisterous playing of a brass band, the musicians all resplendent in native dress, and the happy laughter and shouted greetings of the milling mob below. But Hubert, his peaked cap firmly planted on his head, was chillingly serious as he spoke about his own identity and the forces that continue to be ranged against his culture:

> I am not an Indian. I am a native of the North American continent. It was Columbus who called us Indians. Since his time the white man has done his best to kill off the native people. He took away the language, he took away the country, he took everything away. There are ancient prophecies in my religion which say that he is going to keep on doing it too. If they left me alone right now where I am without taking anything more away I would call it justice. But we are not going to get justice. And the white man is going to turn the native people's mind so that he is going to work against his own people.[38]

In other areas of Canada the breakdown of native society has led to the church becoming an alternative community, a group apart; and a strenuous conformity to the norms of the new way of life gave a sense of belonging and security. The church thus provided a new social network. Nina Burnham, a former chairperson of the Council on Native Affairs and an Anglican representative on the Canadian Council of Churches (1985-7), was our host at Six Nations Iroquois reserve, where she is also a band councillor. Her family has been active in the Anglican church since the horse-and-buggy days of her grandparents. Her grandmother attended the Huron diocesan synod in the 1930s, while her mother was past president of the Ladies' Guild, now the Anglican Church Women. The whole family, men and women, were in the church choir and sang at all the festivities on the reserve. Nina emphasized that

> people identify closely with their church. In a sense they are married to one church only, the church on the reserve built by the old people. This is their identity, the place where they were born and raised, where they feel secure and at home. In the old days the church was the centre of the reserve and

everything evolved from it, politics, religion, and social life. But although this has changed now the church still holds people together.[39]

However, church education also provided an avenue for social mobility in moving out into the wider western world, and in the urban migration the sense of belonging to a religiously based community in which all knew their place, as of old, fell away. Many people told us that urban native people will not participate in urban church life and choose to go home to the reserves for all special occasions such as baptisms, confirmations, weddings, the celebration of Eucharist, wakes, and funerals. Bea Cuthand relates that some churches in Regina have tried picking up native people in buses and vans to take them to church. "That's not our way," she says. "I feel people should come on their own and not be bribed to come and that it does more harm than good."[40]

Willy Hodgson hosted us for ten days in Saskatchewan and she took us to visit her many relations still living at Sandy Lake Reserve and roundabout. Through her we were able to experience the strength of the extended family network which finds its roots on the reserve; but our ability to absorb culture shock was tested to the full by our turning up each night at a different relative's without prior warning. Willy's confidence in native hospitality was amply rewarded but our nerves were somewhat shredded by the end. On the Sunday we joined family and friends at St. Mark's parish church. The church was built at the head of Sandy Lake so that the bell would echo over the water, calling people to worship. Willy's memories of St. Mark's go back to her childhood when the women would sit on the left, the men on the right. Her ties to the place are still strong even after a long absence:

> When we go back to our churches we have a community of people and a community of acceptance. The Christian community opens its arms and embraces us. We never have to worry about that. We walk into our church and we are in total communion.[41]

This is in stark contrast to the racially mixed churches in towns and cities where native people continue as outsiders even after many years on the parish roll. This is Willy's experience:

I feel I am at the fence of the church looking in. The bulk of us do not feel we are even part of this society. We are the original people of this land but we have been disenfranchized in so many ways. Being a second-class citizen stops us from feeling part of most institutions. I have been attending the same parish church for twenty-one years. For about fifteen of those I was mostly invisible. If I hadn't put some energy behind being visible myself I don't think anyone would have known my name.[42]

Chapter 4

Pouring out of Native Wine-skins

Recovering the Ancient Native Spirit

> No one puts a piece of unshrunken cloth onto an old cloak, because the patch pulls away from the cloak and the tear gets worse. Nor do people put new wine into old wine-skins; otherwise, the skins burst, the wine runs out, and the skins are lost. No, they put new wine in fresh skins and both are preserved.[1]

The vintage wine of the good news was brought to the Turtle Island by the European races in their European wine-skins. Today these containers can no longer be expected to hold the wine and would burst if their use was continued in the native setting. The old European wine-skins, however nicely dressed and cured, have to be put aside in favour of their native counterparts if the wine of the gospel is to be rendered palatable and acceptable at the native feast. The fire-water which the early settlers sold to the native people in exchange for furs and food left them derelict only on a physical and emotional level; but the wine of the white man's religion, poured out of his wine-skins, has created a more deplorable kind of drunkenness at a much deeper spiritual level, robbing native people of their soul and their identity. The vintage gospel somehow seems to turn flat and even sour when poured out of alien Caucasian containers. The wine indeed needs new wine-skins made by native people for themselves, and then the good news of Jesus Christ, the keeper of the heavenly vineyard, shall ferment and sparkle.

Some may question the wisdom of discarding European ways of Christian worship and would advocate a judicious blend of the European and the native. But our research of Christian spirituality on the reservations reveals that it is not feasible to put native patches on old European cloaks, muddling the ancient native spirit. The old, worn-out, colonial wine-skins of Europe have outlived their usefulness for the resurrected native spirituality. The new Native Vision Quest of the year 2000 should avail itself of new native wine-skins.

What, may we ask, are these new native wine-skins which are henceforth to hold the wine of the gospel? They are countless, rich, and unique: native myths, legends, customs, rituals, symbols, chants, dances, music, drums, the peace pipe, storytelling, sign language, blankets, robes, vestments, carvings, masks, banners, paintings, totem symbolism, folk games, furnishings, altar cloths, architecture, oratory, languages, funeral customs, sweetgrass, sweat lodges, vision quests, invocations to the Great Spirit, silence, contemplation, humour, wisdom of the elders, community spirit, nature mysticism, healing, prophecy, and so forth. This would be a truly catholic faith incarnated in a liturgy shot through with native colour, scent, sound, and breath. Surely Jesus Christ is the same yesterday, today, tomorrow, and for ever more; and it is the same everlasting gospel, but the shape, form, and manner in which it is preached, received, and lived out is bound to vary from people to people. Yes, the time has come to ferment the ever new vintage wine of the gospel in the new native wine-skins listed above. This sacramental symbol should underlie the church's vision of future mission and evangelism among the native people. The emphasis is not so much on discarding the European ways of worship but on rehabilitating ways which were so ruthlessly jettisoned. Our concern is the recovery of the ancient native spirit.

Those Who Paved the Way

Up until now the native pioneers of the Anglican church have been depicted by white historians as imbibing the wine of the gospel in its unadulterated Caucasian flavour, preaching a message of salvation which called for a radical break with all past traditions and total conformity to the new. However, such assumptions need to be reassessed with care. Neither Henry Budd nor James Settee, the first two native people to be ordained to the ministry, spent any length of time in a protected mission enclave under white supervision. Budd spent many years heading his own mission, while Settee itinerated among his people.

The strength of their ministry lay in their ability to preach in their own Cree language, using their native thought-patterns and imagery, and drawing on their Cree history and folklore. While they also picked up the English tongue and European ways and were critical of many native practices, they were never totally cut off from their roots as was the case with so many later native converts to Christianity. A reappraisal of their writing from a native point of view could well bring to light the very "Indianness" of their teaching and the seeds of a native national consciousness. We have not space to do justice to their diaries; moreover, their writing only gives half their story. We have met several old people who regaled us with a wealth of anecdotes which testify to these first priests' loyalty to their aboriginal identity.

Both Budd and Settee were protegés of the Reverend John West who was sent to the Red River settlement (Fort Garry), south of Lake Winnipeg, in 1820, as a special representative of the newly formed Church Missionary Society and chaplain to the Hudson's Bay Company. West's main brief was to found a school for native children. This became the North-West American Mission of the C.M.S., near where St. John's College stands today. West did not last long in his post, but his school spawned the first indigenous leaders in the Anglican church. He began with two young boys, Henry Budd (Sakace-wescam) and James Hope, whom he had picked up on his canoe journey from York Factory to Red River. James Settee and Charles Pratt were among those who joined them. All four were Cree-speaking but typically they were given English names at baptism. For West the Red River was "a Heathen land, which Satan hath held bound . . . probably since the Creation of the world." Nonetheless, he at least learnt to speak Cree, unlike his successors at Red River who saw the native converts' learning of English as the only sure way to Christianity.[2]

In line with their policy elsewhere in the world, the C.M.S. was concerned to have native agents in the field and so it was that Hope, Pratt, Budd, and Settee were sent out as catechists and teachers to various Indian settlements. Hope ended up at one of the Battleford reserves, Pratt served many faithful years at Touchwood Hills, while Budd and Settee became priests.

In 1840 Henry Budd was sent to open a mission on the lower Saskatchewan River. He eventually settled at The Pas, an old

French trading post and a favourite native camping ground about half way between the Hudson's Bay posts of Cumberland House and Moose Lake. As in so many other parts of the world the way had been prepared by the indigenous people themselves. Messengers of the local chief had been directed to spend a winter at Red River finding out about the book which was reputed to contain the words of the Great Spirit, and had spread the gospel message ahead of Budd. But he himself was a gifted teacher. Adam Cuthand describes how his reputation as "a story-teller of a wonderful news" spread rapidly to other native settlements with people coming from far and wide to hear him. Within two years he had prepared eighty-five people for baptism. By 1848 the number of baptized had reached four hundred. As elsewhere baptisms were the yardstick of a mission's success and great encouragement to the sending body. Theirs was not to reason why a breakdown of native society was leading to mass conversions, nor to confront the causes of this social dislocation.

Budd was ordained deacon in 1850 and priested two years later. Apart from a ten-year stint at Fort à La Corne, where he opened up the Nipawawin mission (now Nipawin), he remained at The Pas. For part of this time he worked under an English missionary, James Hunter, teaching him Cree and assisting him in translating the Prayer Book, while Hunter helped him prepare for ordination. But for the rest Budd was in charge of his own mission. He was as concerned as his white colleagues to implement a civilizing program through various agricultural pursuits. Even though he had only half their stipend his mission station was "a model of neatness and good order," much to the satisfaction of his white superiors. At the same time, all his services were in Cree, and he was said to be "a fluent and forcible speaker . . . gifted with a strong but mellow voice."[3] There is no doubt that the fact that he was a native, drawing on the idiom and traditions of his people and knowledgeable of their ways, enabled them to retain some of their past traditions in coming to terms with the new. He died in 1875 and is commemorated in the Anglican church calender on 2 April.

James Settee was sent further north to open a mission at Lac la Ronge in the Churchill River area. Here too a native called Kayanwas, "The Prophet," had gone ahead with the good news so that Settee found many ready to listen to his teaching. In 1847 one hundred and seven native people were baptized. After his ordination in 1853 Settee went to work among the Plains Cree said to be "the wildest and most savage in the country" at that time. Over the years he was attached to a number of different missions in what are now the dioceses of Qu'Appelle and Saskatchewan, moving from place to place as he was needed. When urged to establish a permanent mission in a favourable place, he resorted to the Bible injunction that "here we have no continuing city." Settee retired to Red River and died in 1902, "almost unnoticed by the Church."

A biographer makes the embarassing comment that although he mixed a good deal with white people, "civilization never spoiled his native simplicity"[4] Settee seemed to retain his native identity in the midst of his busy missionary flurries. He did not allow himself to be converted to white ways, though he converted to the Christian faith. This supreme ability to sift the essence of the gospel from the trappings of western culture marks Settee as a pioneer in the struggle to fight for the integrity of native spirituality in the bewildering labyrinth of modern civilization.

It is an open secret that in the colonial churches non-Europeans always kept their feelings and perceptions to themselves. Even a slight disagreement, whether in secular or theological matters, would have compromised their position. Originality, which held the promise of retaining or reviving indigenous spirituality, was summarily branded a heresy. Their insights were not asked for nor welcomed when offered. Native people have been painfully aware of this silent conspiracy to castrate their creativity but for obvious reasons would never talk about it to white people.

Stan Cuthand pointed out to us the significance of Settee's first baptism as being a community affair. Settee saw the importance of the group as a whole committing itself to Christ, as in the early church and also in conformity with the corporate communal bias of native spirituality. Settee was moving towards evolving a uniquely native theology of baptism. This was something which the missionaries failed to understand in their emphasis on personal salvation. Stan went on to tell how Settee came to set down "The Story of the Four Winds" in his unpublished journal.

Settee had gone to a big feast of the Swampy Crees, at which his grandfather had been chosen leader, to pray and to speak.

There in this great big tent his grandfather was asked to say something that his people would remember, so he told them ''The Story of the Four Winds.'' This is a story of a man and a woman, and of how the four directions to which we raise our pipes came into being together with flint and rabbit. Settee wrote down the story just as his grandfather had told it. Old Testament stories would have been more meaningful to him and his generation than the New Testament ones because they were more like the Cree stories. But this story remained hidden away in his diary until recently. That side of Settee has only just come to light.[5]

Clearly Settee's itinerant ministry enabled him to retain strong links with native traditions and freed him from the straight-jacket of the mission establishment. This needs to be explored and reflected upon.

Native converts to Christianity in different parts of the world have often been the first to record the myths and legends of their people because they have been the first to become literate. Historically they have thus had a pivotal role in laying the foundations for cultural nationalism among the newly educated indigenous elite. But the European hierarchy in the colonial churches has always tried to keep a heavy hold over any possible radical talent in their midst that might threaten the balance of power. In the case of James Settee and Edward Ahenakew the fear of upsetting their superiors could well have put the lid on any seemingly contentious activities during their lifetime. And celebrating their native past could have been explosive. Moreover, it is only since the late 1960s that native literature has received much government encouragement. Ahenakew went as far as he could in getting his *Cree Trickster Tales* published in *The Journal of American Folk-lore* (Vol. 42) in 1929, and in writing articles on health, agriculture, education, and world news for his *Cree Monthly Guide*, which he translated into Cree syllabics and printed and distributed himself during the 1920s. He also assisted in compiling the Cree-English dictionary, left unfinished by the death of Archdeacon Mackay in 1923. But his manuscript, written about 1950 on ''the Cree Indians and the work that has been done among them by our missionaries in Saskatchewan,'' giving an account of native religious beliefs, has never appeared in print.

Ahenakew's long years of service to the church as general Indian missionary for the diocese of Saskatchewan were recognized by Emmanuel College in Saskatoon in 1947 when it conferred on him the honorary degree of Doctor of Divinity, the first to any native person.

Peter Jones was the first person of native blood to be ordained in the Methodist church. Born in 1802 of a white father and a Mississauga mother, he was known as Sacred Feathers (Kahkewaquonaby) and had a traditional upbringing. As a youth he went on a Vision Quest and although he never had a vision nor acquired a guardian spirit, he was steeped in native lore and custom. Only later did he join his father and become baptized in the Church of England. In his book, *Sacred Feathers*, Donald Smith has drawn extensively on Jones's own writings to tell the story of his life: his conversion at a Methodist camp meeting in 1823, his evangelism as ''a missionary to the Indian Tribes'' in a circuit nearly fifteen hundred kilometres in circumference, his translations of the Bible and Methodist hymns into Ojibway, his marriage to an Englishwoman, his fight to preserve the remainder of his people's land, his involvement in schools and agriculture, and much more. Jones is seen as a bridging figure, a bilingual and bicultural go-between who was able to facilitate the Mississauga's adjustment to European culture and their survival as a cohesive group. But even though his part-native identity enabled him to interpret Christian doctrine in terms which his native brethren could readily understand, he was still committed to presenting the gospel in European wine-skins. He is a step further removed from Settee's sense of loyalty to the native tradition.

The Roman Catholic response to their native pioneers in the church has been somewhat different. They have taken a saintly figure, Kateri Tekakwitha, the Blessed Lily of the Mohawks, and made her into a cultic symbol for a Catholic Indian folk religion to integrate Catholicism with native culture and spirituality.

Kateri was born in 1656 in Ossernenon, ''the village of the Jesuit martyrs,'' to a Mohawk father and an Algonquin mother. Her parents died from smallpox during her infancy and she was left disfigured and with poor eyesight. Baptized at the age of twenty-one she had to take refuge at Caughnawaga, the Christian Mohawk village at Sault-Saint-Louis, allegedly because of her resolve to remain a virgin. But claims of persecution because of her conversion to Christianity have been exaggerated. If she was in fact persecuted it was equally likely because of her physical appearance, her ineligibility as a bride, her orphaned status, and her association with the Jesuits whose motives were suspect to the traditional native peoples. Attributing her persecution to her alleged virginity and her new faith is sidetracking the issue much as the Jewish-born German nun Edith Stein was claimed to have been persecuted under the Nazis for her Catholic faith.

For the next three years, until her death in 1680, Kateri became renowned for her extreme piety and asceticism, sleeping on a bed of thorns, being flagellated with willow branches by a friend, and placing burning coals between her toes. Kateri's many biographers (around fifty!) have had a field day in extolling her supposedly Christian virtues, but in fact some of her tests of endurance can be linked with a traditional native upbringing and training to endure physical pain. The vow of chastity was her most radical break with her past. During her last illness many came to her bedside to receive blessings. An Iroquois custom allowed dying people to sing on their death-bed. Kateri preached to her visitors, some of whom were converted. Veneration and devotion to her arose after her death and people claimed healing through her intercession, a tradition which continues to this day. She was beatified in 1980, a first step towards canonization. Her feast day is celebrated on 14 July.

Twin factors have brought on a renewed interest in native spirituality among Roman Catholics in recent times: an attitude of openness to other faiths shown by the Second Vatican Council and the Freedom of Religion Bill passed in the United States in 1978. This Bill made way for a resurgence of formerly outlawed practices such as the sweetgrass ceremony, the Sun Dance, and the sweat lodge, and this rapidly spread to Canada. The founding of the Tekakwitha National Conference at Grand Falls, Montana, in 1977 was part of the new initiative taken by Catholics to find a place for native culture and religious practices within their church. These developments were given the final seal of approval when Pope John Paul II addressed native Canadians in Quebec in September 1984. The pope spoke about injustices in the past, the present need for forgiveness and reconciliation, and the right to native self-determination. He then confronted the question of how native Americans might be loyal to their own culture as well as to the faith-tradition shared by all in the Catholic church:

> Your encounter with the Gospel has not only enriched you, it has enriched the Church . . . the Gospel does not destroy what is best in you. On the contrary, it enriches as it were from within the spiritual qualities and gifts that are distinctive of your cultures. . . . In addition, your Amerindian and Inuit traditions permit the development of new ways of expressing the message of salvation. . . . There can be no question of adulterating the word of God or of emptying the cross of its power; but rather of Christ animating the very centre of all culture. Not only is Christianity relevant to the Indian peoples, but Christ, in the members of His Body, is Himself Indian.

In 1986 the Tekakwitha Conference celebrated the appointment of Father John Hascall, OFM Cap., as their first native president, and Father Donald Pelotte, SSS, as the first Catholic native bishop in North America. Father Hascall is of the Chippewa band of Sault Ste. Marie of the Ojibway nation and has the distinction of being the only medicine man who is also a Catholic priest. Through his example native Catholics have been encouraged to bring their native tradition into the Christian liturgical setting such as the praising of the Creator through the sacred pipe, praying to the four directions, purification through the ceremonies of the sweetgrass and the sweat lodge, drumming and dancing, powwows, songs and stories, and devising new liturgies which can be set in the tribal milieu. The Tekakwitha movement is kept active as far north as the Arctic through regular workshops and courses, pilgrimages to the Kateri shrine, prayer and healing services, youth activities, a newsletter, and the co-ordinating of the many Kateri Circles in native parishes. The Blessed Kateri has thus been pressed into service by the hierarchy of the Catholic church as an overarching symbol to unite all native people under the umbrella of the Catholic church.

Some aboriginal Catholics have been disturbed by these attempts to use native symbols to strengthen the church's hold on their people. A papal visit to the Tekakwitha Conference Center in September 1987 seemed to consolidate this hold. The pontiff described the Blessed Kateri as the best known witness of Christian holiness among the native peoples of North America. . . . Even when she dedicated herself fully to Jesus Christ, to the point of taking the prophetic step of making a vow of perpetual virginity, she always remained what she was, a true daughter of her people, following her tribe in the hunting seasons and continuing her devotions in the environment most suited to her way of life, before a rough cross carved by herself in the forest. The Gospel of Jesus Christ . . . is never in contrast with what is noble and pure in the life of any tribe or nation, since all good things are his gifts.

One wonders if the mordantly anti-sensual lifestyle of the Blessed Kateri would not radically militate against the positively sensual genius of the nation! Kateri appears to be more a product of Latin patristic misogyny than a flowering of Canadian native spirituality.

The Roman Catholic church in Canada has fostered other places of pilgrimage for Christian Indians such as the shrine of the Jesuit martyrs at Ste. Marie-among-the-Hurons in Huronia, and the shrine of Ste. Anne de Beaupré in Quebec. Much publicized papal visits to these sites in the last few years have helped to add to their prestige as holy places and so augment their authority and power as symbols of unity for native Catholics. In this way the Roman Catholic church has attempted to overcome the tribal divisions which have so often plagued the Protestant church. But is this make-believe unity a welcome sign if it is achieved at the cost of co-opting native spirituality into a Roman world, and by trivializing the diversity and uniqueness of the spiritual traditions of different native cultures?

Music and Liturgy in the Church

No account of Indian religious practices is complete without some reference to music, to singing, chanting, dancing, and drumming. And yet one Anglican bishop, noting the total absence of indigenous Indian music in the Canadian church, wondered whether native people had any music whatsoever in their tradition.

Luther Standing Bear points out that ''hard as it is for the white man's ear to sense the differences, Indian songs are as varied as the many emotions which inspire them, for no two of them are alike.''[6] Singing is at the very heart of the native way of life. There would be singing in all the tents before any sort of expedition, singing as they sallied forth into battle, a horse-song before a horse-stealing foray, a buffalo song before a buffalo chase, songs for fishing and songs for hunting, songs for every kind of religious ritual, songs at burials and songs at weddings. A good singer was always in great demand. The mood of the song varied according to the occasion. The Song of Victory was lively and the notes high to express the exultation of the warrior or hunter riding triumphantly home over the prairies. Battle songs were solemn and urgent, to fire young men with courage, while songs of death were full of praise. Among the prairie people a young man would be taught his very own song by a spirit in his Vision Quest and he would use it to call on the spirit for help in times of direst need. This song was more than a signature tune because it gave him his identity and invested him with sacred power. A dying man would be heard singing his song with his last breath.

Luther Standing Bear recalls how the Indians' worship of life was expressed in dance:

> The Indian wants to dance! It is his way of expressing devotion, of communing with unseen power, and in keeping his tribal identity. When the Lakota heart was filled with high emotion, he danced. . . . When his blood ran hot with success of the hunt or chase, he danced. When his heart was filled with pity for the orphan, the lonely father, or bereaved mother, he danced. All the joys and exultations of life, all his gratefulness and thankfullness, all his acknowledgments of the mysterious power that guided life, and all his aspirations for a better life, culminated in one great dance — the Sun Dance. Today we see our young people dancing together the silly jazz — dances that add nothing to the beauty and fineness of our lives and certainly nothing to our history, while the dances that record the life annals of a people die.[7]

For the prairie people ritualistic dances like the Sun Dance were held in the same place every year, ''while ceremonial dances, which were simply community socials in which any dancer could join, were danced on any flat area that the tribe fancied.''[8] They would think nothing of dancing for days on end at the great religious celebrations. The varied dances were not just sportive and athletic in character, but had a spiritual dimension. When the native person danced, he prayed with his body.

For the early missionaries native music and dancing was as much ''the devil's work'' as any other aspect of their tradition. The Jesuits, bent on saving souls, lost no time in using church music as part of their armoury for incarnating Jesus among native people. The composition of ''Jesus Ahatonhia,'' now called ''The Huron Carol,'' is attributed to Father Jean de Brébeuf, about 1641-2. The words were in the vernacular but the tune was taken from a fifteenth century carol, ''A Young Maiden.'' The carol was sung by Christian Hurons each Christmas until the Jesuit missionaries died at the hands of the Iroquois in 1649. John Webster Grant notes that the translation of the hymn is ''by no means literal, and 'Gitchi Manitou' figured in Algonquian rather than Huron theology.''[9] What is important though is the way native imagery is smuggled into Christianity. Jesus is born in a lodge of broken bark and wrapped in ''a ragged robe of rabbit skin.'' ''The hunter braves,'' ''sons of Manitou,'' come and kneel before him in adoration. Manitou is co-opted into the Christian deity, while angel choirs take the place of bird and animal spirits. The first verse reads:

'Twas in the moon of wintertime,
when all the birds had fled,
that mighty Gitchi Manitou
sent angel choirs instead;
before their light the stars grew dim,
and wondering hunters heard the hymn:
Jesus your King is born, Jesus is born,
in excelsis gloria.

The different Protestant denominations were all eager to translate their hymnals into the various vernacular languages as speedily as possible, together with the Bible, prayer books, liturgies, and catechisms. These linguistic feats were a source of much triumph to mission societies. However, there seems to have been little concern to encourage the composition of an indigenous church music which would readily meet the emotional and aesthetic needs of native people, either in words or music. Hymn-tunes from England were transplanted as part of the colonial church legacy to the Canadian Indians.

Native music, drumming, and dancing were banned. In the audio-visual meditation on native spirituality based on the testimony of the late Archdeacon Andrew Ahenakew, "Sometimes We Burn . . . Sometimes We Tremble," he testifies to the powerful pull of his Cree tradition when he heard the drumming of the Rain Dance and the Sun Dance, and his bewilderment at their being out of bounds:

> That's the Indian culture, the best. When my father taught in White Fish Lake there used to be drums. We weren't allowed to go. I was baffled, my two younger brothers were baffled. What went wrong, we would like to have gone. Our hearts were there but we weren't allowed. So that's the way we were raised.[10]

Not all missions were that strictly regimented. Adam Cuthand recounts that on the Little Pine Reserve his father was a great singer in the Sun Dance *and* an active Christian, but much was driven underground. The dances were held across the river out of the missionary's way. "The only pressure came from the white lady teacher at the mission school," he recollects with a laugh, "she knew what was going on but she couldn't stop it even though she tried." His brother Stan maintains that his father's generation did not see a conflict because they never went to school. They only accepted from the church what was meaningful to them and ignored the rest. Smitty Atimoyoo, a contemporary of the Cuthands at Little Pine in the 1920s, remembers the teacher's anger as the children went running down the hill after school singing native songs. Forty years later Adam was publicly quoted as encouraging the return of the once-banned Indian dances: "The Indians took on Christianity and threw away the drum. Dances can play a major role in bringing to the eyes of each new generation the cultural heritage that is theirs by birthright." The lady teacher, now retired, was horrified to read these words. Referring back to the Sun Dance at Little Pine each summer, she stated her case: "I felt that it was against all that we were trying to teach the pupils and their parents. Little Pine was a small and ignorant reserve — superstition was rife."[11]

When the Cuthand brothers were asked about the possibilities of introducing native church music into the Anglican church, Stan retorted that the church in the prairie reserves is controlled by a conservative element. They want it to remain the same no matter that young people are leaving it in search of something more authentic. The Cree hymns are all translations and yet native people have this rich tradition of music which remains untapped in the church. Adam believes that drums and singing could easily have fitted into the liturgy of the church. He recalls a baptism service in Toronto in which he successfully used a drum at the bidding of an African bishop when the organist did not turn up, and the efforts of a Chinese priest in the Huron diocese to use drums and Indian singers in the liturgy. But he notes the problems:

> We have been so brainwashed that a drum is seen as being evil. There are also difficulties with Indian-style singing because they use notes which are quarter tone. People who are not used to it say it is just like coyotes howling.[12]

Choirs and brass bands were the church's answer in finding a cultural replacement for the native musical tradition; and the schools provided the training ground for this musical transformation. Annual competitions of both choir and band helped to reinforce the new anglicized identity. The church bands seem to owe their popularity to their being a form of strongly rhythmic music which was acceptable to missionary sensibilities. In some native areas today leadership of choir or band is as much prized a status symbol as leadership of any social institution. One old Iroquois lady at the Six Nations Reserve recalled her excitement at hearing the brass band striking up the old marches: "It kind of hits you in the heart when the drum goes Boom, Boom, Boom."

The Reverend Percy Tait, chief and priest at New Aiyansh, plays the drum in the Church Army band. The brass band was introduced into the Nass Valley as part of the Church Army tradition in order to channel enthusiasm during an Anglican revival in 1893.

Evangelical hymns and jolly tunes were belted out with trumpet and drum on every public occasion, social and religious, and this tradition continues to this day. At a Nisga wedding we attended in New Aiyansh in June 1987 it was the brass band which opened the reception with a hearty rendering of popular musical items. But, as Percy recollects, past associations with the drum were suspect. At a Church Army training course in the mid-1930s the English instructors would not allow the drum to be played. However, it was back in use as soon as the instructors left. Percy has no hesitation in using it himself:

> The drum fits into the pulse of a person's heartbeat and so releases joy. You fit into the rhythm of creation through the drum. But people's emotions can be manipulated through changing the rhythm of the drumbeat and this would be wrong.[13]

Others in the church agree that drumming quickens their blood and awakens a longing for their native roots. One person confessed, ''The beat of the drum tells me that I have come home. I need to belong some place because it seems that I have never belonged.'' Another said, ''Even if we go to church we still long to join in the dancing when we hear the rhythm of the drum.'' Now a growing number of native Christians are taking part no matter what the church's stand. Dr. Oliver Brass, president of the Saskatchewan Indian Federated College at the University of Regina and a former minister in the Free Methodist church, describes the emotional impact of his first experience of one of the four Winter Sings that precede a Rain Dance:

> There we were, in a smoky room in a house full of people, the women on one side and the men on the other. There was a lot of singing around the drum, the men singing songs that had been given them directly through revelation or had been handed down to them. They burnt sweetgrass and sage, passed round pipes and made speeches. I realized that day that I was looking at the heart of Indianness. I knew that I was Indian, that I was brown. But I had never seen the heart of Indianness until that day.[14]

The musical vacuum in the native church has been filled with revivalist songs, charismatic choruses, Salvation Army hymns, and gospel songs, all to the accompaniment of guitars or brass bands. "Amazing Grace" is a favourite in Ojibway, Mohawk, Cree, and Nisga. Translations of British hymns continue to be sung in the many native languages, usually very slowly, and falteringly where the language has been lost to everyday use. Among the Dene and the Inuit there is a certain amount of authentic native church music, mostly without words. This is difficult to write down in a western musical idiom. But where are the native mass settings, praises, and chants for use in church worship?

The Catholic church has been the most innovative in developing an indigenous native liturgy. Starkloff notes that as a result of a cautious dialogue in certain places there has been some measure of adaptation although genuine inculturation is still far off. Native elements which have been incorporated into Catholic worship include "the drums, cedar and sweetgrass incense, water blessings, ceremonial dance, sign language, costumes and the prayers of elders at the eucharistic liturgy." In some places funeral rites have become "typically native, with modern additions," and aspects of the native name-giving rite have been linked with the rite of baptism. At the Kisemanito Centre at Grouard in Alberta, the Oblates have inspired an indigenous mass in Cree with indigenous music. Some of Starkloff's more radical suggestions are that a sweat lodge could become the environment for the sacrament of reconciliation, and the eucharist could be celebrated within the setting of the Sun Dance.[15]

The Reverend John Alexander Mackay, C.M.S. missionary and archdeacon of Saskatchewan, was responsible for rendering the Anglican liturgy into Cree. The prayer book and hymns were a straight translation using Cree syllabics as well as Roman script, Mackay's part-Indian ancestry no doubt facilitating his fluency in the Cree idiom. This work was begun in the 1890s, and there have been some modest revisions since then, but a major overhaul is necessary together with the composition of a Cree liturgy which reflects their own spirituality. Adam Cuthand speaks of the difficulties in capturing the essence of Cree expression in translation. This is where the elders can play their part.

Ian Mackenzie suggests that indigenization is not just a matter of using native symbols or native music or even native language. Where native communities have received the tradition of the 1662 prayer book service and selectively made it their own, other forces may be at work. So for example, foot washings on Maundy Thursday and the veneration of the cross on Good Friday, genuflecting, using the sign of the cross and holy water may have become outmoded elsewhere in the church but can be very much part of the Christian spirituality of a specific community and a symbol of indigenization. What is happening underneath is that they have made a connection between the outward expression of these new Christian symbols and a whole sub-set of ceremonies and symbolic meanings drawn from their historic native tradition. In the Nass this is done publicly and consciously with people continually seeing a continuity between who they are now as Christians and what they have always been since time immemorial. The old covenant is thus incorporated with the new.[16]

A new bilingual Nisga liturgy, modelled on the Qu'Appelle liturgy, was created by the Nisga people and the Reverend John Blyth in the early 1970s and is in regular use. This liturgy made a tremendous impact when it was used at General Synod in 1986. It was the first time that there had been any native input in Synod's worship. Part of the service was in English and part in Nisga. The lesson was read in Cree and the gospel in Inuit. This was a tremendously affirming experience for the native people involved.

The Book of Alternative Services of the Anglican Church of Canada was published in 1985. The intention was to give more flexibility in worship, to have liturgy be more inclusive in terms of the breadth of Anglicanism (from Catholic to Protestant and all things in between including Eastern Orthodox), and to incorporate more of the rich tradition of the church, particularly pre-Reformation. At the same time the concern was to modernize the liturgy in terms of language and concepts. The introduction to each service is explanatory and provides good teaching. But although we were assured that the *B.A.S.* is distinctively Canadian, this is not immediately obvious. Nowhere is native spirituality taken into account in any way whatsoever. In the Prayer for the Nation (p. 678, no. 10) there is a reference to uniting "us who came from many nations with different languages." But what about "us who were the first nations"? Perhaps this is partly covered in the prayers for "the oppressed in this land," "the unemployed," and "the poor and neglected." The calendar has a wide selection of heroes of the faith including a number of African martyrs, a couple of English missionary pioneers in Canada and the first Canadian bishops. Henry Budd is the only native person commemorated. Native people we questioned about the *B.A.S.* were distinctly unenthusiastic. They find searching through the pages for different parts of the eucharist cumbersome and they miss the familiar wording of the *Book of Common Prayer*. The fact that there has been a Cree translation of the *B.C.P.* for about a hundred years has allowed the Cree to make that liturgy their own. It has become indigenized.

Ritual and Symbolism

> We Indians live in a world of symbols and images where the spiritual and the commonplace are one. To you symbols are just words, spoken or written in a book. To us, they are part of nature, part of ourselves. . . . We try to understand them not with the head but with the heart. . . . What to you seems commonplace to us appears wondrous through symbolism. This is funny, because we don't even have a word for symbolism, yet we are all wrapped up in it. You have the word, but that is all.[17]

Native people are said to have responded more to the Anglican and Catholic missionaries because their sacramental tradition was closer to their sense of ritual drama than the teaching of the Methodists and Congregationalists. As we have seen the Catholics have gradually brought many of the ancient native rituals into the liturgical life of the church. This folk religion may well look "pagan" to some, but by establishing points of contact with the past, native Catholics have been able to express a genuine native spirituality which has been stifled in the Protestant churches.

In the Anglican churches of the Six Nations Iroquois Reserve we saw intricately designed ceramic communion sets made by a local native potter. In one of the oldest churches brightly coloured stained-glass windows fill the walls, celebrating different aspects of the native heritage. These include symbolic themes such as totems of local tribes, vivid Mohawk imagery, an Indian madonna and child, and famous local people such as a woman potter and Pauline Johnson, the Mohawk poet and theatrical performer whose passionate verse voiced the wrongs suffered by her people. The history of the Six Nations Reserve is depicted in a series of memorial windows in Her Majesty's Royal Chapel of the Mohawks. Built in 1785, this was the first Anglican church in Ontario and is the only royal chapel in the world owned by native people. Not surprisingly, the colonial links with the church and the British Crown are a central feature in the stained-glass memorials and the queen of England has reinforced this element with a royal visit to the chapel.

In Anglican churches on other reserves we saw beautifully beaded collection bags, intricately embroidered banners, carvings in local wood and stone, symbolically designed altar cloths and liturgical vestments, paintings and murals graphically depicting native scenes and imagery, and stained-glass windows with both historical and symbolic iconography.

The Jesuit mission of the Immaculate Conception in the West Bay Reserve on Manitoulin Island boasts a twelve-sided teepee-like church structure. This is intended to capture the ethos of a ceremonial lodge where people come to commune with the Great Spirit. Instead of the usual rows of pews there is a series of carpeted circular bleachers, descending into a well-like area with the altar in the centre. The church walls rise, as in a teepee, to an opening at the top. A sacred native bird symbol adorns the ceiling and a series of paintings of the stations of the cross surround the walls. These are the work of an Ojibway artist, Leland Bell. Baptized a Catholic, he is no longer a practising Christian and had considerable qualms in carrying out the assignment. He fears that attempts to blend native spirituality with Christianity may produce a synthetic religion. Bell respects other faiths and wants others to respect his. "We have a culture and a philosophy," he argues. "We have to find it and stop skimming the surface and go down deep into our culture."[18]

Another danger is that the indigenization and translation of religious symbols can go wrong. The totem pole carved by native prisoners and presented to the World Council of Churches gathering in Vancouver in 1985 is a good example. A totem pole is a way of expressing family and clan history. This one told in symbolic figures of West Coast Indians the biblical story from Adam to Jesus. But totems are not religious symbols which can be freely used out of their historical context; the translation of symbols from one culture to another is tricky. The totem pole was moved at great expense to Geneva only for the local community to resist having it erected in their midst because they considered it idolatrous. Dominated as they are by the iconoclastic Calvinist tradition of Swiss Protestantism, they have problems with liturgical art at the best of times.

The Nisga in the Nass Valley have made the greatest contribution in the Anglican church towards drawing on the riches of their native ritual and symbols in a native expression of Christianity. This is a comparatively recent development made possible by the resilience and integrity of Nisga culture and the encouragement of a succession of sensitive priests and bishops who were ritually adopted into Nisga families and accepted as blood sons. Over the years traditional native rituals have become blended with quaint Victorian customs in the ceremonial life of the Nisga villages. This well illustrates the dialectical process which takes place between innovation and incorporation of new elements from the incoming culture on the one hand, and continuity with elements of the indigenous tradition on the other.

Until the 1960s much of the native part of Nisga community life went on outside the church. For example, after a death white clergy would attend the funeral feast but not the settlement feast which followed and related to customary practices of the clan concerned. But the ritual adoption of a number of priests into Nisga families initiated a more intense church involvement in every aspect of Nisga life. This was eventually given the official blessing of the church as being not only compatible with, but a good expression of, the Christian faith. The real breakthrough came in 1969 with the formal adoption of Douglas Hambidge into a family in the Raven clan at the time of his consecration as bishop of Caledonia. Later on his new ''mother'' gave him a ceremonial button blanket cloak of red and black felt, with the raven crest of his clan outlined in shell buttons on the back. The blankets had been hidden away for a long time and were never used. When Bishop Hambidge subsequently asked if he might wear his blanket at a wedding service at Aiyansh, this was seen as an affirmation of the Nisga as native people and it triggered off a whole process of cultural revival.

Initially there were some tensions in the community as they wrestled with the question as to whether the blankets could be used as liturgical vestments or whether they were part of their "pagan" past which they had put behind them. The fact that authority for affirming their old tradition came from the bishop counted for much as he had a spiritual status with them. Once the question was successfully resolved by the community, the priest and lay readers in Aiyansh had blankets made too and it became the norm for them to be used liturgically. This led to the recovery of many of the traditional ceremonials both within and without the church. Other Nisga villages followed suit with the exception of Kincolith. The movement also spread to the Haida, Tsimshian, and Kwakiutl people, and it has become quite common for native elders and local people to wear blankets again. There is no question of "going back to beadwork" as it were. The recovery of the Nisga tradition is in a contemporary form and a true Nisga would say "we are what we are now, not what we were in the past." Archbishop Michael Peers, like Archbishop Ted Scott before him, was ceremonially adopted by all four Nisga clans in April 1987 and his blanket has the four main clan symbols emblazoned on it. This singular honour was said to have been given the primates in gratitude for the Anglican church's support to the Nisga since 1968. But the symbolic meaning goes deeper in that the Nisga have thus incorporated the primates into their community.

In the coming together of native spirituality and Christianity among the Nisga, old and new symbols have been used in a number of different ways. Obviously old symbols can retain their original meaning within a Christian context. At the church funeral of a Nisga chief the elders wore their traditional head-dresses and blankets, and the chiefs sprinkled the casket with swan's down as in the tradition, instead of holy water as in western usage.

Old symbols can also serve a new purpose in church, such as the use of blankets as liturgical vestments; while the sacred names given the prelates are redolent with a native imagery which is given a new Christian content. Archbishop Hambidge was given the Nisga name *Wal-aks* — Bearer of the Living Water, and Archbishop Peers, *K'al Wilimhlkws K'amligi Hahl Haahl* — Servant of God.

At St. Peter's in New Aiyansh the use of a bentwood box as a tabernacle for the reserved sacrament is yet another example of how old symbols acquire new meaning. This type of box, made from a single bent cedar plank and carved or painted with clan emblems in red and black, is normally used for storing food such as dried meat, fish, or berries for the long winter months. Its sacramental usage for the Bread of Life thus draws on the ancient symbolic concept of preserving life. The stylized design on the box at St. Peter's includes the crests of the four main Nisga clans as well as the liturgical symbols of chalice and host, thus incorporating the whole community within its Christian imagery. Again the old idea that the Great Spirit is involved in every aspect of Nisga life finds Christian expression in the priest being asked to invoke God's blessings on every new venture in the community, with a judicious use of holy water and incense, whether this be for a new car, the corner post of a new house, or the opening of a new restaurant. Similarly, there will be a special service for the blessing of new basketball uniforms, the blessing of the team before a big match, or the commissioning of new officers in a concert band.

People do not easily shed their past cultural background, especially in more remote areas like the Nass Valley. Even though native people have taken on the symbols of the western form of Christianity, with the passage of time these may well become filled with an indigenous meaning. Such a process is slow and may be quite unconscious so that it is often difficult to identify. The beautifully carved crucifix in St. Peter's, made by a local craftsman and representing Christ as an Indian, is a more obvious example. Less evident is the way in which the bishop's crozier has been invested with the symbolic authority of the chief's talking stick. Traditionally this stick gives the chief jurisdiction and the right to speak. For the Nisga the crozier has the same significance. This is reinforced by the use of copper on the crozier, copper being a sign of authority and prestige of a chief. The sharing of food is something else that takes on new significance in the native context because there is the conscious recognition of the sacramental nature of feasting. A feast is necessary to give authenticity to any major community event as much in the life of the church as in the village.[19]

Archbishop Douglas Hambidge, now bishop of New Westminster and metropolitan of British Columbia, maintains that the Nisga are strong as church people because they are strong as native people.[20] At New Aiyansh the Reverend Percy Tait embodies in his ministry the interweavings of the different threads of the bicultural tapestry of Nisga spirituality. As a former fisherman and logger, he has lived life to the full. Now as chief councillor and Anglican priest he is continually relating his theology as much to his people's past as to their present experience, to their Nisga culture and to the western trappings of their lives, to social concerns and to justice issues, and the whole in relation to the Bible.

Being Native and Christian

More typically, those native Christians who have tried to keep in touch with their roots have followed a dual system in which their native and Christian practices have been kept totally discrete. We interviewed a number of Cree clergy and lay people in all the mainline churches in the prairie provinces. Almost without exception they have not only started attending the annual Sun Dances on their reserves but have found this to be an authentic spiritual experience. During the Sun Dance they will hoist a flag on their tent to show that they are fasting for the day. Even if they do not dance they become part of the supportive ritual. At the same time the compartmentalization of religious systems is in danger of leading to a sort of spiritual schizophrenia. The Reverend Jimmy Isbister is one who sees the need to overcome this problem by discerning what is good in his native past and relating it to his Christian faith:

> I feel that there is a part of my Indian culture which I cannot leave. If I did I would be leaving a part of God's creation. There is always evil and good in any religious tradition. It is what we do with it that counts. If you are judgemental of the Indian tradition you will find a lot of faults but if you try to understand it you will find much richness. The Bible says you will be guided in discerning right from wrong. When the elder prays in his own way he never forgets anything or anybody. Somehow this feeling of community involvement is very Chris-

tian but in a sense Christ is not there. So what has to be questioned is where does Christ come into all this? How does he fit in as the representative of the Creator? Why did he have to die on the cross? Why did he have to suffer?[21]

Some Cree elders suggest that many symbolic aspects of the Sun Dance can be linked with Christianity. The sweetgrass is folded in the form of a cross symbolizing the four directions. The pole at the centre of the dance performance could represent the cross of Christ, the bunch of leaves on the pole, the crown of thorns.

But other elders told Jimmy that they see Christ as a white man's God because it was the white men who put him to death. The Indians had nothing to do with it and so they do not identify themselves as being a part of that destructive measure for God's creation.

These people have been part of Christianity but have remained part of Indian tradition too. What I find is that the spirit of Christ is not embedded in their minds. They only relate to the Godhead and not to the three persons of the Trinity. The real spiritual awakening happens when you bring in the cross of Christ. The Indians still have an Old Testament tradition where offerings are made on the people's behalf. They do not look at sin as being their business. They themselves are their business. But as Christians we have a personal responsibility in bringing our sins to the foot of the cross. The question is how to meet the challenge of Christianity and still remain an Indian.[22]

Reg Henry, speaker of the longhouse, expresses surprise at being frequently asked to speak at Christian funerals on the Six Nations Reserve. According to him, Christians often realize what they have missed on their dying bed and their last request is for an Indian presence at their funeral. But Reg feels uncomfortable speaking in the presence of a minister of religion. He does not believe it is possible to be Indian and Christian, and is emphatic in saying, "You cannot believe in two different areas. It has got to be one or the other. You can wear Indian beads and Indian clothes but being Indian has to go much deeper than that."[23]

Nonetheless, third-generation Christians at Six Nations, like

Nina Burnham, find great solace in incorporating native customs into the funeral rites of a family member. When Nina's aged mother died they brought her body home for a special wake as in the native tradition. They held a feast with the speaker of the longhouse in attendance. After he had spoken and blessed the food, Nina and her sister handed it round until all was distributed as in the native way. One dish was set aside with a portion of each kind of food as sustenance for the journey of her mother's spirit. Before sunrise next day this food was taken to a quiet place and left beneath a pine tree, this tree symbolizing peace for the Iroquois. Longhouse people believed that the speaker's blessing on the food will ensure that animals will leave it untouched. "Being an Anglican has not left me totally westernized," confesses Nina. "We still have our strong feelings in relation to our traditional longings."[24]

We were greatly privileged to attend a post-funeral feast held at Freda Ahenakew's home in Muskeg Lake Reserve, Saskatchewan. Freda's baby grandson had died the previous week and the funeral and wake had already taken place. The feast was explained as a celebration in which glory was given to the Great Spirit and to the ancestors, and it was held to end the mourning and free the spirit of the deceased. In no way was this traditional native ritual seen as being in conflict with the family's Catholic faith. The rites were led by Eli Bear, an elder from Saskatoon. The food was set out on rugs in the open and the family were grouped around in a wide circle. Eli first blessed the food with the burning of sweetgrass, and then accepted an offering of variously coloured cloths and tobacco with invocations in Cree. Afterwards we were all served with bannock, tea, and dumpling soup. This food had to be consumed on the spot as it had been sacramentally blessed. There was a complete absence of formality during the proceedings, yet the large number of small children present impressed us with their quiet and reverential behaviour.

In all these many different native rituals it is the elders who provide constant guidance and instruction. Traditionally, the feast has always given them a forum where they had the right to speak. In the old days this included criticism of the chief and could lead to heated debate. But in the westernized world the only recognized platform for the elders is in the political arena. Adam Cuthand is one who feels that the church has failed them by not providing a suitable forum where their voice could be heard, and that it is much the poorer for it. "The church does not like to be challenged," he dryly observes, speaking out of many years' experience as an Anglican priest. "It does not think in terms of enrichment. That is the problem. The church is still very English. It is pretty hard for the elders amongst us to make any input from our Indian tradition."

At the Kisemanito Centre at Grouard in Alberta, the Oblate order of the Roman Catholic church has initiated a continuing dialogue with elders in the local Cree communities with the specific intention of establishing a truly native Catholic community. We visited Father Jacques Johnson OMI, vicar provincial for the Oblate order and former director of Kisemanito Centre, at the Oblate headquarters in St. Albert, near Edmonton.

When Father Jacques first went to Grouard in 1978, the many stories he heard about evil spirits and curses, and the prevailing climate of fear prompted in him a negative response to native religion. But with time he came to see that "bad medicine" had nothing to do with native spirituality. He learnt to appreciate the native heritage, more especially the many parallels with the Old Testament tradition, such as a monotheistic vision of God, a profound sensitivity to the spirit world, a creation-centred spirituality, an ethic of sharing, respect for prophets and elders, a belief in the direct revelation of God through dreams and visions, sacred signs and symbols, holy places, the healing gifts of medicine people, a moral view of man, a Deuteronomic sense of sin and retribution, sacrifice, fasting, the belief in eternal life, and the idea of covenant with God and with other people sealed through gifts. However, Father Jacques is concerned that many native people continue to separate their native and Christian spiritualities. "We seek to dialogue with them," he says, "so that bridges may be built between the Indian way of praying and the Christian way, thus enriching both traditions and working toward that unity that Christ prayed for."[25]

In a moving testimony Father Jacques shared with us his own personal Vision Quest over the years, his experiences in the sweat lodge, his fasting, and his praying with the peace pipe. For him the coming together of Indian and Catholic symbols in full respect of each other is "a very happy marriage":

We need to accept the people as they are, respect their culture and promote what is good in their tradition. We have to learn from the elders and the native people themselves how to pray in their way, how they are spiritual beings. Then we can build on that. Of course this brings in doubts and fears as we are uncertain where this will lead us. But from the start at Kisemanito we felt we had to become Indian just as Paul felt that he had to be Cretian for the Cretians, and Roman for the Romans.[26]

Father Jacques acknowledges that native people have always had a strong belief in the Creator, but in accepting Christ their understanding of God has to move to a perception and an experience of him as Father. This is a radical step. "God is not a mere Creator. He wants to be Father to us and as proof he sent his Son to be our brother. That is why a medicine man prays to Jesus in the sweat lodge, calling him our brother." Father Jacques believes that Christianity has brought native people liberation, particularly from fear of evil spirits, and he cannot see them going back to their native ways without Christ. But he warns that there must be discernment of spirits and challenges them to go to the one Spirit, Jesus Christ, who brings love, not fear.

Chief Harold Cardinal has worked closely with Father Jacques in facilitating a spiritual dialogue at Kisemanito. He is both a political and spiritual leader among the Cree in Alberta and seeks the rebirth of the native people. Cardinal debunks the sort of thinking which sees it necessary for native people to make a complete about turn from having given up their traditions to become Christians, to now having to give up Christ to embrace their own traditions: "Our communities are already suffering and certainly do not need to be put through a kind of (tug-of-war) to see which man of prayer they should follow." According to him, the elders believe that just as they have been given a certain knowledge and "a vision of our Father," so has the church:

And they recognize that it is almost time . . . to begin bringing these two traditions together so that we may be able to enrich each other; and, hopefully, through that process, come to a better understanding of who we are as human beings and also to a better understanding of Our Father and what He

wants of us in the world. There is no reason for us to fear each
other. If we in fact pray to the same Father, why should we
have to check whether your prayers are more valid than ours?
. . . The ceremonies that we have . . . are all really united in
their common reach to Our Father. For those are the celebrations that Our Father wanted of his many different children
on this continent and across the earth.[27]

However, as Cardinal judiciously indicates, any coming
together of traditions cannot happen overnight. He argues for
a systematic approach. For native people this would mean seeking "something that might heal the hurt and wounds that still
exist within our communities . . . a vision that would bring healing and harmony."

Symbols of the Salmon People

Quadra Island, off the northeast coast of Vancouver Island, was
the setting, in the late 1970s and early 80s, for dialogue between
the Salmon People of the Kwakiutl culture and the Christian tradition. The moving spirit was the Reverend Ron Atkinson, the first
United church minister to be called by the native people
themselves to Cape Mudge village in 1972. He remained there
four years and then, after a three-year absence, returned in 1979.
Ron had been director of an experimental group in liturgical
development in Toronto. At Cape Mudge his strong sense of affirmation encouraged his congregation to recover the symbols and
spiritual richness of their Kwakiutl culture within the ambience
of the church. This was not without initial difficulty though,
because missionary indoctrination had labeled their past traditions as pagan. It was only when Ron returned for his second
term that his ideas took hold.

The native way of stillness and silence was part of the Quadra
people's new offering to the liturgical life of the church. Counter-
poised to this was the traditional dancing and singing in their
own language which once more found expression at funerals. Ron
did not encourage the return of the potlatch because this was seen
as a statement of power.

The native people of Quadra are dependent on fishing, so the

Sunday service was held in the evening to accommodate early morning fishermen. At the service an Indian basket was passed from family to family to make their seasonal offering, while during the salmon season in April salmon was cut up and shared with the elements during the eucharist.

In 1979 the native congregation opened their church to everyone in Quadra, as a ''spiritual community of respect,'' and together they worked to restore their fifty-year-old church building and to develop a parochial program to express the commingling of their different religious traditions. First came a stained-glass window, designed by Russ Fucco and placed in the west wall at the back of the church. With its powerfully elemental background of sea, land, moon, and sky, the window is both a natural depiction of a local fishing boat making a set, and an interpretation of the last chapter of the gospel of St. John, with the ship under the cross riding the waves thanks to the power of the Holy Spirit.

Next in line was a richly coloured altar cloth made by the women of Cape Mudge from a traditional red and blue blanket of Kwakiutl design. More than two thousand shell buttons are woven in a wealth of intricate symbolic patterns. The tree of life is placed in the centre, a symbol common to both Kwakiutl and Hebrew cultures. The sacred number four of the native people finds a place in the four corners of the cloth. At the same time, a button-blanket robe was presented as a surprise gift to Ron to wear on behalf of the community on special liturgical occasions. Other examples of native imagery in the church include an Indian carving of the head of Christ and a print showing Jesus receiving shamanistic powers from the thunderbird. But pride of place goes to the bas-relief sculpture in yellow cedar which fills the reredos wall. This replaced a cross, which was carried ''out into the world'' and planted in the ground in front of the church.

The cedar carving, by Bill Reid and Jim Hart, represents a diving and leaping salmon moving to fulfil a complete circle. Ron notes that this visual imagery is frequently found in the early church where it was used to depict the fall of humanity, of all creation, and redemption through the death and resurrection of Christ. In the native setting an even more ancient idiom amplifies the image with other resonances: the cycle of life and death in the migration and reproduction of the salmon in the changing seasons. This suggests the natural way in which all things turn and return in the sacred cycle of the cosmic order. Ron expands on the symbolic meaning of the carving as an interplay between like and unlike energies: "a quiet dialogue between symmetry and diversity, strength and grace, male and female, motion and stillness, simplicity and complexity, power and elegance." Further, there is the fish symbol used as a password by persecuted Christians in the early church, and the imagery of fishing as a symbol of spiritual life in the gospels. "In this carving, an ancient spiritual and natural symbol with roots in both northwest coast and Mediterranean history expresses both divine and human life, eternal and local reality." But above all this visionary work of art should be freed from definitions which might constrict its meaning for our contemplation.

The service to dedicate the carving in April 1984 was followed by the traditional First Salmon Ceremony, revived after a seventy year break. According to legend, the Salmon People who lived in villages at the edge of the horizon would change form from human to fish at certain times and swim across the sea to present themselves to the people living on the land. In the ceremony the first four salmon caught were cooked and shared. The remains were gathered together in a newly made cedar bark mat and returned to the sea. This was called treating the salmon with respect. The legend relates that after the supernatural salmon had been returned to the water, they became whole again and swam back to their village at the edge of the horizon. When they reported that they had been treated with respect, the Salmon People would return once more as salmon to the villages on the coast.

The Salmon Ceremony at Cape Mudge began in the church with Kwakiutl songs and prayers and a recounting of the legend of the Salmon People. According to native legend, twins are Salmon People born on land and so it was twins who led the procession to the beach. They were followed by the elders, all robed in button blankets. Four salmon had been roasted over an open fire. After everyone had had their share, the bones were laid reverently inside a new cedar bark mat and returned to the sea. The twins lowered the mat into the sea from a herring skill while a native leader beat the drum on shore and chanted. Ron Atkinson regarded the revival of the ceremony under the aegis of the church as a celebration of the unity and cyclical continuity of all chains in creation, a theme that is common in both native and Christian spiritual traditions.

At the time the response of the United church as a whole to the spiritual dialogue on Quadra Island ranged from indifference to hostility, except for exceptional people like Lois Wilson, who later became moderator of the church. The Kwakiutl people's feelings are expressed by Alberta Billy, who took a leading part in the changes. Alberta's family are into their fifth generation as members of the United church. She is scathing in her criticism of the church's distortion of the gospel:

> They have misused the real teachings of Christ. Jesus was a simple man but we constantly put him on a pedestal. This is not what he wanted. His teachings were so basic. They fit all mankind. Christ taught the truth, and this is what Christianity should mean, the truth. But to me the traditional teachings are far more valuable than what Christianity has turned out to be for us. The old people accepted Christianity because they saw it as another form of teaching. Like all indigenous people we were divided. Some found it easier to fit into the wider society and become white Indians. Others held onto the peace and harmony with creation which was their spirituality. These are the ones who must now speak to us.[28]

According to Alberta, the distortion of the gospel can be reversed by making it relevant to native people, as has happened on Quadra Island:

> The affirmation was important. We needed to see the blanket on the altar table because the other covering had no meaning for us. We needed the carving of the salmon because this symbolizes the cycle of our life. It describes who we are. Everything is in full circle. Indian people should not wait to get permission to do things in their church. They should just go ahead and do it as we did. We were not trying to divide ourselves from the non-native Christian teachings. We were saying this is who we are and if you value who we are you must accept it. The church finally realized that that is what we meant. The revival of the Salmon Festival was very significant not just for the good of the people but for the good of the church too. But

really this is just touching the tip of the iceberg. Our work is just beginning. In rediscovering who we are we must listen to the traditional teaching of the old people. Each community must work it out for itself because each place has a different basic teaching.[29]

Chapter 5
A Concelebration of Native Identity

Native Americans on the Spiritual Warpath

A major factor that has blighted a free flowering of native spirituality within the church has been the constant chaperoning of native peoples by white missionaries, bishops, priests, and others in authority positions. These laboured under the illusion that they were destined to guide and tame a non-European, hence to them inferior, mode of spirituality. Political subjugation consolidated spiritual subjugation. A people with unique spiritual gifts lost control over their own destiny and had white labels foisted on them to describe their identity. So native people became Anglican, United church, Roman Catholic, Pentecostal; Metis, Treaty, or non-Treaty; Conservative, Liberal, Socialist. The native American was totally deracinated. Converted to an alien creed, divided across tribal boundaries, refugee on his own ancestral lands, despoiled and demoralized, the native person lost track of his ancient Vision Quest. His tribal identity, nourished by his corporate spirituality, was threatened by the individualistic thrust of western Christianity. Afoot were a myriad secularizing factors, such as school education, urbanization, westernization, that aimed at defeathering the native person and assimilating him into the mosaic of white society, thus destroying all links with his past.

The prerequisites for the renaissance of a Native Vision Quest are first and foremost freedom of the native psyche from spiritual colonialism, a regeneration of a ''pan-Indian'' consciousness across the boundaries of tribes and nations, and the establishment of rituals, institutions, and festivals where native people, unchaperoned by whites, take charge of their own destiny and celebrate their own Indianness.

One of the most important examples of this development is the emergence of the Pan-Indian Ecumenical Conference. Perhaps for the first time in history it created a ''pan-Indian'' spiritual consciousness, sinking all the petty tribal feuds that have bedevilled native unity in the past and have prevented them from confronting the might of the white settlers. Here at last native people staged the show entirely on their own initiative without having to live up to any white labels. They saw themselves as a secular and spiritual power, a movement that surged from ''sea to sea,'' a communion by the native people, of the native people, for the native people.

Equally sovereign in character was the phenomenon of the Church Army which grew among native Anglicans in the diocese of Caledonia independently of the national body in Canada. Although initiated by white missionaries, the Nisga Church Army soon became an authentic native institution, warp and woof with the native ethos.

Of a piece with the spiritual sovereignty engendered by these structured movements is the more fluid but nevertheless grassroots movement that flourished around that quietly charismatic figure Andrew Ahenakew. An ordained Anglican priest and a full-fledged medicine man, Andrew recovered the Native Vision Quest which was the groundswell of his healing ministry touching many native lives. ''He cast out the spirits with a word and cured all who were sick.''[1] The Venerable Andrew Ahenakew unashamedly claimed his healing powers to be of authentic native origin and character. Though in Anglican Holy Orders, he was uncompromisingly a medicine man. In Andrew we see not only the beginning of the self-affirmation of the Native Vision Quest but also its restatement in ways relevant to the spirit of the Christian church.

The Pan-Indian Vision Quest

''People are taking a pride in their Indianness.'' So said Chief John Snow after the fourteenth annual Pan-Indian Ecumenical Conference at Morley in 1983. But, sadly, the Morley Conference had by then lost its initial impetus and was barely limping along. At its peak in the early 1970s several thousands made the pilgrimage to the Stoney Indian Park at Morley each summer and through them thousands more were touched by the vision of a pan-Indian spiritual consciousness. This swept across the country like a prairie fire, empowering native people to affirm their Indian identity and igniting a myriad local celebrations of "Indianness," which have since spawned all manner of cultural movements. There have been recent attempts to breathe new life into the Morley Ecumenical Conference; but no matter what the future holds it has already achieved much in helping to catalyze the renaissance of a Native Vision Quest across North America.

As already mentioned, pan-Indian consciousness first took shape in 1919 with the founding of the League of Indians of Canada. But early attempts at organizing native people nationally were seen as a threat to the status quo and were frustrated by the heavy hand of the Royal Canadian Mounted Police together with the Indian agents. Later pan-Indian organizations received official recognition by federal and provincial governments, but "Red or Indian Power" did not surface as a motivating force until 1970. The upsurge of a more aggressive native consciousness is associated with the civil-rights movements in the United States in the 1960s and the penetration of the American Indian movement into Canada in 1969. Like Black Power, Red Power attempts to give native people a positive self-image as the basis for mobilizing political, socio-economic, and cultural action. But there are also some conspicuous differences, more especially in that Red Power sees the reserves as a viable community base for native people and has fought for comprehensive control. The more militant followers of Red Power in Canada have remained limited in number, but there is no doubt that native anger against the dominant society might yet trigger off a wider response and find an outlet in violence.[2]

While the pan-Indian ecumenical movement was not directly tied to political developments, they provided the impetus for an upsurge of cultural nationalism and it is no coincidence that the First Indian Ecumenical Conference was held in 1970. A steering committee met in Winnipeg in 1969 and plans went ahead for a conference the following year at the Crow Indian Reservation in Montana. The idea was to bring together about one hundred and fifty native American spiritual leaders of every religious persuasion, including traditional religions, from the United States and Canada. There was to be an old-style grand council, but on a scale hitherto unknown. All were committed to healing the religious strife and factionalism endemic in modern native communities as a starting point in restoring the social fabric and cultural identity of their shattered national life.

Chief Andrew Dreadfulwater, a Cherokee religious leader from Oklahoma, expressed a common mind in saying: "We should have started something like this a long time ago. We have almost let all this religious squabbling smother our spiritual power and destroy us as a strong people." His sense of urgency was echoed by Bernard Second, medicine man of the Mescalero Apaches of New Mexico: "This may be our last chance. We will have to save our communities and revitalize them. We are, by nature, a people who look to our religious traditions to guide us." The Reverend Ernest Willie, an Anglican priest and a Kwakiutl Indian from British Columbia, took pride in the fact that "we are basically a very spiritual and religious people and this is just the beginning of more general religious movement. I feel a religious mood growing, especially among the young." For Ernest Tootoosis, a Plains Cree from Saskatchewan and a follower of the Sun Dance, the need was not only to strengthen the medicine men but also to teach whites "how to live in our sacred land without polluting it and destroying ourselves in the process. When we had the responsibility of caring for this land, it was a Garden of Eden."

Forty-seven tribes were represented at the Conference — Apache, Cherokee, Chippea, and Creek; Choktaw from Oklahoma; Blood, Cree, and Stoney from the prairie provinces; Micmacs and Mohawks from the eastern coast; Nisga and Kwakiutl from British Columbia; Seminoles from the Florida Everglades; Dog Rib Crees from the Northwest Territories; Shawnee, Squamish, Tlingit, and Yuchi, and many others. An unexpectedly large number of young native people came as observers, auguring well for the future.

The gathering coincided with the Crow Fair and this was a popular side attraction. Formal sessions were held over four days (four being a sacred number for nearly all Indian tribes) and a number of resolutions were passed. A steering committee was elected, almost equally divided between Canada and the United States and representative of the breadth of their ecumenical understanding. It included two leading members of the Native American church, a Shaker church member, a famous Baptist missionary, two Baptist laymen, one Catholic and three Anglican priests, a medicine man, and various native ceremonial leaders. Native Americans have of course never recognized the border between Canada and the United States. Even so they were greatly encouraged to find that despite their widely different tribal backgrounds, they had a common purpose. This sprang from a basic agreement about the nature of all creation and man's need to respect and live in spiritual harmony with Mother Earth. As the final report reads:

> Everyone agreed that modern Indian religious life must be a furthering of the historic continuity of time-honoured Indian values and philosophical concerns; that both modern Indian ceremonies and Indian Christianity must be part of that continuity; and that both native ceremonials and Indian Christianity can be mutually supportive or parallel and co-operative or integrated according to the desire of the particular tribe involved. Most felt that the work of future Conferences would be to evolve a way of implementing this process.[3]

Important as resolutions are, they cannot hope to capture the essence of what was a profoundly spiritual experience for all concerned. John Snow, chief of the Wesley Band of Stoney Indians at Morley and an ordained minister of the United church, expresses his sense of renewed hope after the historic gathering:

> I returned to my home reserve with a feeling of encouragement and realization that there were many Indian leaders who were concerned with the revival of our cultural, spiritual and religious heritage. I was aware then that, in order to revive our religion, we would also need to retain our language and culture.[4]

Chief Snow had offered the hospitality of his tribe in hosting the next conference. So it was that the Stoney's new park on the Bow River became the home of the Indian ecumenical movement. None of this would have been possible, however, without financial assistance from the mainline churches.

The Anglican Church of Canada was the largest contributor through grants from the Primate's World Relief and Development Fund and the Anglican Church Women. Providentially the Hendry Report had just been published and the church was eager to demonstrate its commitment to new native initiatives. This was followed by a General Synod resolution in 1970 endorsing the request of the Ecumenical Conference for all religious bodies and governments to declare 21 June a National Indian Day of Prayer. The United Church of Canada was equally supportive. Incidentally, 21 June was chosen because it was the longest day of the year and had always been a feast day for most native people. All native people were urged to worship in their own fashion on that day and where possible to take part in special ceremonies.

The Anglican Church of Canada continued to be the main sponsor in subsequent years despite the reservations of some bishops, nervous of the implications of certain conference resolutions. A task force was appointed by the Program Committee in 1972 to investigate. They resolved that the conferences should continue as long as native people so desired "with no reservation from the Anglican Church." This was a major step forward in loosening the hold of white domination. The Program Committee also agreed to support other key resolutions of the first two conferences including one which petitioned denominational authorities "to permit Indians the freedom to use native languages, traditions, dances, legends and their ancient religions as instruments of expression of the Christian life." The church had come a long way in giving recognition to pan-Indian consciousness.

Initially, financial assistance was also given by the Canadian and American Catholic Conferences, the United Church of Canada, the Protestant Episcopal church in the United States, and a number of individual churches and people. But the Catholics and the Episcopalians soon fell by the way and declined to give further support, as did the Presbyterian church in the United States. According to Dr. Harold Turner, the issue here for the Protestant bodies was all-Indian ecumenicity, independent of white controls, and developing in Indian ways, as against a white-mainline-churches-promoted ecumenism, which was much narrower, initiated from non-Indian sources, and organized and administered more on white cultural patterns than on Indian. Turner notes that some denominational bodies had started to include token native people in an advisory capacity, but these were not necessarily the natural spiritual leaders and were often the ones most against traditional religion and culture. However, for the Indian ecumenical movement, the time had come for the church as a whole to accept the Indians' own leaders, "not the ones *we* pick and train *for* them in *our* manner."[5]

Turner attended the Second Ecumenical Conference in 1971. What impressed him most was "the shared depth of concern for the spiritual renewal of the Indian peoples as having priority over all other approaches to the solution of their problems." He believed that the native ministers present could well handle any possible issues of syncretism and unorthodoxy which would occur to some. As he observed:

> Whether they had been formally appointed by denominations is beside the point, for it is the authentically Indian initiative and manner of operation that is the invaluable feature of this movement. When Indian spirituality in any form has found itself and can speak with confidence, then a new dialogue can commence with the white Christian community.[6]

Turner's advice to white churches was to allow the Indian leaders to speak while they listened. During this necessary discipline of silence, the need was to give financial support without tags of any kind. The United and Anglican Churches of Canada honoured this resolve.

The one hundred and fifty delegates at the Second Ecumenical Conference were even more widely representative than before and embodied grassroots religious leadership which had both the social responsibility and the power to effect radical change. One-third hailed from the United States despite the fact that their national church bureaucracies had refused any financial assistance. There were also nearly seven hundred observers, among them many young people. The Conference followed much the same format as before with informal group meetings and discussions, personal testimonies, a sharing of concerns, admonishments to young people to return to their native traditions, talks on history, language, culture, and spirituality, prophecies, healing rituals, and traditional native ceremonies. An important new development was the holding of Christian services and these were well attended. This was the first Conference to be held at the Stoney Reserve at Morley, establishing a pattern for all future gatherings there.

Morley nestles in the Rocky Mountain foothills midway between Calgary and Banff. The camp site is on a grassy plateau, flanked by pine trees and aspens, with the Bow River coursing strongly through the wide gorge below. Half a mile away are the buffalo grounds, the mystical heartland of the community. Towering mountains are an ever-present backdrop, while eagles circle high up above. In the shelter of the aspens is the arbour, a latticed framework of poles which is the spiritual centre of the Ecumenical Conference. During the annual gathering the arbour is covered with freshly cut branches and a sacred fire is kept burning there night and day. The Conference has always been held mid-summer and in the early days the meadow would come alive with a huge teepee encampment. The camping area, dance pavilion, teepee, and arbour areas are all designated as sacred grounds. People are expected to be decently dressed and the use of alcohol and drugs is strictly forbidden. The spiritual leaders say that alcohol has been the white man's way of killing native people and they preach total abstinence as the only solution.

By the Second Conference sufficient trust had been established for different tribes to share the secrets of their spiritual life and to perform their religious rites in public. The Navajo began with a Blessing Way Ceremony to sanctify the meeting ground. The major traditional religious leaders of the Plains Cree tribes led a Sunrise Ceremony giving thanks to the Creator with pipe, sweetgrass, and sage. The Cherokee and Seminole delegation laid down the sacred fire in the arbour at the start and put it out at the finish, while the Stoney people held a Buffalo Welcoming Ceremony (something which had not been done before and was precipitated by the buffalo herd breaking loose). The gathering ended with the shaking of hands in the Creek and Cherokee manner and pilgrims gathered up ash from the sacred fire in order to take blessings home with them.

Some white observers, conditioned to following a tightly packaged conference programme, found the absence of formality disturbing. There was no agenda, no carefully prepared speeches or papers, no clearly stated objectives. The meetings were conducted native-style with people being encouraged to come forward and speak from the heart. And open their hearts they did. They felt free to express their joy at being there, to share their pain and their sorrow, to impart wisdom, to philosophize, to talk about their native culture and religious customs, and to voice concern about present problems such as environmental pollution and alcohol and drug abuse. Much of the discussion might have seemed backward looking to non-native observers. Much was critical of white oppression, now and in the past. This was painful for some to hear. Many of the speakers could only manage broken English. Others needed translators. What was important, though, was that they had come together from all over North America to try and recover their spiritual identity and, in celebrating their "Indianness", were liberating themselves from the shackles of white domination.

Numbers of resolutions were passed and although many of the same concerns were expressed as in the previous year, active steps had been taken to initiate change. A recurring topic was the distress caused by archeologists in desecrating native burial grounds and sacred places. Another burning issue was the education of native youth in various aspects of traditional lore and custom, this being seen as providing a vital stabilizing force in their lives. But the main concern was to establish the Conference on a permanent footing and to develop regionally so that native people of every religious affiliation could carry on with the work of piecing together their fragmented sacred world.

Chief John Snow spoke as an ordained minister and organizer of the Morley Conference when he articulated the growing alienation of native Christians from the church: "We as native people have given Christianity every opportunity to flourish, and although it is sound theoretically, it just doesn't seem to work."[7] This is his challenging vision:

> I still see a need for the Church in our native society, but a reformation is needed within the Church. The mission of the Church can achieve some of its original goals by studying Indian religion with an open mind, by evaluating its position, and by starting a new kind of mission to the Indians.[8]

In embarking on this reformation Snow called on the church to "first develop its own understanding of what it means to be an Indian in today's society." At the same time, his people were trying to rediscover their native heritage, and it was to the few dedicated native religious leaders and medicine men and women who had kept the sacred fire burning over the past one hundred years that they had turned to rediscover their spiritual identity.

However, for all the idealism of the Indian ecumenical movement, there were also stresses and strains which constantly threatened its continued existence. The first Conferences had a strong Christian presence and the various ministers of religion valued the fact that they were able to function ecumenically with Christians of other denominations as well as traditional native people. Anglicans and Baptists shared services together, and Adam Cuthand recalls his pleasure at concelebrating mass with a young Roman Catholic priest from the north. But, according to Adam, there were power struggles among the traditional religious leaders which sometimes created tension:

> They did not trust each other. They were afraid that one might have a bigger power, a bigger magic, than the other. I just ignored it, but I was conscious of the presence of a power of evil because of the struggle between them.[9]

But Adam got on well enough with one of these leaders to be invited to sit beside him during his ceremony. He asked Adam to pray and to explain to people what was going on in English. Another medicine man, however, was stridently vocal in his rejection of the native clergy. Andrew Ahenakew describes the pain which this animosity caused him after he had been picked to go into the Circle of religious leaders, rather against his will. He was then co-ordinator for Indian work in the diocese of Saskatchewan and a member of the steering committee of the Indian ecumenical movement.

> One Indian from Paw Maker Reserve spoke with a harsh tongue and he said, "No more of these white-collared clergy in our Circle. They destroyed us so much with all that condemnation." I happen to sit there for two days listening to this kind of talk, and I was hurt right to the core of my heart. There was one moment there when I thought I would just get up and go home. But then something compelled me to stay. . . .

Anyway, I survived that ordeal. I stayed there till the end of the meeting, and I stood back at those kinds of meetings and talks ever since then, and I withstood everyone of them.[10]

As the nationalist wing gained power on the executive of the Morley Conference, the overriding mood became ever more aggressively Indian and non-Christian. A strong contingent opposed the continued participation of whites, while others fought for a less exclusive position. The fundamentalist Pentecostalist group in their turn actually complained that much of what was happening was anti-Christian and satanic.

Intimidation by members of the American Indian Movement is said to have been largely responsible for the ultimate demise of the Pan-Indian Ecumenical Conferences. Linked to this were the neverending financial problems. When the funding churches eventually discontinued support, the Stoney people were left to foot most of the bill. This they were able to do for a time because they had suddenly found themselves sitting on millions of dollars worth of natural gas. But by 1983 the situation had changed drastically. Money was tight. Regional celebrations of native culture had become much more common, making the need to go on a costly pilgrimage to Morley unnecessary; and churches had promoted their own ecumenical gatherings over which they had greater control. Numbers at Morley had dwindled to a few hundred and the sacred fire had to be put out two days early because of lack of interest. Whether recent efforts to revive the Conference will succeed remains to be seen.

The Reverend Jayant S. Kothare shares these treasured memories of his experiences at Morley:

I had the privilege of attending the Indian Ecumenical Conference four times, and each visit was a blessing and an enrichment of my spiritual life. I had never slept in a teepee before. What became clear to me was how one's consciousness gets cabined by living in the square boxes we glorify as homes. The circular perimeter of the teepee, with its poles rising to meet in the mid-point above and the fire glowing in the centre, was an initiation into the cyclical awareness of time and space. The holy fire was a constant reminder of the spiritual fire within. An elder who visited us in our teepee talked reverently about

Grandfather Fire, only to be fondly countered by a liberated native woman who was quick to identify the Sacred Fire as Grandmother.

The grounds of the Stoney people of the Wesley Band have a fey mystical quality about them. On one visit, I had just spent two excruciating weeks in the cement jungle of Calgary before trekking to Morley. The contrast between the high level of spirituality there and the low tide in commercial Calgary made a particular impact. I would spend most of my time walking around, meeting and talking to people. These were ordinary native folk with extraordinary insights into the dilemma of modern civilization and the possible ways of healing Mother Earth and her children. In each native person, man or woman, I discovered a prophet, a philosopher, a poet, a mystic, and last but not least, a martyr. They were all refugees of the decadent American Dream which threatens to desecrate the native way of life.

I engaged in literally hundreds of conversations, which all revolved around the spiritual experiences these people had had. They all rebelled against western materialism. But there was a sensual, earthy, incarnational quality to their experiences, so unlike the earth-negating pseudo-spirituality prevalent among the bohemian white people disenchanted with materialism. Every native person I met at Morley seemed to know intuitively that mystical insight was not the prerogative of a chosen few but the birthright of every individual who was willing to live in harmony with creation. It was a democratic mysticism. When I asked Ernie Tootoosis to tell me more about the great Indian figures like Sitting Bull and Seattle, he smilingly retorted: ''All Indians are equally great. All equally unique and important. It is the white man's idea that this one is greater than the next.''

When I listened to the elders holding forth in the sacred arbour, this theme of democratic mysticism was repeated again and again. Spirituality and justice issues were mentioned in the same breath with no contradiction as you would find in the traditional teaching of the church. The elders taught without any air of superiority or ploy to lock us into set patterns of thinking, so unlike the dogmatic, non-experiential, non-dialogical teaching that goes on in church Sunday schools, confirmation classes, adult Bible studies, or from the pulpit. The elders, humble and radiant, seemed to channel the truth rather than impose it on us. At the same time, there was an unstaged climate of reverence and trust between them and their listeners, imbibing the traditional sacred teaching of their ancestors without a trace of credulity or slavishness.

During one visit it rained for days on end and the sacred dances could not be held. A cold spell set in. I was walking the grounds wrapped in my shawl and looking quite distressed. An elder told me that the spirits had rained out the sacred rituals because a large number of unspiritual people with ulterior motives were attending the Conference. He also prophesied that these undesirable visitors, discouraged by the weather, would leave that very day and that the following day the sun would shine and the festivities proceed as planned. The prophecy came true.

The time spent at the four Conferences was probably the most enriching time of my life as a Christian minister. I had experiences which one normally would not have in the white man's straight and cerebral world. I met Andrew Ahenakew and his wife Alice. They were busy day and night with their healing sessions. I did not realize then what a great medicine man he was. Looking back, I am touched by his humility. A lesson for the leaders of the white church riddled with the disease of hierarchical power-broking! His wife Alice talked about healing and other spiritual issues in a matter-of-fact manner. "We do nothing. The Great Spirit does everything," was the kenotic message.

I met a man who sat perched on a mountain ledge looking intently at a far-away mountain top. On being asked what he was about, he coolly confided to me that he was trying to commune with the network of sacred energies that were being transmitted by the mountain. He spoke of the mountains as people, as ancestors who watched over those gathered there. I met another who claimed to commune with the huge tree beside his teepee, and others who communicated with birds and animal species.

Being on the grounds with native people of diverse nations afforded one an opportunity to sense what it must have been like being part of native society before it was disrupted by the white man. Associating with native people on their reserves had always depressed me. It was like looking at tigers in a cage. Sharing their space at Morley was quite different. It was an experience of Christian fellowship in the truest sense of the word, although most native people would balk at that way of referring to it. I have never before been with such large numbers of people, yet felt so little tension, stress, panic. People looked each other in the eyes. There were long silences and lively banterings. No formalities, no unctious courtesies. The whole congress was one huge experience in sharing the Peace of Christ.

The dances, the sweat lodges, and the peace pipe ceremonies were all sacramental, and the church would do well to recover its sacramental vision from the native people. The silence and the hand gestures of those involved in the sacred native ceremonies reminded me of the ritual gesturing in the Christian service, as in blessing, crossing oneself, laying on of hands, and so forth. The native people seemed to use silences and gestures more eloquently than Christians do their creeds and formularies. The robes and blankets of diverse hues and shades — red, blue, black, etc. — corresponded to the liturgical vestments in the church. Children were not shunted away as in Sunday schools, but were allowed to stay and even play during the festivities. The solemnity of the occasion was such that the children naturally conducted themselves with surprising dignity.

The bottom-line of the spirituality of the Conference was experiencing the truth first-hand, and sharing it, reconciling and integrating varied insights, seeking the voice of the Great Spirit in everything that went on around. Nobody preached. Nobody judged. Nobody was in exclusive possession of some exotic spiritual truth. Everything spiritual had to be earthed, made incarnate, and shared through a sacramental relationship with everybody around. The feeling of sacredness that permeated the entire proceedings of the Conference was infectious. There was no set agenda. The sacred festivities did not start nor end at any particular hour. There was this ongoing celebration of the Holy in and through every act, word, and gesture. Eating a buffalo steak was as much sacramental as smoking the peace pipe or taking part in the Sun Dance. There was a good deal of humour, integrity, respect, joy, and sadness.

On the negative side, I must note that the Conference did unwittingly spawn a small breed of self-styled medicine men who had little grounding in native spirituality. They set up their lodges, attracting, among others, young white people who had come to shop for cheap spiritual goods. Another cause for friction were the numbers of native Christians mostly with Evangelical-Pentecostal leanings, who were not interested in the revival of native spirituality but only the mobilization of native people under the banner of the Evangelical church. But the ecumenical spirit of native spirituality at Morley was too strong to be clouded over by these negative elements. The Conferences I attended have opened my whole being — body, mind, and soul — to the Numinous and the Holy as no experience in the church setting has ever done for me either before or since.

The Church Army on the Nass

Where will you find electric guitars and altar calls among native people in the Anglican church? Tambourines, testimonies, and tears? Uniformed officers and healing with holy oil? High church sacraments, charismatic choruses, and powerful evangelical preaching? All this and much more are the outward and visible signs of the Church Army in the diocese of Caledonia; and externally there are many similarities with the national body in Canada. But the inner reality shows that although the Church Army had its origins in England, the native peoples of the northwest coast of British Columbia have made it uniquely their own whether they be Nisga, Tsimshian, Haida, or Gitskan. It is a native expression of worship and of faith controlled by the people themselves and is in fact the only truly indigenous movement in the Anglican Church of Canada. Not surprisingly there have always been those clerics who criticized it as being ''un-Anglican,'' and even ''unchristian.'' But bishops who in the past tried to hasten its demise had to back down smartly when confronted by the implacable opposition of Nisga communities. Anglicanism is the Church Army in the Nass Valley. The one cannot exist without the other.

Caledonia's Church Army was founded in the early 1890s and

over the years there have been periods when it became separated from the established church, functioning as an independent body. But in the last twenty years the Army has been brought firmly back into the Anglican fold through the vision of successive bishops and the empathetic support of local clergy, undergirded by a heavy infusion of Anglo-Catholic sacramentalism. While he was bishop of Caledonia, Archbishop Hambidge was quick to identify the spiritual strength of the Army as a united community-based evangelical task force and it was he who formalized its position as a much-valued diocesan organization. He explained to us that because life in a Nisga village is all one and coterminous with the church, the Army is regarded as an integral part of their community. Where clergy have this understanding, the whole life of the village will hang together. Otherwise the Army will be divisive, operating as a separate entity from the church. Archbishop Hambidge sees the Army as a good example of native Christianity.

In the heyday of the Protestant mission era the battle for the supremacy of religious symbolism led to the symbols of native spirituality being totally overwhelmed by those of Caucasian Christianity, together with the inculcation of the Protestant ethic of hard work, right living, and capitalist accumulation based on individual enterprise. The original native ethic of communal ownership and sharing was displaced by a new Calvinist ethic of the successful Christian who made it in the white man's bric-a-brac world of buying and selling. But the American prosperity cult has found ready soil among some native people as a result of their growing fascination with material power which missionary teaching has led them to connect with the God of the white man.

The ancient native spirituality had its own symbols of power and this manifested itself as a spiritual healing and restorative power available to the whole community. The Protestant ethic distorted this concept of spiritual power. Ninety-five years ago the Church Army was established on the Nass in order to confront the blatant Protestant equation of an individual's material prosperity with divine grace. The Church Army did accept the power symbol of material prosperity but it linked this European Protestant symbol with the ancient Nisga symbol of communal ownership of material blessings received from the spirit world. In this way the time-honoured symbols and values of sharing and healing continued to hold sway and nourish Nisga spirituality but now under the thin disguise of Christianity. Nisga Christianity has taken on this uniquely native character thanks to the Church Army.

Mission work among the Nisga was begun in 1860 by William Duncan, a young lay worker of the Church Missionary Society, with a brief visit to the Nass. Two years later he founded the Christian community at Metlakata, but a permanent mission was not established until the coming of the Reverend Robert Doolan to Quinwoch village in 1864. Three years later the mission was moved downstream and established as the Christian village of Kincolith on the north bank of the Nass estuary. This was a time of social dislocation for the local inhabitants, aggravated by the white man's booze and new diseases, and many found refuge in the churches.

First reports of religious enthusiasm came from Metlakata in 1877 when the converts responded to the highly charged sermons of a newly arrived missionary with all-night meetings and extravagant displays of emotion. The native-directed worship was said to be "more in the tradition of native custom than Anglican usage," with visions and supernatural communications being the order of the day. Duncan was away at the time but returned forthwith to stamp out the religious excitement in no uncertain terms. Significantly, the leaders of the revival were drawn from the chiefs. They were sternly reprimanded and the new missionary transferred, but bitter feelings remained.[11]

A second revival was inspired in 1893 by a great fire at Kincolith which destroyed the church and many houses. The Reverend William Collison reported an outburst of religious excitement which quickly spread to all the encampments along the Nass, infecting native Christians and traditionalists alike. Services for prayer and Bible study were held daily and often continued well past midnight. Men and women were found preaching and praying out of doors and evangelizing at the fisheries and camps: "As the canoes passed up and down the river and along the inlets, songs of praise might be heard in both the Indian and the English languages."[12]

Collison's main concern was to contain this religious zeal and to prevent abuse. The Church Army, founded ten years earlier in the Church of England, seemed to fit the bill. Modelled on the

Salvation Army, lay people were organized under the leadership of captains and sisters and went out into public places to evangelize with brass band and drum. The members had to be confirmed communicants and their object was to strive for "Conversion, Consecration and Loyal Churchmanship." Collison's suggestion of founding a branch of the Church Army on the Nass was greeted with unanimous approval by the leaders of the revival. In no time a senior Christian had been appointed captain and the first band of twelve men admitted as members. Branches were soon set up in every Church Missionary Society station in the area. The women's groups cared for the sick and visited back-sliders among the female converts. Through the Church Army, therefore, a large group of native Christian leaders became actively involved in mission and evangelism.

This was possibly the only part of Canada where the C.M.S. policy of the Reverend Henry Venn was realized in laying the foundations of a self-extending, indigenous church. But it was not as yet self-governing or self-supporting. Collison made sure of that. He retained tight control and his list of rules for the Army was fearsome, sin being equated with traditional customs, and the potlatch, settlement feasts, and other ceremonials being expressly forbidden. Only those in good standing could preach, the missionary was the arbiter of disputes, and a serious infringement of the rules was punished with excommunication.[13]

For the first Nisga converts the Church Army provided a tightly knit community-based social structure that replaced what was lost through their conversion. Their grey Army uniforms and band music identified them as a group apart. However, in cementing this new identity they were often as strenuous as the missionary in trying to root out customary Nisga practices. There are gruesome stories of bloody feuds between Church Army members and the rest of the community at funeral feasts and of divisions within families lasting years. At the same time, the Army has always preached a total abstinence against drink and has served as a unique form of Alcoholics Anonymous with a strong local Christian base.[14]

When John Hannen, present bishop of the diocese of Caledonia, first went to Kincolith in 1971 he was shocked by what he considered to be almost heretical behaviour in Church Army meetings. But he persevered in an attempt to bring the Army back into the church, and although evangelicalism was not his preferred theology, he began to see the Army's potential while they in turn came to see that the church valued and accepted them as full members rather than as second-class native Christians in a separatist sect. As bishop at the time, Douglas Hambidge formalized the reconciliation and gave the Army due recognition by ensuring that the officers were properly licensed to him as their head, hosting an annual conference in the cathedral, and bringing the Army into active service as a diocesan organization.

In June 1987 Janet visited the diocese of Caledonia to find out more about the Church Army and Nisga spirituality. Fortunately, while she was in Terrace she was invited to accompany Archdeacon Ian Mackenzie to an ordination in Fort St. John and to make the return trip with Bishop John Hannen. This involved a twelve- to fourteen-hour journey each way (depending on the driver!). Leaving Terrace they drove through much of the night. Coming back they started at three o'clock in the morning. As they flashed past range upon range of snow-draped mountains, rumbling, tumbling rivers, mist-heavy lakes, and the ever-changing greens of field and forest, Janet kept the tape recorder running almost non-stop. She likes to think that her enthusiastic questioning, punctuated by squeaks of excitement at the sight of unfamiliar creatures of the forest melting away into the dark, or a black bear foraging for breakfast by the roadside, did yeoman's duty in keeping them awake and the car on the road. Ian was fortified with chewing gum and coffee spilling out of paper cups, Bishop John with throat lozenges! Janet was richly rewarded with fascinating tales of ministry among the Nisga, of weddings and funerals, fishing and hunting, hazardous journeys across flooding rivers and cracking ice, and, above all, of the people themselves and the vitality of their communal life in linking the old with the new.

According to Ian, there were two religious traditions in pre-Christian society on the Nass, the hereditary chieftains and the shamans. Both had control over sacred power. The tribal chiefs derived their authority through religious law and custom on a communal base, while the shamans exercised a more individualistic authority through ritual practices. The chiefs were continually being challenged by the shamans, and when the missionaries first came there were serious power struggles going on between them. Significantly, some of the first converts were chiefs. They reasoned that Christian law was almost the same as their law; but, more importantly, they saw an opportunity to direct the power of shamans who converted to Christianity to their cause by adopting them as their priests and in so doing eliminate their Nisga shaman enemies. This is in fact what happened.

However, the chiefs had not reckoned with the missionaries wanting to keep jealous guard of all religious power. No wonder that the first revival at Metlakata led to a battle royal between Duncan and the chiefs. What was at stake here was control of sacred power, with the chiefs threatening to gain authority from the rival power base of religious enthusiasm within the Christian framework. Horrors! Collison's response to the second revival at Kincolith was masterly because in founding a branch of the Church Army there he was able to deflect the power struggle into constructive channels. The Army satisfied the Nisga need to have direct access to and some control over sacred power, while Collison was able to retain overall control by maintaining a rigidly enforced disciplinary code. The Church Army is in a sense a continuation of the shamanistic tradition. It is to be expected that there would be power struggles between it and the established church over the years because of the lay leaders and priests being an extension of the rival religious traditions. Today all community activites are led by the hereditary and elected chiefs; but the priests are expected to work closely with them and be present at community functions and meetings so as to articulate unity in village life. It is a very serious matter for a priest to go against a chief.

Each parish has a Church Army corps with six officers elected at an annual meeting and licensed by the bishop. In addition the local corps may elect a number of other officers to lower ranks; they are licensed by the parish priest. All the officers have particular functions and the highly prestigious leadership posts are much sought after as status symbols. The first and second captains and the first and second lieutenants are in charge of the services in the village, organizing and running the meetings, preaching, and arranging for visiting preachers. The parish priest has no say except if he is called in to settle a controversy. The secretary-treasurer takes care of business matters, while the field captain is in charge when the Army goes off on a gospel trip to another village. The sergeant major organizes the missions away from home and he may be supported by a colour sergeant and a drum sergeant. Originally these posts were filled by men. The women had a similar organization of Church Army Sisters but with lesser status. Today women may be elected to the Army ranks.

Most corps have twice weekly services, on Wednesday evenings and Sunday afternoons or evenings if there is no evening prayer. One of the Army rules is that their service must not clash with divine worship. An afternoon service can last from two to three hours but the evening one can go until midnight or later. The emphasis is on evangelism and emotions run high as in a revival meeting with lots of rousing music to get the spirit moving, tears flowing and arms upraised in joyful surrender to Christ. Brass bands are very much part of the Army image, and they have a dual function in that they will double as the concert band for social and ceremonial occasions.

Gospel songs and charismatic choruses are belted out to the accompaniment of drums, electric guitars, an organ or piano, cymbals, tambourines, accordians, and every sort of brass instrument. The noisier the better. Some choruses like ''Walk in the light'' have been translated into Nisga but the music is all western. During the service different people are chosen to start the hymns or choruses, to read the lesson, to preach, and to pray. An elder usally says the opening prayer and one of the officers may preach. The sermon is followed by an altar call and then singing takes over with testimonies in between. Army officers run the service, the priest having to wait to be asked to take part, whether this be to preach, say the offertory prayer, or give the closing prayer and the blessing. He would be invited to preach only at the start of the service, a rather shattering experience for those accustomed to relying on well-prepared sermon notes.

The regular service follows much the same pattern as a non-native Army meeting in the sense of chorus-singing, altar call, and sermon, except that it is likely to be much freer with more speaking in tongues, extempore prayer, raising of arms, being slain in the spirit, and even trances. This is what has horrified those who insist on everything being done ''decently and in good order,'' although nowadays the charismatic movement has familiarized most people with the more emotional pentecostal practices. And this is where there seems to be strong links with the old shamanistic tradition of the Nisga, as for example with the altar call and the kind of wailing that goes on at confession of sins. Says Ian Mackenzie:

> An altar call might be for returning to Christ because you have fallen away, or for recommitment, or because the Spirit has moved you to go up. It might also be a way of expressing contrition for something you felt you had done wrong that week. Sometimes people will go up to the altar at every meeting. They will speak in tongues and pray and weep and give themselves to Christ anew. It is a very cathartic experience emotionally.[15]

Bishop Hannen also sees the testimonies as being very much part of a more native approach to Christianity. For instance, the Nisga will not presume to admonish directly according to prescribed rules and regulations, as in white society. Rather, exhortation will take the form of testifying, speaking obliquely out of their own experience; and this practice continues in church life.

> In the Church Army testimonies often include an expression of repentance and an asking of the collective community for forgiveness. Again it is traditional for Nisga people to say, ''I have been far from God. I have fallen away from him. I am sorry. I repent. I have done this, that, or the other and I ask the community, the church, you people, to forgive me and to pray for me.'' This might be accompanied by many people coming up and recognizing the act of repentance and restoration to the life of the church by prayer and the communal laying on of hands for that person. This public restoration is very much part of the native tradition.[16]

Bishop Hannen contrasts the white way of expressing repentance — either by hiding under the umbrella of the general confession in the eucharist or in the offices, or by making a private confession to a priest. In the native tradition someone who brings disgrace on himself in the community disgraces his family as well. This has good biblical roots. Until there is reparation, forgiveness, and restoration his sisters will drop out of the church choir and his brothers out of the concert band. They will accept guilt for what he has done as being their sin, and having offended the community will hang their heads in shame. Repentance and restoration will of necessity involve the whole community. The penitent's tribal family will hold a big feast at which he will publicly confess his sin and ask for forgiveness. He will then be bathed and cleansed in sight of everybody, and there will be speeches of encouragement by the elders. Only then can his family resume their responsibilities and take their place in village life again. In the Church Army lesser offences would be expressed in testimonies. Major offences, however, would involve the church and the Army in the act of forgiveness at the feast, pehaps through music and prayers, but definitely through participation in the ritualistic setting in which to redress insults, injuries, and grave misdemeanours.

It is important to remember that the Christianity of Nisga people is directly fed by their indigenous tradition and spirituality. Salvation or redemption for them means not just forgiveness for moral lapses, and consequently a place in one of the heavenly mansions; but a rebuilding of the whole community, a healing of broken interpersonal relationships, a reconciliation, a resolution of tribal feuds, a restoration of losses, the strengthening of the tribe as one big family.

The laying on of hands in forgiveness, restoration, and healing seems always to have been part of Nisga tradition and is continued in the Church Army. Their liberal use of holy water probably dates from the coming of the Anglo-Catholic clergy into the diocese, while anointing with holy oil was more likely introduced earlier by Pentecostal sects. But these new sacramental gestures would not have found favour in what was a typically evangelical church life unless they had found resonance with native thought-patterns and practice. Many people carry phials of oil around with them. This can cause problems in the church where priests customarily do the anointing. Healing and laying on of hands are done especially on gospel trips where one whole village on the Nass will visit another for a week at a time. This is an important part of the Church Army tradition and seems to have pre-Christian roots too.

In former times the Nisga moved to the fishing areas in the spring and only returned to their villages in the fall. Their rich ceremonial life thus came to a climax in the winter months and would include shamanistic performances and inter-tribal feasting. The Church Army has to some extent followed this pattern, with villages taking turns to visit each other on gospel trips. They might go from Aiyansh to Greenville or Kincolith to conduct a mission. In the old days they would think nothing of walking thirty miles or more downriver on ice. Under the direction of the sergeant major, a troupe would be sent ahead to set up camp along the way. The journey itself would initiate a process of renewal, with people getting back into confessing Jesus Christ as they went. As one of the Nisga priests says, ''By the time we got to the first camp site everybody had been converted.'' The visiting Church Army would be welcomed into the host village with their field captain taking over the running of the services and revival meetings. Their purpose was to strengthen Christian life and there would be mass conversions, the gathering in of those who had fallen away, renewed promises of commitment to Christ, healings, and the rest.

Bishop Hannen sums up the Nisga spirit of the Church Army in these words:

> All these kinds of elements are part of the Nisga heritage. There has not in a sense been a recovery of traditional patterns, because they have always been there and to a greater or lesser extent have continued to be expressed in the fullness of community life. They may well have got overlaid with English Victorian Anglicanism but they have never been totally displaced.[17]

Andrew Ahenakew: Priest and Medicine Man

Andrew Ahenakew was the first to acknowledge that his upbringing had cut him off completely from his native spirituality. Born in 1904 and brought up on Sandy Lake Reserve, he had come under the stern teaching of the Anglican missionaries and had been forbidden any association with native ceremonials. Not so Alice, his wife. Her foster-parents gave her a thoroughly native upbringing. This was to be of paramount importance when Andrew was confronted with his calling to a healing ministry as a native medicine man. Andrew was farming at Sandy Lake at the time of his marriage in 1930 and he continued farming while working as a lay reader in St. Mark's Anglican church. After many years of faithful service he was ordained priest in 1960. For the next sixteen years until his death, on 16 November 1976, he ministered at Whitefish, Sandy Lake, and other reserves in northern Saskatchewan, being appointed archdeacon in 1971.

The Ecumenical Conferences were a turning point in Andrew's life. For the first time he was confronted with his own "Indianness." This was a shattering experience as he recalls in the personal testimony which he gave to a gathering in Winnipeg shortly before his death. This is recorded in his own moving words in the audiovisual presentation, "Sometimes We Burn . . . Sometimes We Tremble."

> I went to all the ecumenical gatherings since Crow Agency, and every time I went there I learnt a little more. You know what was wrong there with me at first, some people call it brainwashed, some people call it that you are not living the real way, or what your life is, as an Indian. I don't know which is which but I always tried and I tried but there was something lacking. I went to Morley the last four years since it started and I saw great men at work, really praying, really working the spiritual word and . . . to my mind, two of the greatest doctors are medicine men.[18]

The two men were George Cattleman and Victor Youngbear, and Andrew was proud to wear their collars, handed to him after their deaths. But trained within a rigid Anglo-Saxon framework of missionary strictures, he struggled to accept the authenticity of his own vocation as a medicine man. Archbishop Hambidge recalls Andrew's shock at the Indianness of a Nisga Church Army celebration which he attended prior to his turn-around. He wore his surplice when all the other priests including the bishop were wearing blankets and he was deeply shaken when the bishop asked him to speak Cree during the service. He had no problem in speaking Cree to his own people but he resisted being Indian elsewhere.

Much of the traditional native ritual has to do with healing and a healer acquires his power through a vision. Alice Ahenakew recollects that even before Andrew was called as a medicine man he was a man of visions. Dreams and visions are central to every aspect of native spirituality and no fine distinctions are made between the waking and sleeping states. Both are part of the same reality. They are the medium of communication with the spirit world and the way in which a person enters into harmony with creation. The Vision Quest is in itself a process by which dreams and visions can be induced and youths are trained to anticipate and deal with them physically, psychologically, and spiritually. The youth must be consciously aware that during the Vision Quest he might be specially chosen for a new role such as a medicine man and be blessed with healing powers. The sharing and interpretation of dreams are an integral part of the healing process for native people. All this has to do with social and spiritual integration and a deracinated native might well rediscover his cultural identity through dreams and visions.[19]

However, although visions had long played an important part in Andrew's inner life, he had always given them a Christian interpretation. The ones that Alice remembered were to do with him as a priest being taken up into the presence of the heavenly, in an "out of body" experience. As she told us:

> In the morning he said he had had a vision. "I left the world," he said. "I went zooming up. All at once I came to a place that was just like a rainbow. I was way up there and it was sparkling all over. It was just so beautiful. And I just stood there looking," he said. "All at once I saw the Lord coming, and he came and stopped here. And he said my name. Then he told me, 'This door is open for you. You can come in and you can go out.' "[20]

At Sandy Lake Andrew had another vision in which he took off and went up into the air. When he looked down he could see his body far below. He finally reached a place looking like a big saucer. There was a building and somebody came to the door to find out what he wanted. Andrew asked to see his mother and father. They came, and he talked to them. Then, at his request, his sister was brought to see him. The person who fetched them was not the Lord, but somebody else. "The guy told Andrew, 'You are not ready to come here. You have to go back. There is a lot of work to be done.' So he had to come back, down to earth," said Alice.

Another time he told me he went away again in the night when he was sleeping. He came to the Lord, and the Lord said, "Look at all those stars." There were stars all over, some of them really small, some of them really big. And the Lord said, "That is just like the people down on earth. Some of them have a big life and others hardly any. We need a lot of workers. You have to go down there and go back and help those people that are barely shining."

As a convinced Christian Andrew had no problems in accepting the authority of these dreams and visions as coming from God. His vision from the spirit world of the Great White Bear, however, "came suddenly one time" after he had started going to Morley, and it posed a crisis of conscience which he found hard to reconcile. The bishop of Brandon had asked Andrew to go to Moose Lake to check on a native man about to be ordained priest. At that time Andrew's younger brother, Walter, had just been sent home, dying of cancer. As Andrew takes up the story, he remembers that he left home for Moose Lake with a very sad heart:

Eventually I reached The Pas, Manitoba. There I was, billeted in a motel right there by the river and I prayed that night alone, a stranger in a strange town and very lonely. I went to bed, I don't know what time, but I think it must have been about 1 o'clock, 2 o'clock, somewhere around that time. I saw something coming from the river way, from the north. When I looked again I was sitting on the bed. I knew I was sitting on the bed but I guess I was sleeping. That motel seemed to have no walls. This creature came right towards me. He stopped about six feet from me, maybe a little closer, and he looked at me and smiled. A beautiful creature, a creature of God. And he spoke to me.[21]

Alice adds that the creature was suspended in the air. In his account, Andrew goes on to describe his amazement when the animal spirit, a great white bear, told him that he knew he was alone, that he knew his brother was dying of cancer, and that he had come to help him. Andrew wondered how this could be.

''Well,'' the creature said, ''Don't misunderstand me.'' He said, ''I have been sent here by the higher power. I'm sent to come and instruct you to make medicine, which will be yours. If I tell you what to do and if you listen.'' I thought to myself, how can I listen, when I'm a clergyman, to this creature?

The bear could read his thoughts and told him that even though he did not believe now, he would believe later and would do this big thing. The bear smiled, showing teeth four to five inches long, and continued: ''I'm sent here to come and teach you how to make this medicine. I'm willing to give my body to be killed so that you can take me and use me for that medicine.'' He promised that if the medicine was given to Andrew's brother, he would live. When Andrew showed disbelief, the bear pressed him to give his reasons. Andrew explained that he had no way of going up to the Arctic Circle from where the bear had come, nor was he a hunter. The bear replied:

''Well, I'll make that simple. You have several species of my family in your country of different colours. These brothers of mine are moving around your forest. Use them. Do as I tell you. . . . Make this medicine and when you put it in a bottle, when it has settled down, you'll see a gold colour, about half a thickness of your small finger, on the surface.''

Again Andrew expressed his disbelief and again the bear told him that though he did not believe now, he would believe later. The bear then explained that the creatures of the North Arctic Circle had been created perfect at the beginning of time. But the people on earth were dying of all kinds of sicknesses such as cancer, sugar diabetes, and tuberculosis. With the medicine that he was going to teach Andrew to make, many of them would survive. And he told him exactly what to do using the fat from across the bear's back and the tongue. The bear then took his leave, saying that he had a long way to go and was in a hurry. Andrew's bewilderment is tangible as he describes the bear's leaving:

I thought he was on the ground, but, when he turned around, there, a beautiful thing, I can still see it, he was moving around just like the sun. And when he was racing away he was going up from the earth and he was going still further up into the air towards the north pole. That was the last I saw of him. I woke up. I put the light on. I looked at my clerical collar. It was on the table. I thought to myself, Andrew, are you going crazy? How are you going to do it, to be a priest in the Anglican church and to be a medicine man? So I went to sleep again.

The next morning Andrew put the vision from his mind and went on with his business at Moose Lake. On his return home his wife was immediately aware that something was wrong, so he told her the whole story. She was excited and urged him on. "You have got to do it," she said, "you are gifted." But he resisted, fearful of what the bishop would say if he found out, and at a loss to know how to get hold of a bear. In the meantime his brother was getting worse. Although Andrew searched all over for the necessary ingredients, it was the wrong season. When his brother finally died, he lost interest. But Alice kept after him and refused to give up. Eventually, they heard that somebody had got a bear at Montreal Lake. They went there posthaste, only to find that the bear was just skin and bones and no good. Another couple of months passed and then news came of another bear, north of Battleford. This time they were in luck. The bear was in prime condition and they obtained all the right parts.

They brought the stuff home and Alice insisted that as Andrew was the gifted person who had been shown what to do, he must be the one to make the medicine. It had to be made in the small hours of the morning, when all was quiet and nobody was around. Alice laughs as she remembers Andrew's vain efforts in the kitchen.

He tried to make the medicine but he could not do it. Andrew was the sort of guy who did not even know how to make tea, let alone a meal. I had to do everything for him, so now I told him I would take over. The next night I made it. I went ahead after he had gone to bed. When I had finished I poured it into a little bottle. The next morning I got up and brought it to him.

"That is exactly the way the bear showed me," he said, smiling, "it has to be gold on top."

The bear fat and tongue had to be cooked in an enamel pot and boiled right down to oil. Even the cracklings, or Indian popcorn, were used, being ground up and used as a paste. Alice and Andrew were the first to sample the medicine. "We hardly used to go up them steps," says Alice. "We soared all over after we had taken the medicine ourselves. We thought, My goodness, this medicine is really good."

By this time Andrew's other younger brother, Austen, had been hospitalized with cancer. But Andrew did not take him the medicine. As an Indian he had to wait to be asked. However, he did tell his sister everything and when Andrew next went to the hospital his brother asked for the medicine. "If you can't help me, I'm done," he said. So Andrew gave Austen a little bit and warned him not to take too much as it was strong. Austen insisted on keeping the bottle, much against Andrew's wishes. "What if the doctors find it," he worried. "They will put me in jail. I am not supposed to bring any medicine here." But Austen promised to hide it. And then he nearly killed himself by taking too much. He was very sick for two days, but having survived the ordeal he became well enough to jump out of bed and go home. Later he was ill with gallstones. He refused to have an operation, taking Andrew's medicine instead. Two weeks later he was back at work, cured.

News of Austen's recovery spread like wildfire. All of a sudden Alice found strangers turning up at the house, at all hours of the night and day, bringing gifts and asking Andrew to treat them. Alice recalls the first one, a man with a huge suppurating wound on his leg, which doctors had been unable to cure the past thirty years. Andrew prayed and rubbed a little medicine on the wound. The man took medicine away with him and within three weeks the wound had healed. Another time a convoy of cars came from Regina early in the morning with a two-month-old baby girl, crying pitifully and dying of cancer. Andrew treated her at once and she slept peacefully for the first time. Three years later, after Andrew had died, they brought the girl back. She had recovered completely and was running around. Another man at

Little Ponds was covered with cancer sores and could not move. He too was healed by Andrew. The medicine could make a person feel really ill for a couple of days, and he would want to sleep. But after that improvement would be rapid. Once people knew that Andrew needed certain parts of a bear for his medicine he was kept informed of any bears that became available.

Alice was amazed by the many miracles that appeared to take place. "He healed so many people whom I did not believe he could heal." But it was often tough on her. She would have to get up at all hours of the night to give the endless stream of strangers tea, and find blankets so that they could doss down in her living room. People came from all over Canada and the United States. Most were native people but there were some whites. Andrew never once made them wait. "Sometimes I used to get tired," confesses Alice. "I used to think, why do they have to come in the night. But not him. He would get up at once, and I used to get up and help him. But sometimes I did not want to get up."

The teepee where Andrew took people for healing stood alongside the Ahenakew's house at Sandy Lake. The poles are still standing but the covering has gone. People had to take their shoes off when entering the teepee so that their bare feet were in contact with Mother Earth. They had come from the earth and to the earth they would return. The soil was thought to be strengthening, cleansing, and healing. Some were bare from the waist up too and watches had to be taken off. The medicine must never touch metal.

At the start of the healing service Andrew burnt sweetgrass in a little pan and went round the circle purifying each person in turn with the smoke, praying all the while in Cree. Adam Cuthand was present on two occasions and recalls that Andrew broke down completely when he started to pray. Fortunately, they had been warned beforehand. When he came to he murmured, "Thank you Father." After that came the anointing with Andrew rubbing medicine on the people's legs and praying in his own way. He always went clockwise because that is the native way of following the direction of the sun. The next time round he laid hands on each person's head in turn, saying, "Be healed in the name of Jesus." At the end they were all given little bottles of medicine and instructed in the oral dosage. A more greasy medicine was used for anointing. The services were a lengthy business with an average of fifteen people in attendance. Adam says that he always prayed with the people he sent to Andrew from Winnipeg before they left home. The healing had to start in preparing for the journey as they emptied their minds to focus on their purpose in going.

It is customary for a native person to take a medicine man gifts. According to Alice, it has to be four things — clothing, a blanket, tobacco, and pieces of material — and could include money. This is in the nature of a covenant with the healer, sealed through gifts. The Ahenakews did not use the gifts themselves but would have a big sale from time to time in aid of the church.

Andrew was only too aware that his gifts of healing had been given to him by a higher power. When one man tried to give him the credit, saying, "You saved me," he replied, "No, my friend, it's not me. My hands are used, my heart, my whole being. I'm weak. I'm just nobody. But the source, that's the thing that's helping you. Not me." But even so he was deeply troubled by the thought that his work as a medicine man was against the church's teaching. Alice explains that this was because the church had done so much to stop native people practising their healing ministry in the past. She vividly remembers the hurt she felt in seeing her people being forced to burn their medicines on a big fire. Where she came from they had only used good medicine. Her grandfather had had that power. The problem was that some people got hold of bad medicine and did great harm. Says Alice:

> In the Vision Quest the wicked spirits come first and try and crowd out the good spirits. Some of these people go with the devil spirits. They get bad medicine and know how to hurt people. If you have a good spirit, smoke your pipe, and the wicked spirits will shy away. You must wait for the good spirits to come, to give you good gifts, like the gift of healing.

Because of the church's attitude towards native spirituality, Andrew justifiably feared that he would have to quit his ministry as an ordained priest. Finally, he plucked up courage to go and see his bishop. He takes up the story once again:

> This thing was bothering me. I was hiding this from my bishop about a year and a half. And my bishop and I always talked with each other, because I was archdeacon under him. So, it troubled me. So I went over. I had my collar. I took the bottle.

And he said, "Oh, you've come over." "Yes," I said, "I've come here for a special reason." "Well," he said, "whatever it is we will talk about it."

When Andrew told the bishop he had been keeping a secret from him for over a year, the bishop expressed surprise and disappointment. Andrew then explained:

This is really a secret of my own, but it's a gift, I may say, or a spiritual gift, I don't know what you will call it. But Bishop, there's one thing I am here for. I have a guilty conscience because of this gift, a personal gift, a spiritual gift, that's the way I feel. If, Bishop, you don't like it, and if I'm smearing the white collar of my brother clergy, that's the last thing I'll do. If you tell me to take my collar off I'll take it off today.

The bishop gave him a long hard look, then asked for his story. Andrew told him every last detail, claiming that "this is a spiritual experience which was put aside by a lot of denominations. This was the real thing long ago, but now it's not." Luckily, the bishop was a man of vision himself. As Alice recalls, the bishop gave his full support, saying: "This is in the Bible, go ahead. You are gifted. Do not push it away." Towards the end of his life, Andrew had this to say about his healing ministry practised in a Christian context:

So my friends, this is the story of Andrew Ahenakew, who was angry when the Indian cultural men told him that the Indian way of worship is real. It is real. I helped them . . . but again I didn't help them, but the great Creator, God. People come there with trembling hearts, heart diseases, mental diseases, half-crazy. Withered hands have been made whole. Legs are walking again. One fellow I can see now from Fort LaCorn having all kinds of great big blisters on his heels. Now he's walking again. I thought that perhaps I should be bold enough to say the true experience I've had this last two and a half to three years. But, my friends, with all this thing, with all this gift, your strength starts to get low and your cup is empty. But it's full again the next day. It refills itself. This is the experience that I have. . . .

So with the Christian faith, my friends, this is what can really happen. I found that experience. And today I tried to tell you about this man making a Sun Dance, purifying himself. We have to purify ourselves, my friends. Andrew Ahenakew is always humble, and I've lived a pure, clean life all my life. I was a chosen vessel. I didn't know until the day that it was appointed that I should be helping my people and their needs. This is the story Our God is alive. You people, it is up to you to use that faith and make it work. . . .

We preachers are human beings. The spiritual world is so great. Sometimes we burn, sometimes we tremble, sometimes we are so weak. But give us time to help other people. We're telling them. We're giving wisdom, and we will speak.

The spiritual struggle of Andrew Ahenakew typifies the problem of confrontation between native spirituality and Christianity, and Andrew had to bear the brunt of the hostility from both camps. He was spurned by native people because he was a Christian priest, while Christians suspected him because he was a medicine man. For Andrew it was a crisis of identity and conscience. He was blessed with vision after vision and with his Christian upbringing gave them a Christian interpretation, until he was surprised and stunned by the white bear vision. This he could not reconcile with his Euro-Christianity.

Andrew's first vision is symbolic of his diffident attitude towards his native spirituality. He sees a door, which is an archetypal symbol for an uncharted, unexplored territory. He hears the words: "This door is open for you. You can come in and you can go out." He was thus being guided by higher powers to come through the open door. This is suggestive of his openness to the gifts of native spirituality. All he needed to do was to enter into the sphere of that spirituality. There was no fear of his being trapped there for the voice assured him that he was as free to go out as he was to come in. The second vision also features a door, except that this time there is a person, identified as a higher being, waiting there to guide him. He makes contact with his ancestors and seems to enter the realm of dream time.

In the third vision Andrew sees clusters of stars, large and small, in the sky and is urged to work for the smaller stars so that they may grow big. The stars apparently illustrate the spiritual and cultural landscape in which he finds himself, the big stars representing the entrenched Christian church and the small ones, the waning of native spirituality. The star itself is an archetypal symbol for the birth of Christ, and the appearance of stars in the sky conjures up the scene of the heraldic shepherds of Bethlehem waiting for the Messiah. The vision breathes a mood of numinous expectancy on the part of Andrew and his people who are looking for a spirituality that would rescue them from alienation in the church-dominated world. The vision seems to commission Andrew to revive and strengthen native tradition.

Through the first three visions Andrew was systematically being made sensitive to his aboriginal tradition. However, the visions did not present any threat to his Christian mind-set. He could see them as coming from the God of Christian revelation. The big shock came in the vision of the white bear, whom Andrew irresistibly describes as ''a beautiful creature, a creature of God.'' The vision occurred when Andrew was in a highly vulnerable state of mind. His brother was dying of cancer, and his bishop had sent him away from home on diocesan business. Andrew had doubts about his own integrity and identity. To add to this, he felt very lonely in an unfamiliar place, ''a stranger in a strange town.'' The nocturnal hours spent in an impersonal setting triggered off an agonizing sense of forsakenness. This promoted Andrew to surrender himself to God in prayer, and the vision ''came suddenly,'' while he was apparently wide awake.

This fourth vision is strikingly Indian in character. Andrew, much against his best intentions as an Anglican priest, makes contact with the white bear spirit. There is a protracted debate between the two, Andrew being uncertain as to whether he should honour the bear's directions. He is disturbed by the conflict between the spirit of the white bear and the God of Christianity. The entire teaching of the missionary church militated against the spirit world of the native people. There was no room for dialogue. The missionaries had taught that Christianity was right and native teachings were from the devil. Andrew is in a dilemma: ''How can I listen, when I'm a clergyman, to this creature?'' But the bear does not see any contradiction. He assures Andrew: ''Even though you don't believe now, you will believe later.'' The bear neither condemns Christianity nor upholds it. There is no missionary zeal to convert Andrew. Instead, the bear offers to teach him how to make medicine.

Then comes a pronouncement whose Christological component

has been sadly overlooked. The bear, smiling and sporting inches-long teeth, says: ''I am willing to give my body to be killed, so that you can take me and use me for that medicine.'' This sacrificial, eucharistic element in the bear vision focuses on the essence of Christian spirituality. In an indirect way, the bear was affirming Andrew's adopted spirituality without giving his blessing to the triumphalist Christianity of the white church. The friendly, powerful, and gentle bear offers himself as a sacrifice for the healing of humanity and so represents the spirit of the Lamb of God more authentically than the blonde, austere Caucasian Jesus of expansionist, colonial Euro-Christianity.

The medicine which the white bear offers with his sacrificial death is meant to atone for the sinful lifestyle of the newcomers to the country and to heal the hurt which their unwholesome western culture has inflicted on native people. Says the bear to Andrew:

> When this world was created, all creation was perfect at the beginning of time . . . but you people, your people, are dying of germs, all kinds of germs, your people are dying. But with this formula that I am going to teach, a lot of them will survive. I'm sent here to come and teach you, and you are to do it.

The white bear vision brings the conflict between missionary Christianity and native spirituality into sharp focus for Andrew. He wakes up, looks at his clerical collar and says to himself: ''Andrew, are you going crazy? You are crazy. How are you going to do it, to be a priest in the Anglican church and to be a medicine man?'' This conflict was probably not completely resolved to the end of his life. The tenor of his ministry from then on may be best summarized by his own apt phrase, spoken in his revealing talk to the group in Winnipeg: ''Sometimes we burn, sometimes we tremble.'' But just as it raised issues of conflict between the church and native spirituality, the white bear vision also underlined the theme of sacrificial atonement which is the essence of the gospel of Christ. Thus, the bear vision implicitly spoke for compatibility between native spirituality and the spirituality of Christ. The real conflict is between the Christ of the gospels and the Christ of the white missionary church. The bear vision brings the contradiction to a head and shows the way out.

Chapter 6

The Quest of Hope in the Canadian Church

The Christian church began among the native American as a missionary venture with the frontier mentality to christianize the "wild, wild West." Blinded by the blinkers of Eurocentrism, the church failed to realize that it was a people with a unique spirituality from which it would have benefited immensely had it been humble and true to the spirit of Christ. However, the Canadian church remained white, European, colonial. Now it has to rethink its image, refashion a viable theology of mission, renew itself with a transfusion of native spirituality, and restructure its ties with the native people. A creative impetus in this direction came with the publication of the Hendry Report in 1969; and things have not been the same ever since.

Although the established church had always claimed among its loyal membership a sizable percentage of native people, its theology, structure, and vision had hitherto hardly reflected the native presence. With the arrival of the Hendry Report, the nameless ghosts in the ecclesiastical closet were, for the first time in the history of the Canadian church, named, if not exorcized. A healing process of renewal began. Increasingly the church set out to question and confront itself. A rare show of repentance was on the horizon. Studies of native spirituality at church-funded seminaries were begun and new methods of training for ministry were pioneered among native ordinands. Whatever the sins of the past, the church in Canada across the mainline denominations showed signs of being poised on its own Vision Quest. Among native peoples there was hope for the future in the church.

The Hendry Report: Before and after

Up until the Second World War there was little contact between native and non-native people in Canada, nor concern for the native people's plight. Many, if not most, whites assumed that native people would eventually die out and were therefore not a force to be reckoned with. But after the war this "out-of-sight-out-of-mind" syndrome was no longer tenable. The native population was on the increase. On many reserves they faced the prospect of a total economic blight brought on by the erosion of their natural means of livelihood by hunting, fishing, and cropping. The white takeover of their ancestral lands only aggravated this situation. The resulting urban migration created new demands on existing social structures, while European schooling and a wider initiation into the white man's world fostered new expectations on the part of native people.

A study undertaken by the Anglican church in the early 1960s highlights this post-war period "as the re-entry of the Indian into the stream of Canadian life and history." Efforts were made to monitor the changing conditions of native people, but the church, hampered by a chronic shortage of manpower and money, was slow to respond to the new challenges. Growing concern during the 1960s led to successive investigations as the church tried to re-evaluate its missionary stance and explore the possibilities of native intitiatives. The rise of "Red or Indian Power" precipitated awareness that the native people had emerged as a major political force. A report to the Anglican General Synod in 1967 calls for "forgiveness regarding Anglican participation in the perpetuation of injustices to Indians." But reconciliation cannot be bargained unilaterally with words and there can be no Christian forgiveness if restoration and healing of the Body of Christ does not follow on from this repentance. Nonetheless, an equivocal admission of white guilt had been rendered and the church was challenged to reorientate its social policy towards indigenous leadership.

A conference on church and society in Montreal the following year, with the theme "Christian Conscience and Poverty," led to Dr. Charles Hendry being commissioned to make a thorough investigation of Anglican church policies and programs. His report, *Beyond Traplines*, was accepted by General Synod in

August 1969. Hendry charted the specific steps which needed to be taken to implement change. Top priority was given to the necessity for a change in basic attitudes toward native peoples, both within the church and within the wider society.

Incisive as this report is in social analysis and recommendations for action, it has certain limitations. There is no attempt to ground its prophetic vision in the Scripture. Nor does it offer any theological tools by which the church can seriously enter into dialogue with native spirituality. Without theological and spiritual dialogue any new relationship with native peoples must fail to be sufficiently radical in its thinking and praxis. Unlike the whites, the natives regard social and political life as a direct expression of their spirituality. Says Archbishop Hambidge:

> An understanding of Indian spirituality encourages an understanding of all other aspects of Indian life. When the church sees life as a whole then it also recognizes that justice issues are as much concern as the religious life. A Halleluia religion is not enough. The church must be involved with political and justice issues as well.[1]

Ultimately, what is at issue is the relenting of power and sharing of privilege as much in the religious realm of the church as in the secular realm of the society at large. It is as important to honour the political rights of the native people, and to grapple with economic issues affecting them, as to affirm their spirituality. The development of a bi-cultural policy in the Anglican church in New Zealand, founded on the principle of total partnership in protecting the spiritual as well as the secular interests of the Maori minority, could provide a viable model in setting up new structures in the Canadian church. Of course, the prerequisite is to trace the spiritual context of seemingly non-spiritual socio-economic issues. Hendry, the social scientist, cannot be faulted for not providing the theological bedrock for his prophetic vision. Subsequent reports spawned by the Anglican church have not materially filled this lacuna. We in our own modest way have tried to make up for this deficiency.

In previous chapters we have dealt with the salient issues raised by Hendry. For him, the really crucial question was:

Does the Church mean what it says about wanting to minister to Canada's native peoples? Or will it be content with token measures? In man-in-the-street language, the time has come for the churches "to put up or shut up." The Church must face the fact that — whatever have been its merits or deficiencies in the past — present social programs are having little effect on the massive poverty and alienation of the native people.[2]

It is not our brief to trace all the repercussions which the Hendry Report triggered off. One thing stands out clearly; the church went through a conversion experience and saw the need to commit itself to being "a transforming influence" in Canadian society. According to Peter Hamel, consultant on national affairs to General Synod, "action was taken to redeem past errors of commission and omission. . . . The old Anglican style of phrasing its protest so ambiguously and so politely that no one could suffer shock was put on the shelf."[3] The church set about acquiring a new vision in allowing native people space for self-determination.

The Primate's World Relief and Development Fund, established in 1959, was primarily responsible for funding a wide variety of new ventures. A clear need was perceived to expand, deepen, and transform the church's theological premises. This precipitated a move from the do-gooding apologist stance of the missionary era to a profound concern for working towards justice. This commitment continues to this day. In Canada the PWRD Fund has responded to a wide spectrum of native initiatives.

As an inter-church project on northern development, Project North spearheaded much of the work done by the church as a whole to assist the native peoples in their struggle for sovereignty. It began as a task force on the church in the North, set up in 1970 to sort out the Anglican church's priorities in response to Hendry's recommendations. The task force challenged the Anglican church to move beyond its previous "ambulance" ministry of "picking up the wounded and of protest" to becoming actively involved politically with governments and corporations in confronting social justice issues affecting native peoples.

The first step was the establishment of the Public Social Responsibility Unit by General Synod in 1973. One of the key areas in

the unit's portfolio was aboriginal rights and northern development. In 1975 it facilitated a resolution through General Synod
calling on the General, Provincial, and territorial governments
to halt northern industrial development projects until aboriginal
land claims had been settled and to initiate negotiations on land
claims issues without prior conditions. That same year saw the
establishment of Project North as a coalition of Canadian
churches. By combining forces they could command greater
resources and carry more clout as an action group. Initially, the
coalition involved the Anglican, United, and Roman Catholic
churches. Later, they were joined by the Presbyterian, Lutheran,
Mennonite, and Evangelical Lutheran churches in Canada. Project North's major objectives were:

> To support the native people in the recognition and implemen-
> tation of their aboriginal rights and claims, and to challenge
> and mobilize the Church and other constituencies in southern
> Canada to deal with the ethical issues related to northern
> development.[4]

In 1976 Project North held a Listening Conference with leaders
of native organizations across Canada to establish its priorities.
Four major areas were identified for action relating to native
rights, land claims and development projects among Dene, Inuit,
and Indians in the north. An increased understanding of native
attitudes towards the spirituality of creation led Project North to
take environmental justice as seriously as social justice. Deep concern for the havoc wreaked by the prevailing ideologies of
materialism and technological progress, in terms of human suffering and ecological devastation, resulted in a call for a
moratorium on all major resource development projects in the
Yukon and the Northwest Territories until land claims had been
settled and implemented.

Project North has had a proud record in public education and
advocacy even if it sometimes crossed swords with northern
bishops of the Anglican church in achieving its ends. Sadly, it
closed its doors at the end of 1987. There were administrative difficulties in holding the ecumenical coalition together, conflicting
views as to its vision, and a loss of interest by the native constituencies it was meant to serve. However, new moves are ahead.

In the 1980s Project North was drawn into the native people's struggle to have their rights recognized in the Canadian constitution, so expanding the scope of its work to include aboriginal rights issues in the south. The just settlement of native claims entrenched in the constitution is seen as being the responsibility of every member of the church. As Chief Rod Robertson of the Nisga says: "My fellow Christians, we the Nisga people, like our bishop, would hope that our struggle is indeed your struggle, that our dignity is indeed your dignity, that our truth is indeed your truth.[5]

Following the Hendry Report, the Anglican church made an effort to put its house in order by increasing native participation in its decision-making bodies and appointing a consultant on native affairs. In the years that followed, Adam Cuthand, Andrew Ahenakew, and John Jeffries did sterling work in keeping native concerns before General Synod. The forming of a Sub-Committee on Native Affairs in 1973 was a further step forward in providing native people with a forum within the structures of the church, even if they had to function under the watchful eye of the Program Committee. Taking stock in 1980, the S.C.N.A. called for indigenization in the church, in which Indian Christianity would come "to a fullness and maturity of its own and not simply an adaptation or imitation of missionary Christianity"; and it stressed the need for a native bishop. This plea has become ever more insistent over the years but the church has been slow to respond. It also stressed the importance of the move towards native self-determination, "from dependence to independence and responsibility":

> It is important for the Church to realize that longstanding policies such as the appointment of clergy to native communities by the Bishop, without prior consultation with the people, will come under question. Orientation to culture and language will be required resulting in a highly specialized ministry.

General Synod responded by elevating the Sub-Committee's status to a Council on Native Affairs with Adam Cuthand as the new consultant. The Council now had direct access to General Synod, giving native people a much more forceful voice in the shaping of church policy. And it has gone from strength to strength. The Council is made up of sixteen to twenty native persons. Four are appointed by the primate and the rest represent those dioceses which have more than a one-third native membership. The Reverend Laverne Jacobs, former chairperson of the Council, took over as national co-ordinator of native ministries in 1987. The council sees its purpose as being two-fold: to increase the visibility of native people at all levels of decision-making in the church, and to make native people at the community level aware of the church's concern by meeting among them and providing an opportunity for dialogue. Janet had the chance to experience the reality of these aims when she had the good fortune to meet with the Council at New Aiyansh, in the Nass Valley, in June 1987.

Janet arrived a few days early and was billeted with the Reverend Percy and Doris Tait. Percy was the host member of C.N.A. and was kept busy fulfilling his many duties as chief councillor and priest of this Nisga village as well as arranging our program. It is quite an adventure reaching the Nass Valley; this gives an idea of the remoteness of many native communities and how out of touch they must feel with the wider church family. One starts off in style from Terrace, skirting a series of breathtakingly beautiful lakes strung out along a narrow mountain valley. Then, abruptly, one's eyes become riveted to the road as tar changes to dirt and the car goes bumping and swaying into the loggers' domain. The area was only opened up to road transport in 1957; until then the only means of communication was by river. Timber trucks still have the right of way and this makes for adventuresome driving as they roar past in clouds of white dust. The road to New Aiyansh runs through an extraordinary flow of lava, solidified into a surrealist lunar landscape of pitted black boulders.

Nina Burnham, from Six Nations Reserve in Ontario, was another to arrive early and Janet and she spent a day exploring the Nass Valley and meeting the people. The small Salvation Army stronghold of Canyon City is entered by a long swing bridge for pedestrians only, with the river swirling far below. Small comfort that the bridge has been known to flip over in a fierce wind. Greenville, further down-river, sports a new road bridge, but watch out for bears in the forest verge. The salmon fishing season had just started. Local fishermen were offloading their early-morning catches, while commercial fishermen were making last-minute preparations to their boats and fixing their nets. Women were hard at work in their backyards, processing salmon for winter stores. Viciously sharp knives were being wielded at top speed and the sliced fish expertly packed into cans. In the smokehouses, row upon row of drying salmon fillets gleamed golden in the smoky gloom. Care has to be taken to keep the wood burning slowly night and day, and the women labour long and hard. Talking to these people one came to appreciate why the C.N.A. sets such store by meeting with them in their communities and entering into their lives, even if only for a few days. The sophistication and ease of access of a centrally situated city venue could never replace the immediacy of experience found in isolated native areas.

Back in New Aiyansh, Doris Tait was slaving away in her smokehouse in between her duties as a community health worker, attending a Nisga Valley Assembly on health care, preparing for a family wedding, providing food for community celebrations, and welcoming the C.N.A. members. They streamed in, travel-weary from all over Canada — Fort McPherson, Old Crow, Moose Jaw, Forest, Canwood, Ohsweken, La Ronge, Easterville, Fisher Branch, Westmount, and Ottawa. They came with stories to tell of native issues and church life in their dioceses, and these reports took up the first part of the meeting. Some had good news. Others found relief in unburdening their disappointments, frustrations, and anger. But no matter the mood, there was always laughter close at hand to chase away the tears, and the very act of sharing was a healing of the many hurts. The formal business agenda followed, with all the procedural exactitude of the western committee system.

The issues in which the C.N.A. have become involved are widely ranging: more native priests, adequate pay for clergy, specialized ecumenical urban ministries incorporating native spirituality, native-language and native-oriented Christian education resource material, a college for native ministry, cross-cultural orientation of non-native church workers, constitutional recognition of aboriginal rights, legal recognition of land claims, housing and unemployment benefits which enhance native self-worth, and ecumenical and international links with other indigenous peoples. But the C.N.A. complains that the native people's voice is still not being heard in the church whether this be in diocesan and national decision-making bodies or in the absence of a native element in the Anglican liturgy. The Anglican church has continued to reaffirm its stand on native rights and to promote native self-determination. Yet overseas partners in the 1986 Partners in Mission consultation stressed the need of the church to strengthen the ministry of native peoples.

The C.N.A. met at New Aiyansh from the Thursday until the Sunday, but all was not work. One evening we attended a banquet put on for the elders by the youth, feasting on local specialities such as fish roes, dried seaweed, and salmon of every description, and being entertained with music. The highlight, however, was the Nisga wedding on the Saturday and this was a marvelous opportunity to share in local village life. Laverne Jacobs was roped in to play the organ during the service and Willy Hodgson, acting chairperson of the C.N.A., gave thanks at the reception on our behalf. Despite dancing half the night through, the C.N.A. were out in full force the next morning for Holy Eucharist in St. Peter's church. Percy celebrated the Mass, Bishop Caleb Lawrence, the episcopal representative, preached, Laverne played the organ, and the rest of us constituted the choir. We were reminded of the Nisga contribution to Indian Christianity with Percy robed in his splendid button-blanket vestments, the Nisga liturgy as the order of service, and Nisga graphics all around the walls.

The ethos of the C.N.A. is well illustrated in the native design of its logo created by Bill Powless of the Six Nations Reserve. This design brings together many ancient native symbols and lays them within a circle at the centre of the Christian cross, thus representing the aspirations of native people to full participation within the church. There is the eagle with outstretched wings symbolizing vision, protection, guardianship, and freedom; the white pine for peace, the green of the tree for new life, and its outstretched branches for shelter; buried weapons for everlasting peace; four white roots for the four directions of the earth; and a blue background for the whole universe. The logo is said to remind "all Christians of Christ's deep love and concern for the more vulnerable people — which is the basis for the Anglican Church's commitment to stand beside the native people of Canada as they face their common struggle for social, economic, legal and political justice."

Native Women in Dialogue with the Church

In March 1981 the ecumenical Women's World Day of Prayer was celebrated with a service prepared by native American women from all over the United States, entitled "The Earth is the Lord's." This was a brave attempt by native women to initiate a dialogue between native spirituality and Christian faith, and to share it with their sisters around the world. But it raised a furor in the Anglican Church of Canada when certain bishops branded the service as being "seriously deficient or sub-Christian."

"Sparks Fly over World Day of Prayer Service" blazoned the headlines in the *Canadian Churchman*. And accusations of ethnocentricity, sexism, racism, and paternalism were hurled at the bishops' heads as various women's pressure groups in the Canadian church took up the cudgels on behalf of the native women. Misrepresentation seems to have added much heat to the ensuing debate. Unleashed were all the tensions that had been simmering beneath the surface in the church. But the crux of the matter was, and remains, theological rather than emotive. What is native? What is Christian? Where do the twain meet, if at all? Where do they overlap? Where do they conflict? These are some of the salient questions.

The native women who composed the liturgy were all Christians, but some were steeped in the traditional ways of native life and were thus able to bridge both worlds. They introduced the theme of creation in the service by noting that native American people are said to be the first ecologists: "Their reverence for nature and their relation of kinship with all creatures of the earth, sky and water enable them to teach us how to live justly, respectfully and in harmony with our world and each other." Authority for presenting a dialogue between two religious traditions stemmed from the Hopi belief that there is only one human race, divided into two groups — light and dark. Accordingly, only when the dark-skinned peoples with their "gift of knowing," and the light-skinned peoples with their "gift of recording and doing," come together at the centre and share their gifts "would each receive a Greater Gift than either alone can ever give."

The service began with a native American prayer, an Iroquois thanksgiving to the Great Spirit, and a reading of selected verses from the story of creation in Genesis 1:1-28. The liturgy then continued in four parts entitled — the sorrow of the earth, the healing of earth's wounds, the offering of gifts of self and substance, and the new earth. Scripture readings provided a biblical framework in developing these ideas. They were taken from Joel 1, Psalm 103:13-17, 2 Chronicles 7:12-15, 2 Corinthians 5:17, Matthew 5:23-24, a paraphrase of Ephesians 1, and Revelations 21:1-5. Appropriate hymns were also suggested.

The native contribution to the liturgy drew on the riches of their myth, symbol, and ceremonial tradition. Significantly, each of the four sections made space for silent reflection. As Black Elk has said, ''Silence is the very voice of the Great Spirit.'' In the first litany the earth was personified as ''mother,'' and she spoke of her sorrow at man's despoiling of the world. After each of her indictments came the refrain, ''Are you listening?'' and the people's response, ''We are listening, Mother Earth.'' The theme of sorrow was continued in the mystic oratory of Sealth (Chief Seattle) on surrendering his tribal lands to the United States government in 1854, a poignant testimony to the suffering of native people in their displacement. In the second section, the litany and prayers for the healing of the earth were all addressed to the Great Spirit as a continuation of native thought-patterns. Section three began with a meditation on the theme ''who am I in relation to the earth and its people?'', with searching questions to stimulate a repentant awareness. The act of confession was based on Matthew 5:23-4, and stressed the interdependence of all people and their mutual responsibility to present and future generations. An important native insight in the offering was the emphasis on spiritual as well as sacrificial giving: ''In the process of healing, people must offer some part of themselves in a spiritual way through which they will continue their passage through to the cleansing and renewal which begins the new cycle of life.'' In the last section, the Lakota ceremony of praying to the four directions in the form of a cross was adapted for use as a Christian litany with the following explanation:

> Five poles are set up in the form of a cross, one at the centre and one at each of the four directions. In some traditions west is the direction from which come purifying waters, north is the direction of purifying winds, east, being the source of the rising sun and the morning star, is the direction from which

comes knowledge and wisdom, and south is the direction of guidance and the source and end of life.

A person in search of "vision," seeking wisdom and understanding and attempting to reach union with the Great Spirit (Wakan-Tanka) fasts and prays and follows the prescribed ritual. At each of the directions, the person prays: "O Wakan-Tanka, have pity on me, that my people may live." And returns to the centre between prayers.

A parallel was drawn with the apostle Paul, with a paraphrasing of the first part of his letter to the Ephesians. The contention was that he was speaking of Christ as centre:

Let us praise God for the gift given us in Jesus Christ by whose death we are set free. In all wisdom and insight, God fulfilled and made known to us the plan made from the beginning of time . . . to bring all creation together, everything in heaven and on earth with Christ as centre.

In adapting the Lakota ceremony the people were asked to begin by facing a central point, and to return to the centre each time before facing the next of the four directions in prayer. The prayer was again antiphonal with the leader identifying the symbolic ethos of each direction as a focus for their petitions. The concluding litany was composed by Lois Long, a Sioux, and addressed the "Almighty One" as "Wakantanka Tunkasila."

There were various levels of criticism of the service, the harshest being from eleven bishops of Rupert's Land. They had met in Winnipeg the previous week and the question as to whether the service was Christian or not had been raised right at the end of the meeting. After a quick look at a single copy they had expressed the feeling that although the liturgy was "rather beautiful and certainly spiritually elevating," it was not Christian. One bishop volunteered to write a confidential report to be used as they wished. None appear to have forbidden the service, as later alleged, but the fat was in the fire.

The report came into the hands of the *Canadian Churchman* and the bishops were said to have sent a letter to their clergy and laity advising them not to participate in the service unless alterations were made. The native women's cause was taken up by members of the Anglican Church Women's Unit and the Women's Inter-Church Council of Canada among others, and the debate was shifted to wider issues. The bishops were castigated for their put-down of women, of native people, and of the laity for daring to compose a liturgy, swamping the original charge of religious discrimination. In vain did the bishops attempt to refute most of the accusations. The press failed to give them a hearing.

As reported in the *Canadian Churchman*, the bishops maintained that many of the scriptural passages, especially those from the Old Testament, invited an interpretation that was "pantheistic, rather than ethical monotheistic":

> It is our conviction that as a Christian act of devotion this service is, to say the least, sub-Christian; on the other hand, if it is intended for a gathering of Christians and non-Christians, its use can be defended. . . . Christians taking part in such an act of worship need not feel they are being guilty of infidelity to God as Christians know him in Christ.

In the report, the bishops questioned how they could distinguish between the times when the earth was apostrophized as Mother Earth and when she was addressed "as though she were a god." And whether the name "Great Spirit (Wakan-Tanka)" could be "equated with the God of the Christians." The paraphrasing of Ephesians 1:10 was also said to be unjustified. But the main issue was that "Christ crucified is not fully upheld." The report ended by saying that the bishops could not commend the service because of its serious deficiencies as an act of Christian devotion: "Christ is in no sense central in this service and indeed there is hardly any mention of him."

The Anglican bishop of Montreal followed much the same line. He was concerned about the dangers of "syncretism," arguing that the service had a tendency to absorb the tenets of one faith into the system of another. This was not in accord with the New Testament understanding of the Christian faith nor was the New Testament pattern to encourage "pantheism" or "animism." The bishop argued that respect for the earth, while part of a Christian's responsibility, was not the means of salvation. It was essential to hold Jesus Christ "as the Lord of our faith and worship. This is not the nature of this service," he wrote.

In a letter to his clergy in the diocese of Qu'Appelle, Bishop

Michael Peers (now Anglican primate) took a more conciliatory approach in addressing the complex issues involved:

> It often seems to me that we encourage this sort of thing in faraway lands, but are much more uneasy with it on our own doorstep. Perhaps we should do two things — on one hand, be more sensitive to those troubled by these changes in (places like) Africa and the South Pacific; on the other, be more sensitive to those urging the same phenomena in North America.

Nevertheless, he recommended that his clergy should make judicious adjustment if the service was being used in an Anglican church. Any suggestion of prayer "about the dialogue with the earth" should be scrupulously avoided, and the Sioux prayer at the end should be omitted. Changes were also made in the British form of the service, and this was the version used by the Salvation Army in Canada. Some of the Roman Catholic bishops actually forbade the service.

The Reverend James Boyle, ecumenical officer of the Anglican Church of Canada, was one of those who decried the "unfortunate lack of ecumenical sensitivity in the Church." "The task of reconciliation is becoming more and more difficult," he complained. He made an impassioned plea for serious consideration to be given to how the Gospel could be "planted and rooted in a culture different from our own." One result of the controversy was the showing of an audio-visual on native spirituality to General Synod two years later. The Women's Unit of the Anglican church took an even more positive step by bringing together a collection of articles on Christianity and native spirituality as a means of conscientizing non-native people about the issues involved. But nowhere was there any endeavour to grapple with the questions raised in the service by using it as a model for ongoing theological discussions.

For the first and perhaps the only time an entire Christian liturgy using full-blown native symbols was devised and performed thanks to the courage, ingenuity and inspiration of native women. This liturgy is probably the best attempt yet at instituting a native-Christian dialogue.

The United Church Apology to Native People

British Methodists began work in Canada in 1840 as chaplains to the Hudson's Bay Company and missionaries to the native people. They remained twenty years and during this time the native church flourished, raising up its own strong leadership. However, the appointment of a Canadian superintendent coincided with a flood of white settlers and their needs became paramount. The native spiritual leaders were ignored and the creative dialogue which the first missionaries had so painstakingly built up was replaced by ''a coercive, paternalistic approach.'' The sorry pattern of assimilation was followed as strenuously as in any of the other churches, aided by the residential school system and support of government suppression of native culture and language. At the time of union with the Presbyterian church, the concerns of the white congregations remained central. Native congregations continued to be relegated to a dependent mission status without any say in the decision-making structures of the church.

By the early 1980s, the Reverend Stanley McKay, national coordinator of the Native Ministries Council in the United church, had ample justification in depicting the native wing of the church as a dying community. The number of native congregations had dropped in the past twenty years from seventy-seven to about fifty-five. Nonetheless, the cultural nationalism of the pan-Indian movement had stirred up new life, and native initiatives in the church had precipitated a quiet revolution. The Indian Ministry Training Program was begun in the 1970s to train elders in the church and promote their ordination. This snowballed into a standing church committee on native ministry training and the setting up of a new ministry training model based at the Dr. Jessie Saulteaux Training Centre at Fort Qu'Appelle in Saskatchewan.

Native church structures were the next to be shaken by the winds of change. The native congregations were spread across twenty-one presbyteries in nine conferences. But the native people's growing demand for self-determination at every level motivated a move towards forming their own native presbyteries, and, ultimately, a native conference to provide a forum for the concrete sharing of power and responsibility. In 1981 the first all-native United church presbytery, Keewatin, was constituted in northern Manitoba. Three years later saw the establishment of a second one, called Plains, in Saskatchewan. But, as Stan McKay explained at the time, the native church was "still kind of an appendage. We can influence change but we still have very little room in which to experiment." What they have been looking for is a place at the negotiating tables and the chance to have their say in formulating programs and determining leadership policy. Says Stan:

> Native people are people who do not feel at home in terms of the decision-making structure. There is an experience of non-involvement and, in different ways, of being manipulated within the process that must be seen for what it is, structural racism. Despite all the good intentions of the non-Native people the agenda was always set and the process has always moved in ways that excluded us.[6]

The Reverend Bob Hamlin, President of the Manitoba and Northwestern Ontario Conference in 1985, defends this apparent balkanizing in the church: "It's not like apartheid, because it's not a majority excluding a minority, it's a minority choosing to be on their own." In 1987 another native presbytery was set up of Cree and Stoney people within the Alberta and Northwest Conference, called *Inivinuk* (a Cree word meaning "all tribes"). And in the summer of 1988 the All Native Circle Conference was formally inaugurated for the native members at the United church's thirteenth Conference. This is to include all the native United church congregations outside British Columbia. Stan McKay has seen the Conference issue as symbolic of a desire of the native congregations "no longer to thrive as children within the family," but rather "to take on some power and some direction, which we will determine." There is also the need for natives and whites within the church to learn to exchange their gifts. The main barrier, according to Stan, is "our sense of exclusion from the Church's processes through all our history and a sense that you (the white church) are always the ones to give and never need to receive."[7]

Alberta Billy is the woman who challenged the United church to come up with the famous Apology to the native people. We visited her at Cape Mudge, a Kwakiutl fishing village on Quadra

Island off the northwest coast of Vancouver Island. Her home is just across the road from the Kwakiutl museum, guarded by stately totem poles. Nearby stands the church, with fishing boats moored below. These are symbols of the passionate priorities in her life: her total dedication to recovering the spiritual integrity and cultural identity of her people, and her fight for justice with regard to their livelihood, salmon fishing. Alberta is wedded to the sea, assisting her husband on their boat during the season. Her fury over federal government control of the fishing industry knows no bounds: "They have taken over and tell us what we know how to do best! Where to fish, when to fish, how to fish! People are just not aware of what is happening."

Alberta is the youngest looking grandmother we have yet to meet. A warm, affectionate woman, with laughing eyes and a husky voice, she personifies the spirit that gave rise to the Apology. Her campaigning is an expression of her commitment to the survival of her people, not a rabble-rousing political grandstanding. This came across in her mannerisms, directness, humour, courage, dignity, and her total willingness to be just, as much to whites as to her own people. It would be a total travesty of Alberta's stance if we lumped her together with professional church people who make a career out of raising issues. Her vitality expresses a lack of vengefulness and hate. She lives out her spirituality and has an abiding faith in the harmony of the spirit world. The justice which she seeks on the socio-political front for her people is part of this cosmic harmony in the spirit world. The two are linked. Ecology, politics, and spirituality are mere synonyms in the dictionary of her native earth-bound spirituality. As far as the history of the native people is concerned everything seems to be in full circle. Her hope for her people is for a rediscovery of their original spirituality:

> "Reverence for Mother Earth was the centre of our being. We need to go back to our traditional spiritual teaching, and the values of that teaching, to survive as a people. We are trying to regain our identity and become strong once again. Otherwise we will be lost as a people for ever."[8]

Alberta evinces a healthier understanding of Christian confession than do most Christians. For her, true repentance embraces redressal and restoration of the breach. Hers is not only an ethical but a cosmological understanding of sin, confession and forgiveness arising out of her holistic, cyclical native spirituality. The established church has lost this dimension and would do well to receive it gratefully from such as her.

Alberta is not interested in ideologies. Rather, she taught us to look at people. She incarnates what she believes and fights for. There is no split between her being and her value system, unlike what we find in the established white western ethos with its Cartesian split between who you are and what you represent. That is why she is a truly spiritual woman. She gave the United church an opportunity to recover its own spirituality, the spirituality of Christ. In so doing she has restored and rehabilitated the church no less than her own people.

As Alberta describes it, the first step in her involvement in the Apology was the formation of the Coastal Regional Group of the United church by a concerned band of native people in the early 1980s. Young, middle-aged, and old, they came together to form a pressure group within the church. Alberta was not overly enthusiastic about attending their first meeting in Victoria as she had been decidedly unimpressed by her previous experience with an ecumenical task force during the 1970s:

> The task force was supposed to have communication and connection with native people across Canada, and help rectify Indian issues wherever they should arise. But it was set up by white people with only token Indian input. There was no communication and no connection with grassroots people. It failed because white people were still talking at us and from above. Indians were not given much chance to speak for themselves. They would have known what to do but they were not listened to.

Mercifully, the Coastal Regional Group proved different. As a formalized structure within the United church it received official recognition, and together with other native pressure groups it was able to make things happen. A national board was formed and this became the National Native Ministries Council with Stan McKay as co-ordinator. Alberta was the representative for British Columbia and in March 1985 she was one of three chosen to represent the N.M.C. at a General Council executive meeting in Toronto. ''I did not think we were there to do any kind of business," she laughed, "but only as token Indian people. I went to report on what the church was not doing and to remind them of what they had promised to do." But then came the shock. Alberta, with strength and courage coming from the sure conviction that her late grandfather was standing by her side, brought the proceedings to a standstill, by saying: "You know, Mr. Moderator, I have one more item to add to my report. I really believe that the church owes us an apology. We were stripped of our natural native spirituality."⁹

Recalling the experience, she explained that it was done "to free the elders so that they could come back and teach us our stories, our legends, our songs and our dances, and not to be afraid to say 'This is who I am.' They were not doing that because they had structured their lives by the Bible."

What Alberta looked for in a formal apology was affirmation: "Anyone can say I am sorry and not necessarily mean it. What I wanted to come out of the Church was that they realize that they had taken something away from us and that we have so much to offer them. And that in order to survive we all needed to come together."

On 15 August 1986, Moderator Robert Smith made history by leading the United Church of Canada in the Act of Apology to their native congregations, asking forgiveness for the way in which they had long denied them their spirituality. The place was Laurentian University in Sudbury; the occasion, the meeting of the church's General Council. *The United Church Observer* gives a graphic account of the events.

> Hours earlier members of the National Native Consultation had made a final impassioned plea to the white Church for this act of repentance. "No longer can we live on the edge of society or the church," maintained Alberta Billy. "We come to teach, because we must once again mend and keep the cycle flowing." "Just think how much I can share with you about sweet grass," Floyd Steinhauer from Saddle Lake, Alberta, had urged. "Just think how much I can share with you with the peace pipe. My friends, I'm sure we'll live in a better world." But something as momentous as an Apology could not be hurried and the commissioners had needed further deliberations before they had finally been convinced that "it had not been

wrong to bring the Gospel — but it had been wrong not to hear the Gospel from the Native people.''

A statement of Apology was prepared by the General Council and Moderator Smith made ready to deliver it to the native people gathered at Sudbury. He prayed and then robed, using the purple stole for penitence, while the assembly sang ''Amazing Grace.'' He then led the procession of commissioners down the dark winding road to the fire-lit teepee where twenty elders were awaiting him. Seated in a circle, they too had been praying, but in the traditional native manner. Sweet grass and tobacco were the sacramental elements of their ancient ritual. After a long silence, Smith was invited to speak. The air was charged with emotion as he asked forgiveness on behalf of his church. The Apology was read a second time before the massing throng of native people waiting patiently in the grounds beyond. Smith's voice rang out in the darkness as he declared:

> ''Long before my people journeyed to this land your people were here, and you received from your elders an understanding of creation, and of the Mystery that surrounds us all that was deep, and rich and to be treasured.
>
> We did not hear you when you shared your vision. In our zeal to tell you of the good news of Jesus Christ we were closed to the value of your spirituality. We confused western ways and culture with the depth and breadth and length and height of the gospel of Jesus Christ.
>
> We imposed our civilization as a condition of accepting the gospel.
>
> We tried to make you be like us and in so doing we helped to destroy the vision that made you what you were. As a result you, and we, are poorer and the image of the Creator in us is twisted, blurred and we are not what we are meant by God to be.
>
> We ask you to forgive us and to walk together with us in the spirit of Christ so that our peoples may be blessed and God's creation healed.''[10]

''Of course we forgive you,'' the elders said. An old grandmother among them struggled to her feet and held Smith in her arms as she told him, "I have been waiting all my life to hear those words, not for myself, but for my grandchildren." "Of course we accept your apology," the native people echoed, and the soft sobbing of a woman swelled into a wave of weeping as the drums began to throb, expressing the cumulative sense of agony and joy.

The Apology had a mixed reaction in the Church, meeting with sympathy, hostility and indifference from both white and native communities. For many it was a welcome sign that the Church had at last recognized the authenticity of native spirituality, as well as being a symbolic act of the healing of past hurts. Said Bernice Saulteaux, who was present at the Apology, "It is important that some Church people realized that native spirituality is a part of our lives and that it isn't wrong."[11]

Others among native Christians, whose families had been in the church for many generations, could no longer relate to past traditions. One woman we spoke to in southern Ontario maintained that her London Native Conference was against bringing native culture and traditions back into the church because it was associated with unchristian practices, as well as being something that they had long since lost. Furthermore, she could not see the necessity of whites having to apologize for bringing Jesus to them. What they did all still feel sore about, though, was their treatment in residential schools. This type of response betrays the lack of awareness and analysis that the very white attitude which inflicted the injustices on them in secular matters was a reflection of the triumphalist Jesus-religion that they had brought the native people.

Some white people felt that the Apology was an attack on "the faithfulness and worthy intentions of the early missionaries," and that the church was selling out the Gospel. They feared that the native people were altering the place of Christ in the church. However, as Stan McKay patiently explains:

> The place of Christ is not in question, and never has been. That is central to us. But in my involvement in the United Church as a minister over the last 15 years, I have noted we have made the theology of the United Church very inclusive. We have tried to protect it. Sometimes we pretend we understand fully the message of the Kingdom. But the Gospel is very open. And

what the apology has brought into question, is how this experience of Native people can bring some insights into how all people can be faithful.[12]

Elsewhere Stan has spoken of the difficulties which indigenous people all over the world experience in having the value of their spirituality recognized:

> The oppression of indigenous people has gone hand in hand with the denial of their spiritual values and their spiritual pilgrimage. At times, certainly, we could claim that it was not intentional — it was a kind of natural process of innocence — but there are other examples that indicate that there were movers in the whole process who had a vision of the extermination of Native people. Genocide does fit the description of what their goals included.[13]

The educational material that went out before the Apology has an excellent section dealing with the radical nature of repentance, as seen in the Scriptures, and the theological significance of the church making a public act of repentance, besides the humanitarian aspect of such a gesture:

> Repentance does not demand that people feel guilty — ''the poor can't eat guilt.'' Repentance requires us to redress injustices so that people can eat. . . . A recognition of our denial of native culture is not enough to redress the wrong. Repentance of thought *and* deed are required. Repentance requires that we do justly not just think justly. It means that we must ''act'' in such a way that native congregations are given proper recognition, and that a new partnership is established with them.

Certainly, the Apology has meant much to many native people in the United church. There has been an upsurge of interest in incorporating native customs and culture within church worship. Drums are used in church while symbols such as the pipe, sweetgrass, and the talking stick were used in services of the 1988 General Council. Some congregations have responded to the new-found openness in the church by becoming more involved in its life and function. "The fact of being a Native person is important now," reported one minister. "There is definitely a movement of reemerging pride."

At the same time, native Christian leaders warn that the rebirth of native religious ideas and practices has brought their people to a spiritual crossroads. According to Stan McKay, there is entrenched opposition not only from white congregations but from conservative native congregations as well, and this could fracture the native community. Floyd Steinhauer, of Saddle Lake Reserve and native ministries co-ordinator for the United church's Alberta region, is more hopeful. "We are not saying that we are going to bring all the native religion into the church," he explains. "We are saying give us that open chance to express our ways of worshipping." But both men are deeply concerned about the inroads of militant evangelical churches into the reserves, whose white preachers teach that "Christ provides a narrow path to salvation and that native worship must be rejected as paganism and the tool of Satan." McKay regards this is a new wave of oppression. "I see it as slowing the process of dialogue and learning between the cultures."[14]

The formal native response to the Apology was given after the inauguration of the All Native Circle Conference at the Victorian General Council in 1988. After two years the native church elders were prepared only to "acknowledge" the Apology, not "accept" it. After centuries of oppression the healing process had only just begun in the church.

Doing Native Theology

"We want to be Indian and Christian." This was the constant refrain among both native clergy and laity in the Anglican church right across Canada. "What are the theological institutions doing about this?" we asked. "There has been no formal development of an Indian theology because there has been no study of Indian Christianity or teaching of Indian religion in theological schools," we were told. "In the mainstream theological colleges," added

Archdeacon Harry Hilchey, "there has not been much theological reflection on any native issues except in a general way. They have tended to emphasize counselling and training for ministry." So it is that the advanced theological education of natives has continued to be a tool of assimilation. With so little encouragement the wonder is that native church leaders like John Jeffries and Adam and Stan Cuthand have begun working on a native theology by exploring issues like the influence of Christianity on native culture, native spirituality and Christianity, and pastoral ministry to native people.

There have been new signs of hope in the Native Ministries Training Programs in the Anglican dioceses of the north as Janet discovered when she attended a conference on "Native Ministries and Our Future" in Edmonton in September 1985. Co-sponsored by the Council of the North and the Council on Native Affairs, this was the first time that a wide representation of native leaders in the church had met together. They came from the dioceses of the Arctic, Athabasca, Brandon, Caledonia, Cariboo, Keewatin, Moosonee, Saskatchewan, and the Yukon. The purpose of the conference was to enable native church leaders to share their experiences of the Anglican church and to work together in formulating their needs for developing spiritual leadership. The respective bishops were all present, having been requested to take a listening role, but some obviously found it extremely difficult to keep quiet!

Of great interest were the reports on the native training programs for ministry in the various dioceses. In the north most native communities are isolated and could only depend on occasional visits from their missionaries. This necessitated the development of a strong lay leadership from the start; but with time each diocese has followed a different emphasis in training in response to its particular needs.

The Arthur Turner Training School at Pangnirtung was begun in 1970 for Inuktetoot-speaking people in the diocese of the Arctic. It focuses on a Bible-oriented course and incorporates parish work in the curriculum. In contrast, the Henry Budd Christian Training Centre at The Pas serves Indian and Métis people, lay and ordained. Founded in 1980, in the diocese of Brandon, it aims to further the Christian expression of faith within the traditions of native culture and language, and to develop relevant material for theological education and study groups in native parishes. The diocese of Keewatin began an Aircraft Ministry in the 1960s to provide increased contact with isolated parishes, while its Train an Indian Priest Program, initiated in the early seventies, has been used to upgrade native church leadership. Senior catechists of long standing have been selected by their local congregations for training that will equip them for the non-stipendiary ministry as deacons and priests. This program has been criticized for creating second-class "trapper-priests"; but it was a creative response to the expressed needs of the local communities and has blossomed into an enthusiasm for lay training.

The diocese of Saskatchewan has an in-service training program under the umbrella of the James Settee School and uses material from the Cook Christian Training School in Arizona. The courses are designed to develop indigenous leadership for native American churches through Theological Education by Extension and cover socio-political issues as well as theological training. T.E.E. is based upon the belief that learning occurs best when study and practice of ministry are closely related and students are able to go at their own pace and their own level in their own communities.

St. John's College, at the University of Manitoba in Winnipeg, is attempting to develop extension courses for native people with more of a Canadian content and using local native languages. They too have been involved in providing Canadian input for a Sunday School curriculum developed in the Dakotas for native children. An indigenous theology must begin with children. For too long Anglican Sunday school material has perpetuated a white western image. We were told that children are more sensitive and better able to identify oppression than adults and can more readily see the relevance of the Scripture in this regard. Furthermore, as Adam Cuthand emphasizes, traditional native teaching began at an early age: "It was done by example, learning by discovery, storytelling and taking part in worship."

With all these different programs the question remains how to provide suitable theological education and patterns of ministry for a people steeped in an oral culture and a concept of ministry which includes the whole community? Perhaps the most adventurous attempt to find an answer has been the Ministry Development Program in the diocese of Caledonia which has followed the extension method since its inception in 1970. As the lay training program grew, a number of native congregations raised up candidates for the ordained ministry within their own parishes. Non-native congregations then followed suit. This trend was encouraged by Bishop Hambidge as he saw the importance of a community of faith identifying ministry within itself rather than leaving it to individual vocations as was the usual practice. However, this necessitated new patterns of ministry as the candidates had to be given training on the job. The communities also became involved as they took responsibility for the candidate's ongoing nurturing as part of a shared commitment. Another novelty was the inclusion of an evaluation and accreditation of the students' life experience as part of their assessment. Such a system has been found to accord well with traditional native patterns of ministry. As Bishop Hambidge explained:

> It's not appropriate to put some of our priests through the theological sausage machine for seven years, just because someone says that is the best way to train them. Very often it destroys ministry and people. Many of the people who graduate from college, are, in fact, ill-equipped for ministry in a diocese like Caledonia.[15]

While ministering in their villages candidates are encouraged to reflect on their people's experience from a theological perspective and so relate their training to their existential situation. The church-at-large has been apprehensive about these new models of ministry, seeing them as a threat to time-honoured professional standards. But close supervision by a skilled priest has ensured against turning out second-class pastors. The diocese's T.E.E. Centre has now been established in Terrace in conjunction with the Prince Rupert presbytery of the United church and graduates receive a diploma in theology and pastoral studies.

The diocese of Caledonia is a full partner in the Native Ministries Consortium. This includes the Coastal Regional Group of the United Church of Canada B.C. Conference, the Vancouver School of Theology, and the Cook Christian Training School. The summer schools which have been held at V.S.T. since 1985 are part of the group's aim to develop community-based training programs for native ministries under native direction. The courses are tailored to native interests and have covered such varied topics as Christian ethics and aboriginal title, the Indian family, a native view of caring for God's earth, apartheid and native Canadians, and native spirituality and indigenous Christianity. The consortium is now moving ahead to assist V.S.T. in developing a degree program by extension for native people. New courses are being designed to look at the interface between aboriginal and western theology; but the problem remains to find evaluative techniques which respect oral culture and are not exclusively committed to a literate culture. Initially this program will be directed to the Nisga people, but as a pioneering venture in North America it is hoped that it will cast its net wider.

Native ministries conferences have also been held at St. John's College, Winnipeg, since 1984. Led by native people, various themes have been adopted in an attempt to explore the relationship between native spirituality and the Christian faith. Such programs are invaluable as cross-cultural orientation training for non-native clergy.

In his report Hendry picked up the need for specialized training for all those involved in native ministry, beginning in the theological schools. This has yet to happen. Consequently, non-native clergy can have a difficult time serving in native communities. They do not know the language, the people, the culture, or the way of life. Culture shock is inevitable and many fail to adjust. They make unfortunate mistakes and this creates tension and alienation. Their ministry suffers and the native people are the losers. Now native people are themselves pushing to have cross-cultural orientation training made compulsory in the appointment of all new clergy to native communities. Internship to provide field experience is easily arranged, but what about suitable training? Programs in the United States are prohibitively expensive and Canadian programs for people going overseas are unsuitable. The immediate need is for ongoing local programs with a regular follow-up. The challenge to theological schools and universities is to take native theology and church history seriously, and to launch a program of instruction and research which will bring native and non-native people together in a new academic adventure. Canadian theology cannot take its place in the world until it acquires native content.

In recent years the United church has moved rapidly to explore ways of encouraging native people to initiate new theological developments. There is a native ministry program at St. Andrew's College in Saskatoon with native people contributing to the curriculum design. At the Dr. Jessie Saulteaux Resource Centre at Fort Qu'Appelle, Saskatchewan, students alternate between formal studies and practical experience in the field. At another level the church holds workshops with native people to develop indigenous theological material. The style of education is to include images and symbols which relate to native stories, history, the ecology, and the world around, while working at a theological theme. Outside stimulus has come with visits from native peoples from such places as Australia, the Phillipines, Chile, and Nicaragua. The Reverend Jenini Gondera, head of the Uniting Aboriginal Islander Christian Congress in Australia, made a particularly significant impact during his tour in 1986, by telling of his experience of trying to develop an indigenous aboriginal theology relevant to the Australasian setting.

Consensus Native News, edited by the indefatigable Stan McKay, is an exciting publishing venture covering a wide spectrum of interests for native people in the United church. News events; reports of consultations, council meetings and conferences; poetry; stories and legends, native customs and religious ceremonials; biographies of native leaders in the church — all this and more are contributed by native subscribers. They are the theologians.

As we have seen, the Catholic church, fired by the Second Vatican Council, was quicker to try and inculturate the Gospel among native American people than were the Protestant churches. Catholics have also done pioneering work in the building up of local churches in native communities based on the belief that "mission method today must be dialogical, and that proclamation itself can only take place in an atmosphere of free and open exchange." So says the Jesuit priest, academic and missionary Carl Starkloff.

According to Starkloff, a true dialogue respects "tribal religion for its own God-given values," as well as "those who freely choose Christianity" to become the church. Basic to this is the idea that inculturation of the Gospel is "a mutual process of cultural and spiritual transformation." What form the indigenous church will take depends entirely upon the Holy Spirit, "as the transforming element in the culture." But Starkloff warns against the dangers of superficial adaptation of native elements into

Catholic worship. Dialogue is a long and painstaking affair and genuine inculturation must embody the essence of the church in a culture, not just the outward forms of drums, sweetgrass, and ceremonial costumes.[16] Elsewhere, Starkloff has written, "If a white does enter into any form of conversation (with native people), he must do it as a learner, a beneficiary, even as a begger."[17] This is the rationale behind the dialogical method being used by the Catholic church at Kisemanito Centre at Grouard in Alberta, and Anishnabe Ministries Centre at Anderson Lake, near Sudbury, Ontario.

Wasseandimikaning is the local name for Anishnabe Centre. It is an Ojibway term meaning "a place where one's mind is enlightened." However, as Starkloff indicates, the Centre "is not simply a place where things are done; it is a symbol in itself of the movement toward a native church." So although the Anishnabe program is geared to ministry and priesthood training in a local setting, there is equal concern that it should facilitate the building-up of the local church. The monthly ministry training workshops are central to the program and it is in this context that dialogue takes place. The basic community method of study is followed and this has the advantage of relating the Scriptures to real-life situations. As Starkloff so trenchantly observes, "the community literally *absorbs* theology as it *does* theology." Furthermore, this theologizing is brought to full symbolic expression in the liturgy. No longer are native people the passive recipients of an alien westernized Gospel. Rather, the Gospel seed is nurtured in the soil of a local culture and the people find their own identity as Christians, relating their faith to their own experience. The church is alive and well in the native communities to the extent that it is a church *of* and *by* the people. Says Starkloff, "The entire Christian community has much to learn from the local Church's gradual acquisition of a native face and personality, and its contribution to the mosaic of the Universal Church."[18]

The Future of the Anglican Church's Quest

The consultation on "Native Ministries and our Future" in Edmonton in September 1985 was a seminal event for native people in the Anglican Church of Canada. For the first time clergy and laity came together from all over the country. For the first time they acquired a sense of their unity and their strength. This gave them a sense of hope because at last they were beginning to take control of their own future and to affirm the genius of their own particular contribution to the church as a whole.

"It doesn't stop here," said Alvin McKay, a Nisga educator and chief councillor from Greenville, British Columbia, who chaired the event. "There has to be continued dialogue. We have to find ways of articulating our concerns from time to time and at all levels." He suggested that more could be done at diocesan synods and regional meetings. "The real agents of change are the local parishioners," he argued. But a need was also seen for native Anglicans to establish a platform from which their voice could be heard nationally. The consultation decided to approach the primate to convene an all-native national convocation within two years. The idea of a "convocation" was to allow native people to reach decision by consultation and consensus, rather than following the European synodical model with its divisive parliamentary procedures.

The National Native Convocation finally took place in the autumn of 1988 in Fort Qu'Appelle, Saskatchewan. Beforehand a prayer calendar was sent to every Anglican parish in Canada so that non-native Anglicans could begin to identify the native congregations and those ministering to them by name and uphold them in prayer. But the one hundred and eighty delegates of the conference were all native people. There was one lay representative from each native congregation and nearly all of the native priests and deacons. Observers included a couple of Inuit of the Arctic diocese and the primate, Archbishop Michael Peers.

Story-telling was an important way of sharing life experiences, particularly faith experiences. As the Reverend Laverne Jacobs, co-ordinator of native ministries for General Synod, said afterwards,

> Some of these people have never been outside their isolated northern communities before. To be able to share their problems and their faith and to find they are not alone in the church has been a tremendously empowering experience for them.[19]

The final message of the native convocation to the church called for greater financial support of native ministries, a voice in the decision and policy-making bodies of the church (particularly in matters affecting their life and worship), and support in their struggle for aboriginal rights. During the convocation there had been highly charged emotional scenes as delegates vented their anger and frustration at past treatment in the church. There was even a suggestion that they should follow the example of their United church brethren in seeking an official apology from General Synod. But in the end the emphasis of their message was on affirming the centrality of aboriginal identity and culture. It was their conviction that "the God of traditional native spirituality and the God of the gospels are the same."[20]

As native people in North and South America approach the Columbus Day celebrations in 1992 they have very mixed feelings. On the one hand, they feel able to celebrate the fact that many native societies have survived contact with European peoples after five hundred years. But at the same time, the Canadian church must ask itself how it can honour its responsibility towards the first people of land. The Native Convocation has been an important step forward in the Anglican church. However, nothing will be achieved until native people become equal partners in the Vision Quest of the church. We have to live by this hope of equality and unity under "one God and Father of us all, who is above all and through all and in all." Filled with this "hope that belongs to our Christian call,"[21] we pray in the words of Laverne Jacobs:

Great Spirit, whose breath I feel in the wind, whose voice I hear in the birds, whose eyes I see in the children, listen to us.

You are the God of all our yesterdays, all our todays, and all our tomorrows. You know the plans you have for all your people.

As they prepare to gather in the National Native Convocation, show to the native peoples of Canada your will for them in the life of your Church. Give to them eyes to see the Sacred Way you have prescribed for them. Teach them to walk in the footsteps of your Son, Chief of chiefs. May their hearts beat as one with yours.

You make all things new. May they, your Church, and all creation rejoice in the new way you are preparing for them and your Church, in the Name of our Brother, Jesus Christ.

Chapter 7

A New Paradigm for Dialogue between Native and Christian Spiritualities

Theories of Dialogue

Traditionally, dialogue between native spirituality and western Christianity has had the same air as the play between a cat and a mouse, where, in spite of the apparent playfulness of the encounter, the mouse invariably lands in the belly of the cat. This would be an allegory for the assimilationist, inclusivist understanding that the best in native spirituality is already contained in western Christianity, the latter being assumed to be the norm and the whole corpus of the Gospel truth.

Another possibility is that the poor mouse, after a lot of pawing and chewing, eventually would be discarded as inedible. This would be figurative of an exclusivist view of native spirituality as pagan, heathen, unspiritual, demonic, contrary to the spirit of western Christianity, and contrary to God, the Queen, and the Empire, in that order, and so totally unacceptable!

In *Towards a Theology of Inter-faith Dialogue*, a report prepared by the Church of England's Board of Mission and Unity in 1984, a creative stance of dialogue is advocated: ''Inclusivist with an exclusive loyalty to Christ'' (para. 84). The report claims that the inclusivist position logically follows ''after an historical comparison of the truths and fruits of the religious experience of the major world faiths'' (para. 18). This position, transcending both ordinary inclusivism and exclusivism, seeks to honour the insights of non-Christian faiths without undercutting the uniqueness of Christ. This is, by far, the most consistent and balanced solution to the riddle of inter-faith dialogue; and the B.M.U. report deserves to be commended for showing the way. However, in this context a very radical question needs to be addressed. To which Christ do we owe an exclusive loyalty?

The conventional claims of exclusive loyalty to Christ are based on the hitherto unquestioned assumption that the western understanding of Jesus blended with white European traditions of colonialism constitute the Gospel of Christ. When non-white cultures try to integrate Christ into their respective cultural and spiritual traditions, the white theologians are quick to level the charge of syncretism. However, these selfsame theologians are blind to the blatant syncretism of western Christianity which is in fact a package of Graeco-Roman Anglo-Saxon Caucasian traditions superimposed on the Gospel of Christ. Thus when a white churchman talks about Christianity, he is in effect talking about the baggage of western ideas which he legitimizes by invoking the name of Christ. So it is not really a dialogue between the Gospel and "other faiths," but between a syncretistic colonial European understanding of the Gospel and "other faiths." The latter may not openly mention Jesus but could have a better existential and praxis-oriented commitment to the love, grace, and justice of Jesus Christ.

The writers of the B.M.U. report are fully sensitive to this critique that has been levelled against European Christianity. Hence, the expectation of the report is that "God will speak to us through the sensitivities and experiences of devout men and women of other faiths. We expect our own faith to be challenged, refined and at times judged, but we are firm in our loyalty to the revelation of God in and through the life, death and resurrection of Jesus of Nazareth" (para. 84).

Referring to the syncretic-synthetic Jesus of European Christianity, the Lakota medicine man Lame Deer protests:

> You have made a blondie out of Jesus. I don't care for those blonde, blue-eyed pictures of a sanitized, Cloroxed, Ajaxed Christ. How would you like it if I put braids on Jesus and stuck a feather in his hair? You would call me a very crazy Indian, wouldn't you? Jesus was a Jew. He wasn't a yellow-haired Anglo. I am sure he had black hair and a dark skin like an Indian. The white ranchers here wouldn't have let him step out with their daughters and wouldn't have liked him having

a drink in one of their saloons. His religion came out of the desert in which he lived, out of his kind of mountains, his kind of animals, his kind of plants. You've tried to make him into an Anglo-Saxon Fuller Brush salesman, a long-haired Billy Graham in a fancy nightshirt, and that is why he doesn't work for you any more.[1]

It is not just a harmless European version of Christianity that is at issue here. It is not just a difference in cultural perspective. Lame Deer is quick to point out the socially and politically repressive component of western syncretistic Christology:

The trouble is not with Christianity, with religion, but with what you have made out of it. You have turned it upside down. You have made the religion of the protest leader and hippie Jesus into the religion of missionaries, army padres, Bureau of Indian Affairs officials. These are two altogether different religions, my friend.[2]

An academic inclusivism is, however, cold comfort to the oppressed native people of the Americas if European Christians do not realize that a true inclusivism would revolutionize our Christology and also put the mission of the church on a footing of mutuality. David Jenkins, in a paper presented at the Zurich Consultation, in May 1970, on Christians in dialogue with men of other faiths, writes:

We need to be together with all men of living faith and living concern for the sake of the world, so that the unity of mankind and the sustaining of mankind can be promoted, and for the sake of entering into the fullness of Christ, i.e. of discovering and being part of the realizing of *all* that is involved in Christ, the Son and the Word of God. Our mission is to respond to God in Christ for the realization of God's project for the fulfillment (salvation and wholeness) of mankind and the universe. This is an urgent mission demanding a variety of forms of exploration, activity and sustenance. In previous historical and cultural conditions we have supposed that this mission meant the Christian Church and the Christian religion converting men to Christ by converting them to this Church and this religion.

This has further meant that the relationship with other religions, ideologies and their institutions has been one of aggression/defence. It has been necessary to defend the truth of Christ against the errors of the others and attack the others so as to obtain or promote conversion to the truth of Christ, the true religion and the true Church.

We now have the opportunity of learning how much cultural and psychological self-assertion and self-defensiveness have been bound up in this approach and how the truth, the uniqueness and the absoluteness of Christ are not *exclusive* but *inclusive,* that the fullness of Christ lies only "in the End" when *all things* are summed up in Him.

Surrender in Dialogue

A major flaw in the dialogue between Euro-Christianity and native sprirtuality is the position of power from which western theologians like to argue. But you cannot make a tenable case for the crucified Lord Jesus by the supremacist talk of the superiority of the Gospel over all other religions. The only suitable model is that of *kenosis,* self-emptying, and of blessed un-knowing. Western theologians who make categorical statements about the nature of Christ sound as though they have just eaten the forbidden fruit of the Tree of Knowledge. They forget that God revealed himself to Moses only in the thick darkness.[3] It is only from behind the Cloud of Unknowing that we can hope to catch a glimpse of God, the Father of our crucified Lord.

This exercise demands a willingness to surrender our theological position, our cosy credal statements, and our rigid dogma. This means letting go of one's religion, transcending one's spirituality, finding oneself temporarily in a no-man's land, in darkness, in a spirit of total openness. One has to learn to become vulnerable, defenceless, voiceless, and insecure, just as Christ was on the cross. When the Rhineland mystic Meister Eckhart had to deal with medieval churchmen who were too self-satisfied about their spirituality and too sure of the rightness of their ideas about God, he asked them to question their belief system with these famous words: "For God's sake let us take leave of God." Equally, for the sake of the true Gospel, the white church needs to cultivate humility and courage to take leave of its own narrow colonial Gospel in order to make room for the more authentic and credible Gospel of the oppressed.

The B.M.U. report sees vulnerability as a good starting point of dialogue:

> Those who would journey with us into the unfamiliar territory must learn to accept the stance of vulnerability which dialogue brings with it. Our discipleship is revealed for what it is, as our understanding and faith are put to the test. . . . Those who have already begun the journey into such unfamiliar territory have reminded us that theology is always provisional. It is out of our experience in dialogue with our tradition, under the power of the Holy Spirit, that our theology flows. (para. 83 and 82)

An entirely new way of theological reflection has to be explored which does not proceed deductively from one's own pet tradition or religion, but rather follows dialogically from the mutually agreed point of departure. In dialogue one cannot use exclusively Christian terms of reference. It is unfair while denying the same claim to other faiths. In Canada this patronizing attitude has led to native people being regarded as mere candidates for conversion to be minded and guided gently, so that they may eventually discover the Christ already hidden in their not-quite-so-bad native spirituality.

Dialogue with native people demands respect not condescension. Dialogue is not an exercise in one-upmanship, tinkering with idle theological frameworks or lofty philosophical systems. Nor is it an academic wrestling with impersonal formulations of native spirituality. It is rather an act of relating to individual native people without any hidden missionary agenda to scalp them emotionally and spiritually. We should not pre-empt our encounter by drawing circles around them, nor put them in little cubbyholes and categories so that they may continue to serve the interests of our colonial system. Dialogue, to the white Christians in Canada, means letting go of power over the native people and relating to them from a position of powerlessness. Dialogue is a contract between two equally powerful and powerless camps; it is walking in the Indian's moccasins, sharing his pain and shame. It is getting to know Indians as people, not as items on a missionary agenda. Dialogue is not between Christianity and native spirituality, between one set of doctrines and another, but between Christians and native people, between people and people, between individual and individual.

A true dialogue is never conducted in a vacuum. It is always in a socio-political and historical context. It would be ridiculous to carry out any Jewish-Christian dialogue without taking into consideration what happened at Auschwitz, Dachau, and Treblinka. Dialogue with Judaism is a dialogue with descendants of generations of Jews persecuted in the anti-Semitic climate of European Christianity. There is no dialogue with Judaism without confronting the anti-Semitism built into the thinking of the early church and the church Fathers down to the likes of Martin Luther. So also it is equally unthinkable to talk about dialogue with native spirituality without taking into account the systematic holocaust of the native people on their ancestral homelands perpetrated by white races professing Christianity.

A true dialogue is a confrontation with the triumphalistic and Eurocentric character of the church as it has been operative in North America and elsewhere. The main focus should be the quality of our relationship with native people. An ethics of relationship, more than a brutal dogmatics of belief, should be the prime criteria. The only true basis for an honest dialogue between Christianity and native spirituality in the Canadian context will be the nurturing of an ongoing relationship between repentant Christians and forgiving native people, making for a community founded on trust, integrity, and humour. These are the words which Chief Red Jacket in 1805 addressed to missionary Cran at Buffalo, New York: ''We are told that you have been preaching to white people in this place. . . . We will wait a little while and see what effect your preaching has upon them. If we find it does them good, makes them honest, and less disposed to cheat Indians, we will then consider again what you have said.''[4]

The Holy Spirit and Dialogue

The element of humility, which is such an integral part of dialogue, should move the white church to discover and acknowledge that there is a whole range of genuine spirituality that has flourished outside the pale of established Christianity. Simone Weil, the noted French thinker of Jewish extraction, had little hesitation in accepting Christ as the Messiah of Hebrew prophecy. But to the end of her life she refused baptism and to become a member of the Christian church, for the latter seemed to her to somehow narrow down and distort the catholic spirit of Christ:

> In my view, Christianity is catholic by right but not in fact. So many things are outside it, so many things that I love and don't want to give up, so many things that God loves or they would not be in existence. All the immense stretches of past centuries . . . all the countries inhabited by coloured races; all secular life in the white people's countries; in the history of those countries, all the traditions banned as heretical; all those things resulting from the Renaissance. . . . I should betray the truth, that is to say, the aspect of truth as I see it, if I left the point where I have been since my birth at the intersection of Christianity and everything that is not Christianity.[5]

If there had been no truth outside of Christ and his church, we would dishonour the doctrine of the Trinity, which plainly proclaims that there is more to God and his truth than Jesus. Jesus himself heralded the Holy Spirit, which he claimed would reveal additional spiritual truths and insights at the right time and at the right place in the future.[6] The Holy Spirit, not confined to any one race or culture, has this ongoing ministry of revelation, and is manifesting through the medium of native spirituality truths about Christ not as yet known to the church. No Christian can claim to have grasped the whole mystery of Christ. The Holy Spirit shall continue to unfathom the mystery of God becoming human flesh by exploring and exhausting all the diverse cultures and religious traditions of all of God's children. And so for white Christians to expect native people to believe in Christ only as they know and present him is to do injustice to the ministry of the Holy Spirit and the sacred mystery of Trinity.

The Holy Spirit demands that rather than judge native spirituality on the basis of European Christology, it would be more appropriate to judge, question, amplify, and even correct the traditional European Christology in the light of what the Spirit reveals to the church through the prism of native spirituality. Alan Race, in his essay ''Truth Is Many-Eyed,'' observes:

> We (i.e., Christians) have a foot in two camps. We celebrate and share what we know of God through the impact of Jesus in our world. We also wait to hear, learn and be judged by others who tell of a different experience, without defining their experience by virtue of our criteria of the Christ. We participate according to the Christian norm, yet with other norms which are also universally binding.[7]

Native spirituality may be regarded as an expression of the movement of the Holy Spirit outside the established white European ecclesia.

The B.M.U. report rightly presses into service the Logos theology of the Johannine Gospel (chapter 1) to stress God's continuous activity through all the diverse cultural and religious traditions of humanity:

> While Logos theology understands the unique expression of God as being in Jesus Christ (there can be no surrendering of that belief), at the same time it takes seriously other manifestations of the Logos in other places and other times. This suggests that in relations with those of other faiths Christians have to hold to that unique self-expressive activity of God in Jesus Christ, safeguarded and passed down within the Christian church. But equally Christians need to be open to recognise and respond to all manifestations of the Logos. The decisive revelation of God in Jesus has to be safeguarded for that is the canon by which we are enabled to recognise all other manifestations. Furthermore in the encountering of those other revelations, new depths are discovered in that fullest revelation of God in Jesus Christ. (para. 40)

In Black Elk we find an embodiment of this spirit of Logos theology and a practical application of a mature inclusivism with an exclusive loyalty to the cosmic Christ.

The Gospel according to Black Elk

Nicholas Black Elk (1863-1950) was an Oglala Lakota Sioux born on the Little Powder River within the borders of what is now the state of Wyoming. Owing to enforced migrations, his people finally settled on the Pine Ridge Reserve in South Dakota.

Black Elk was a man of many parts, warrior, mystic, prophet, artist, catechist, entertainer, philosopher, and medicine man. Above all, he was a holy man, *wicasa wakan*. Destined to live in the twilight zone of being neither completely Indian, nor completely Christian, he seemed comfortably to bestride both worlds, having integrated the truths of native spirituality and the Christian Gospel. When he died peacefully on 19 August 1950, in his derelict log cabin at Manderson, South Dakota, he held in one hand a Christian rosary, and in the other a Lakota sacred peace pipe which he had never given up smoking in a ritual manner in spite of his close association with the Roman Catholic church. It seems that during his last hours he said the rosary while smoking the sacred peace pipe, thus ritually and sacramentally combining in himself the roles of a Sioux medicine man and a loyal Catholic catechist. His spirituality could serve as a perfect paradigm for our native-Christian dialogue, which is neither inclusivist, nor exclusivist, nor pluralist, but Trinitarian; that is, in accordance with the Holy Spirit or, as Black Elk would have it, in accordance with the Great Spirit.

Black Elk was blessed with his famous Great Vision as a boy of nine years, and it was not until he attained manhood that he realized the importance of what had been revealed to him. It was not a self-centred vision of a self-indulgent stripling, but one that called upon him to be a prophet and deliverer of his people:

> It was the nation that was dying, and the vision was for the nation. . . . I thought much of my vision and wondered when my duty was to come; for the Grandfathers had shown me my people walking on the black road and how the nation's hoop would be broken and the flowering tree be withered, before I should bring the hoop together with the power that was given me, and make the holy tree flower in the centre and find the red road again.[8]

Black Elk considered himself a failure as far as the prophetic role assigned to him in the vision was concerned. But in his death he has now become a force, mobilizing the native peoples of North America under the banner of a revitalized native spiritual tradition. Black Elk speaks, indeed!

In his introduction to the 1979 edition of *Black Elk Speaks*, Vine Deloria Jr. prophesies that the two books, *Black Elk Speaks* and *The Sacred Pipe*, dictated by the Lakota holy man to two sympathetic white men will become ''the central core of a North American Indian theological canon which will some day challenge the Eastern and Western traditions as a way of looking at the world.'' Hence, we have no hesitation in presenting Black Elk as an authentic representative of the pan-Indian native spirituality and an ideal point of reference in the native-Christian dialogue. Commenting on the breadth of Black Elk's vision, Vine Deloria Jr. writes: ''The universality of the images and dreams must testify to the emergence of a new sacred hoop, a new circle of intense community among Indians far outdistancing the grandeur of former times.''[9]

Black Elk perceived the vulnerability of the native civilization vis-à-vis the whites. He was also a witness to the rapacity of the white culture. Both were flawed, yet both had good things to commend them for the benefit of humanity. Black Elk tried to imbibe all that he could from the white culture, retaining the best of his own tradition. His whole life was an exercise in dialogue between these two seemingly polar traditions. On the one hand, his own people seemed in disarray:

> The nation's hoop was broken, and there was no centre any longer for the flowering tree. The people were in despair. They seemed heavy to me, heavy and dark; so heavy that it seemed that they could not be lifted; so dark that they could not be made to see any more.[10]

On the other hand, the materialistic culture of the *Wasichus* (i.e., a Sioux term for any one selfish or exploitative normally reserved for white people) did not exactly commend itself for emulation:

> I could see that the *Wasichus* did not care for each other the way our people did before the nation's hoop was broken. They would take everything from each other if they could, and so

there were some who had more of everything than they could use, while crowds of people had nothing at all and maybe very starving. They had forgotten that the earth was their mother. This could not be better than the old ways of my people.[11]

After looking at the two embattled cultures, and weighing them in the balance, Black Elk found that there was strength in both and that they could mutually correct and complement each other. As a Lakota, he inherited the catholic vision of his people:

It is the story of all life that is holy and good to tell and of us two-leggeds sharing in it with the four-leggeds and the winds of the air and all green things; for these are children of one mother and their father is one spirit.[12]

But this harmony was broken:

Once we were happy in our own country and we were seldom hungry, for then the two-leggeds and the four-leggeds lived together like relatives, and there was plenty for them and for us. But the *Wasichus* came, and they have little islands for us and other little islands for the four-leggeds, and always these islands were becoming smaller, for around them surges the gnawing flood of the *Wasichu*; and it is dirty with lies and greed.[13]

The *Wasichus* did not share the Lakota vision of a cyclical and harmonious world, yet they possessed a sense of history, of time, and of alienation that lay behind the apparent harmony in creation. The *Wasichus'* Christian religion focussed on the alienation in the world and sought a way to overcome it. This realism about sinfulness was as necessary as the vision of harmony characterizing native spirituality. If the native people ever hoped to recover their harmony, it was imperative that they took seriously the dynamics of sin, duality, alienation and disharmony. The inter-tribal wars, the utter vulnerability to the onslaught of European culture, the low status of women in certain tribes, the hierarchical structure of power in some societies, the practice of bad medicine alongside of good medicine, a primitive technology which failed to invent the wheel although the circle was the prime symbol of native spirituality — these, among many others, are instances of the fallibility and fallenness of the Indian nation. It would be a colossal injustice to the native people to romanticize them as noble savages. They have been neither savages nor noble. To classify them as such would amount to robbing them of their precious irreducible humanity. As members of the human race, they share in the sinfulness to which we are all heir.

It is unhelpful to lump together all whites as sinful exploiters and to see them all as instrumental in bringing suffering to the native people. The sinfulness which the native people saw in the *Wasichus* was also present in themselves. This awareness of the basically sinful nature of humanity was a gift of the *Wasichus'* religion. This universal vision seems to have appealed to Black Elk who probably came under the influence of Christian missionaries in 1889 after returning from a sojourn in Europe, where he had had ample opportunity to study western societies and watch at close hand the working of the Christian church.

Unfortunately, the missionaries failed to communicate to the native people the Christian doctrine of the innate fallenness of all creation, because they equated "Indianness" with sinfulness and set up the white man as a paragon of infallible Christian virtue. Preaching the fallenness of all people, the white race included, would have been an excellent opportunity for the missionaries to proclaim to the native people Christ's Gospel of the brotherhood of all people — natives and whites — under the fatherhood of God in Christ his Son. Sadly, this opportunity was missed. Christian sin was presented only in its individualistic and moralistic sense. A cheap brand of grace was offered as the reward for Christian obedience. An ethics of trivialized sin led logically to a soteriology of trivialized grace.

In Black Elk we see the burgeoning of this profound sense of universal fallenness, of which the fallenness of his own nation was but a small chapter. His was a prophetic voice that cried not just for the native people, much less for the Lakota, but for the entire human race, nay, all creation. He depicts his Great Vision in these memorable words:

> Then I was standing on the highest mountain of them all, and round about beneath me was the whole hoop of the world. And while I stood there, I saw more than I can tell, and I understood more than I saw; for I was seeing in a sacred man-

ner the shapes of all things in the spirit, and the shape of all shapes as they must live together like one being. And I saw the sacred hoop of my people was one of the many hoops that made one circle, wide as daylight and as starlight, and in the centre grew one mighty flowering tree to shelter all the children of one mother and one father. And I saw that it was holy.[14]

The prophetic symbology of Black Elk's Great Vision highlights three major archetypes: the broad circle or hoop containing many smaller hoops, the mighty flowering and withering tree, and the centre out of which the cosmic tree grows. His prophetic eye perceives two distinct scenarios. When the centre is lost, then the hoop is broken, and the tree withers. Black Elk approaches Jeremiah in his lamentation over this vista of universal fallenness. But he is also promised a vision where he sees the centre restored, the broken hoop mended, and the tree flowering again. With the majestic felicity of an Isaiah, he celebrates this universal regeneration. His symbology of the tree in the centre of the cosmic hoop calls to mind a similar imagery traced in an Easter sermon on the theme of the cross of Christ preached by Hippolytus, the renowned father of western liturgy:

This tree, wide as the heavens itself, has grown up into heaven from the earth. It is an immortal growth and towers between heaven and earth. It is the fulcrum of all things and the place where they are all at rest. It is the foundation of the round world, the centre of the cosmos. In it all the diversities in our human nature are formed into a unity.

It is not far-fetched to detect a link between the cosmic tree in Black Elk's symbology and the cosmic cross of Christ in the imagery of Hippolytus. A world-tree growing upward through the centre of a multi-tiered universe as the *axis mundi* was a universal symbol among most Indian nations. Black Elk draws upon this powerful symbolism of his own native sacred tradition and deftly integrates it into the tree symbolism that runs as a golden thread through the corpus of the Judaeo-Christian Scriptures. The Tree of Life which stands at the beginning of time according to the book of Genesis looms again at the centre of the heavenly city of Jerusalem at the end of time according to the apocalyptic vision of St. John the Evangelist. In between these two the tree rises into universal destiny as the tree on which Christ was nailed and pierced.

Black Elk's telling imagery of the withering tree approaches the rich symbolism of the cross, conveying the sense of the total desecration and ruination of all creation. There cannot be a more sweeping and graphic portrayal of the Fall. Although the tree symbolism was already present in the native tradition, Black Elk's originality lies in bringing the tree out of the cosmic dream-world into the arena of time and the historic actuality of alienation. Black Elk the medicine man did all but identify the tree as a cross, as the tree of redemption, which Black Elk the catechist had incorporated into his belief system. Seldom has the imagery of the cross been so effectively evoked with such economy of brush-strokes! Black Elk envisions a flowering tree which withers and blossoms again, thus representing in the native way the archetypal symbolism of Eden, Calvary, and Easter. But he does not just use native symbols; he connects the cosmic tree of the dream time (a mythological awareness of recurring time sequences) with the tree of the Christian *kairos* (the moment of God's incarnation and intervention in history). In so doing, he allows both traditions to enrich each other mutually. One is incomplete and inadequate without the other.

The dream time of the native American people, and all the aboriginal peoples of the globe, and the *kairos* of the Christian church need to be understood as two indispensable and inseparable facets of the new universal creed for the humanity of the year 2000. (The term *dream time*, borrowed from the Australian context, is equally applicable to the native American scene.) Both Christians and native people have to learn from each other. One cannot fully comprehend the mystery of the tree, that is, the cross of Christ, unless one sees it rooted in the centre of the cosmic circle. This is the unique native contribution to a fuller understanding of the Gospel.

European Christianity did not visualize the cross in its cyclical setting. The cross set in the centre of a circle will be an apt representation of the cross of Christ as Hippolytus visualized in his Easter sermon. This would bring the linear, angular cross into the circular cyclical world of native spirituality. The latter believes in the interconnectedness and sacredness of all parts and aspects of the world. This profound sense of the wholeness and holiness of the created world would also make for an equally profound sense of sin as a departure from this wholeness. This whole mystical approach of the native genius could rescue the Christian doctrine of sin from being privatized as an act of personal immorality. Sin as well as redemption is to be seen on a cosmic scale. Set in the context of the aboriginal dream time, the cross of Christ becomes a universal cosmic symbol pointing to the fallenness on every conceivable level. This concept of dream time is best defined by Joseph Campbell:

> All life on earth is to be recognized as a projection on the plane of temporal event of forms, objects, and personalities forever present in the permanent nowhere, no-when, of the mythological age, the *altjeringa*, ''dream time'', when all was magical, as it is in dream: the realm that is seen again in dream and shown forth in the rites.[15]

Life in the temporal world is seen as a projection of the eternal principle. The material world, no less than the inner realm of mind and soul, is amenable to spiritual transformation. The linear theology of the western church confines redemption only to the spiritual realm. However, to the native person, sin as much as redemption concerns every layer of the created world. Black Elk's imagery of the tree, set in the centre of the cosmic circle, is a happy marriage between the linear and the cyclical modes of spirituality. It bridges in one sweep the age-old gulf between the dream time of the aboriginal peoples, of the left brain, of the unconscious, of the animal kingdom, of mystics, of poets, of lovers, of childlike innocence, on the one hand, and the linear time of the Judaeo-Christian church, of monotheistic Islam; of the right brain, of Graeco-Roman civilizations, of historians, of prophets, of neo-Marxists, on the other hand. Dream time and linear time interpenetrate and impregnate each other. Placed within the sacred circle of the dream time, the Christian cross becomes a symbol of a truly catholic, holistic, incarnational spirituality. Man becomes truly redeemed, ''so that not only himself but his whole world and his whole way of life within it will be joined inseparably, through myths and rites, to the field of the spirit.''

Commenting on the cyclical spirituality in the southeast Asian world, Kosuke Koyama, in his *Waterbuffalo Theology*, writes:

God is the Lord of the monsoon rain. He sends his monsoon for his purpose. The biblical view of history is not circular. It is linear. But life in Thailand is strongly influenced by the circular movement of nature. The circular nature is not of demons. It is, as we understand, from God. We see the glory of God both in history and nature. Circular nature shows God's glory as much as linear history. Both are purposeful. Yet, as we have seen, circular nature finds its proper place *within* linear history. In this proper location, circular nature finds its purpose. When two images, circular and linear, are put together, why can we not have the image of an ascending spiral view of one unified history-nature?[16]

This emphasis on the marriage between cyclical and linear is refreshing. Yet, it falls much short of the integration of the two polarities as envisaged by Black Elk. In the first place, it is wrong to subsume, as Koyama does, the cyclical under the linear as if the latter was the dominant theme in spirituality. The circular finds its purpose in history, as much as history needs to find its proper place in the circular. It is equally fallacious to claim that the biblical view of history is not circular, but linear only. It is the typical European distortion of Christian spirituality. In Black Elk, Christian spirituality is once again seen as laying equal emphasis on the cyclical dimension of nature and the linear dimension of history. If the native people needed, as missionaries claim, to learn the linear view of history, then white Christians need even more to absorb the cyclical sense of nature.

A Christological Reflection on Black Elk's Visions

Black Elk was blessed with two cardinal visions in his life. The first one, known as the Great Vision, came when he was still a small boy. He received the second one as a young man during a Ghost Dance, hence the name the Ghost-Dance Vision. His conversion to the Catholic church came later. Neihardt's version of the Ghost-Dance Vision in *Black Elk Speaks* does not contain any Christological terminology. Presumably, Neihardt omitted any such language indicative of Black Elk's religious affiliation. However, his field-notes for the book, which are undated and stored at the University of Missouri Library, Columbia, Montana, retain the original Christological terminology just as the Sioux seer dictated it to Neihardt:

> Then I went to the centre of the circle . . . and there again I saw the tree in full bloom. Against the tree I saw a man standing with outstretched arms. . . . The man with out- stretched arms looked at me and I did not know whether he was white or Indian. *He did not resemble Christ. He looked like an Indian but I wasn't sure of it.* He had long hair which was hanging loose. On the left side of his head was an eagle feather. His body was painted red. *At this time I had nothing to do with white man's religion and I had never seen any picture of Christ.* . . . This man said to me, ''My life is such that all earthly beings that grow belong to me. My father has said this.''. . . As I looked at him his body began to transform. His body changed into all colours and it was very beautiful. All round him there was light. Then he disappeared all at once. *It seemed as though there were wounds in the palms on his hands. It seems to me on think- ing it over that I had seen the son of the Great Spirit himself.*[17]

If the original field-notes contained such seminal Christological observations by Black Elk, then why did Neihardt remove them? Firstly, he was an anthropologist, not a missionary with any religious agenda, and apparently he did not find Black Elk's reference to Christ consonant with the other components of the Ghost-Dance Vision, which were ostensibly so typically native. Secondly, Black Elk himself did not seem to be categorically asser- tive about the Christian core of his Ghost-Dance Vision. Thirdly, here at the age of sixty-eight years he is only reflecting on this vision after having been a catechist for nearly twenty-eight years. Hence, Neihardt might have suspected that the medicine man was merely reading Christian themes into his originally authen- tic Lakota vision as an after-thought, and thereby merely blurr- ing rather than clarifying it. Neihardt, therefore, was perhaps anxious to rescue the Ghost-Dance Vision from unnecessary Christian interpolations and present it in its pristine form.

When Neihardt met Black Elk in his teepee on the reserve, the medicine man was anything but an official representative of the church. Nearing the end of his life he was a sad, defeated, forlorn man living in squalor, and in full view of the shame of his vanquished people. There was not even the semblance of Christian triumphalism. Black Elk, the testimonies of his christianized daughter Lucy Looks Twice and son Benjamin Black Elk notwithstanding, had by this time developed a critical attitude towards the established Christian religion. Small wonder that when he revisited the site of his Great Vision, he intoned the following prayer, which Neihardt records: "Hear me, not for myself, but for my people: I am old. Hear me that they may once more go back into the sacred hoop and find the good red road, the shielding Tree!"[18]

This explains why Neihardt set little store by Black Elk's Christian convictions and saw fit to present his Ghost-Dance Vision devoid of Christian references, which he probably saw as concessions made by Black Elk in his weaker moments.

In the heyday of the Ghost Dance movement, Black Elk, like many of his people, was tempted to interpret his Ghost-Dance Vision as prophesying the coming of the Indian messiah: "I heard the gossip that was everywhere now, and people said it was really the Son of the Great Spirit who was out there." [19] However, Black Elk is sceptical about the reports of miracles allegedly performed by the Ghost Dance messiah. A great struggle ensues in the heart of the mystic. There seems to be no way for him to unfathom the mystery in the welter of all the rumours of his day. "I was puzzled I did not know what to think."[20] Finally, Black Elk allows himself to be invited to lead in a Ghost Dance, and what he saw there inclines him to identify the red man of the Great Vision of his boyhood and the Messiah of the Ghost-Dance Vision of his youth with the native prophet, who had managed to fire the imagination of his desperate people with messianic expectations:

> I was surprised and could hardly believe what I saw; because so much of my vision seemed to be in it. The dancers, both women and men, were holding hands in a big circle, and in the centre of the circle they had a tree painted red with most of its branches cut off and some dead leaves on it. This was exactly the part of my vision, where the holy tree was dying, and the circle of the men and women holding hands was like the sacred hoop that should have power to make the tree bloom again.[21]

His experience at the Ghost Dance leads Black Elk to wonder if the Ghost Dance prophet "might be the Red Man of my Great Vision, who turned into a bison, then into a four-rayed herb, the daybreak-star herb of Understanding."[22] Throughout his life, Black Elk had been looking for clues to decode the Great Vision as well as the Ghost-Dance Vision, and identify the mystery man who had stood at the centre of the visions. Black Elk himself sounds a little diffident about his own interpretation when at the end of his account of the Ghost-Dance Vision he says: "All through this I depended on my Messiah [i.e., Ghost-Dance] vision whereas perhaps I should have depended on my first vision which had more power. And that might have been where I made my great mistake."[23]

The ecstatic and apocalyptic character of the Ghost-Dance Vision was misleading. It created false expectations of a native prophet who was not to be. It also did not clearly point the way to Christ. However, the Great Vision with its strikingly kenotic and sacrificial symbolism truly evoked and prefigured the spirit of Christ and was thus more reliable as a signpost to Christ. That is why Black Elk conceded that the Great Vision, though devoid of any explicitly Christ-like imagery, was Christologically more relevant. Using the typical shamanistic terminology, Black Elk certified the Great Vision as having more power. The image of the man standing against the tree, which dominated the Ghost-Dance Vision, was not part of the Great Vision. It was, however, full of authentic Christological symbols. Black Elk sums up the rich symbolism of the vision as follows:

> I saw that there stood on the north side of the starving camp a sacred man who was painted red all over his body, and he held a spear as he walked into the centre of the people, and there he lay down and rolled. And when he got up, it was a fat bison standing there, and where the bison stood, a sacred herb sprang up right where the tree had been in the centre of the nation's hoop.[24]

Black Elk himself proceeds to interpret this very vision when talking to Neihardt: "I know now what this meant, that the bison were the gift of a good spirit, and were our strength, but we should lose them, and from the same good spirit, we must find another strength, for the people all seemed better when the herb had grown and bloomed.''25 Indeed this colourful vision shot through with such suggestive imagery was open to diverse interpretations. We do not know what the young Black Elk made of it when he first narrated it to Whirlwind Chaser, the medicine man of his nation. But a closer look at the Great Vision would unearth unmistakable symbols of sacrificial nurture and atonement which are at the heart of the Christian Gospel. First we have the image of the man painted blood red with a spear in his hand. Then the man lies down and turns into a fat bison to feed the starving Indians. Finally, the bison slowly transforms itself into a herb that is destined to nourish the people.

All these three archetypes—the man, the bison, and the herb — across the human, animal, and plant kingdoms, carry a powerfully Christological symbolism in them. The Indian brave, painted red and carrying a spear, first standing and then lying down, symbolizes a figure who spills his blood and is not afraid to be pierced, and who is ever willing to lay down his life for the people. The fat bison standing in the centre of the universe under the tree to feed the starving camp is, indeed, the native counterpart of the Christian imagery of the sacrificial Lamb of God taking away the sins of the world. So also the herb, growing right in the centre of the nation's hoop, where the tree had stood before, is an imagery analogous to the Johannine symbology of the Vine and the Bread of Life. The geographical and the spiritual centrality of the three archetypes is evocative of the centrality of the Christ figure in the economy of Christian salvation. All three conjure up the self-immolating cosmic Christ, sustaining and fulfilling all creation. It is a measure of Black Elk's mystical genius that he captures the essence of the Christian *kerygma* in this boyhood vision which, like the White Bear Vision of Andrew Ahenakew, focusses on the mystery of sacrificial atonement on the part of the Great Spirit for the whole creation. The same kenotic and sacrificial imagery is at the heart of the Lakota legend of the Buffalo Calf Woman bringing the sacred pipe and turning into a buffalo calf.

Though graphically clear about the contours of his visions, he was fallible about the exegesis. It is a measure of Black Elk's integrity that in the end he openly admits that he had misconstrued the identity of the man of his visions. Black Elk lived long enough to see the course of history debunk the myth of the Ghost Dance prophet. He realized that he had made a great mistake in interpreting the man in the Ghost-Dance Vision as the native prophet. If he was not the messiah of the Ghost-Dance Vision, nor the Red Man of his Great Vision, then the only possible candidate for that honour would be Christ, whom Black Elk, by the time he met Neihardt, had accepted as the Messiah for his people as much as for the *Wasichus*. The messianic figure of the Ghost-Dance Vision had to be interpreted in the light of the sacrificial symbolism of the Great Vision, and of the Gospel of the sacrificial Lamb of God, Jesus Christ.

Black Elk's singular importance for us Christians engaged in the dialogue between native and Christian spiritualities lies in the fact that he, a full-fledged Lakota medicine man, finally identified the man in both his visions as the Christ figure. The man with outstretched arms standing against the tree was the Son of God with his arms wide open on the cross. The man's body transforming and being full of light and finally disappearing, the heavenly Father vouchsafing the sovereignty of the Son, the wounds in the palms of his hands — all these details strikingly evoke the scene of the Transfiguration of Christ on the verge of his descent into the valley below, on his way to the cross in Jerusalem. The man in the Ghost-Dance Vision is a genuine native version of the transfigured Christ. Misled by the false claims of the native prophet, Black Elk had misread his own vision. Once the confusion had been cleared, he recognized Christ as the key to unlock the symbolism of his visions. He was granted these visions long before he heard about Christ. He was indeed a mystic set apart for the great dialogue.

The Cyclical Theme of History

The linear understanding of history, which has dominated traditional European Christianity, as also Jewish and Islamic spirituality, labours under a preoccupation with the end-time, a series of events culminating in a goal in the historical process. All of history is seen as heading towards that particular end-moment, which stands out as the summation of all the less important moments preceding it. As opposed to this linear thinking, the cyclical view of history regards every moment as equally important, unique, and sacred.

In the cyclical view of history, the passage of time is not secular, and does not lead up to a finale which could be regarded as holy. All time is sacred. Every instant is sacred. As such, every moment becomes an end-time moment, a climax, a spiritual revelation in itself. You live fully, not just for the end-time. Rather you live in and for every moment, for each moment is a messianic moment. By the same token, each act becomes a spiritual act. Black Elk once said to Brown: "Hunting is a meditative act." Interpreted, this means hunting is not just secular and meditation is not just spiritual. Hunting is as spiritual as meditation itself. The secular is the spiritual. You cannot prioritize meditation over hunting. When there is no priority of one act or moment over another, time stands still, as the saying goes. All life becomes an unbroken flow of spirituality. This paradox of time progressing yet standing still is the unified linear-cyclical theme of Black Elk's spirituality of the cross set in the centre of the circle.

The kingdom of God which is to come is already within you. The kingdom is to be sought as much in the end-time as in every present moment. And bestriding these two temporal modes is the Messiah, Jesus Christ, who says: "Before Abraham was, I AM."[26] Jesus does not say: "I was." God, the Father of Jesus Christ, is not only the God of linear history, as the church would have it, but also the God of cyclical history. Yahweh, the God of Israel, clearly reveals himself to Moses on Mount Sinai as I AM.[27] Jesus employs the expression "I AM" without the predicate to refer to himself as the One who remains the constant denominator through the web of linear history. In Jesus, the future and the past are telescoped into timeless reality, which has been identified as dream time by the aboriginal peoples of the world. It is an experience of a transcendent kind which has been sadly forfeited by the cerebral, pragmatic, linear traditions of white established Christianity. It is an ongoing experience transcending yet interpenetrating all time. Says Jesus: "I tell you this now, before it takes place, that when it does take place, you may believe that I AM."[28] Jesus identifies himself as I AM, which is a silver thread running through all temporal history.[29] Jesus talks about being there before the creation of the world.[30] In John, ch. 8, vs. 56-8, we find an interesting encounter between Jesus and the Hebrews, who were trapped in the religion of linear consciousness: "Your father Abraham rejoiced that he was to see my day; he saw it and was glad." The Jews then said to him, "You are not yet fifty years old, and have you seen Abraham?'' Jesus said to them: "Truly, truly, I say to you, before Abraham was, I AM.''

Biblical scholars try to explain these non-Hebraic sounding passages in John as an influence of the Gnostic tradition prevalent in John's times. But it would be more natural to see them as a flowering of the Wisdom tradition of the Old Testament, which was later stifled by the linear tradition of rabbinical Judaism. No amount of sophisticated form criticism could help us unravel the mystery of God's name, I AM, which Jesus aptly invokes to point to his own transcendent identity beyond linear time and linear space. I AM is the realm of sacred time and sacred space. This is the dream time of the aborigines and of the mystics. The church has lost contact with this experience and may do well to listen to the voice of Chief Luther Standing Bear:

> The man who sat on the ground in his tipi meditating on life and its meaning, accepting the kinship of all creatures and acknowledging unity with the universe of things was infusing into his being the true essence of civilization. And when native man left off this form of development, his humanization was retarded in growth.[31]

The cyclical time was very much part of the pristine spirituality of the Hebrew people, before they overstressed the linear understanding of time. The Old Testament notion of time initially focussed on repetitive, paradigmatic, and archetypal thought-patterns: the story of the Hebrew people is cycle after cycle of God's institution of a covenant, humanity's breach of the covenant, God's retribution for the breach, repentance on the part of the people, and then, as the last link in the chain of the respective cycle, God's forgiveness and institution of a fresh covenant. Linear time, however, governs the pattern of a progression of unrepeatable events, culminating in the final one, terminating the entire chain. But the Old Testament concept of the history of salvation is as much cyclical as it is linear. Coinciding with the never-ending cycles of God's salvific acts is the institution of rites and ceremonies that are celebrated year after year or period after period to mark the cyclical time. These rites help us relive the paradigmatic events in the cycle of salvation. The Passover festival kept year after year to commemorate the event in linear time is a classic example of the Hebrew love for cyclical time. This is how rites and sacraments mediate between historical linear time and cyclical dream time.

The Christian church inherited from the Hebrew tradition the recurrent rhythms of history. The celebration of Sunday as the day of the Lord, symbolic of the resurrection of Jesus to be memorialized week after week, is a prime instance of the keeping of cyclical time. The feasts commemorating the birth, death, resurrection, and ascension of Christ, as well as the outpouring of the Holy Spirit, are celebrated year after year. The seasons of Epiphany, Lent, and Trinity recur with cyclical regularity. Feast days of the saints are observed annually. Equally cyclical in spirit is the tradition to regard each celebration of Holy Mass as a reliving of the events of the Holy Week. It is a rite especially instituted by Christ himself to remember (*anamnesis*) again and again the Passion and Sacrifice which happened two thousand years ago at Golgotha as part of linear history, but which is very much part of cyclical history, being embedded and constantly relived in the spiritual struggle of the Christian community.

The linear understanding of the Passion and the Resurrection is meaningless unless it is accompanied and nourished by a cyclical awareness of these historic events so that they are internalized and incarnated in the life of the church in each generation. Meister Eckhart was banned from preaching and was tried for asking the question: "What use is it that Christ was born in Bethlehem, suffered at Calgary and rose on the third day, unless and until the same Christ is born, suffers and rises in our hearts today?" In banning and banishing him and other mystics of his ilk, the established church banned and banished forever the cyclical awareness of salvation history. Salvific events occur not only out there in historic time and geographical three-dimensional space; they happen in the stillness and vacuum of sacred time and sacred space, which is the dream time of the contemplative spirituality of the aboriginal peoples of the world.

The Feast of the Ancestors

An important place where the church can begin to celebrate its long lost cyclical spirituality is in the intercession with and for the saints. By saints one may understand both the distinguished Christian men and women who have been canonized by the church, and the departed ancestors. Traditionally, Protestants have raised a barrier between the living and the dead, whereas catholics of all shades have always accepted a two-way communion and communication between the two realms as a possibility. On the whole European Christianity with its Cartesian split of body and soul, looks askance at any attempts to bridge the two. The Hebrews, who did not labour under this schizophrenia, had a healthy understanding of the continuum of the embodied and the disembodied beings. To them, even the seemingly disembodied had a body, a spiritual body to clothe their departed spirits. And thus both the living and the dead could dwell in one realm. The author of the Epistle to the Hebrews, who wrote for the benefit of the Jewish Christians, seizes upon the Hebrew idea of the continuum of the living and the dead, both worshipping God together.

> But you have come to Mount Zion and to the city of the living God, the heavenly Jerusalem, and to innumerable angels in festal gathering, and to the assembly of the first-born who are enrolled in heaven, and to a judge who is God of all, and to the spirits of just men made perfect.[32]

In worship, the two realms merge together, as in the Sanctus. Then we, the embodied, join voices and minds with all the company of heaven in singing the three-fold ''Holy'' that is forever intoned by all those who have gathered before the mercy throne in heavenly Jerusalem. We are united with the community of saints, whatever we may mean by the term *saints*, whether they be the ascended beings or the departed ones or the Christians alive in our midst. We are ''surrounded by a great cloud of witnesses'' as Hebrews 12:1 has it. This mystical sense of the continuum of the past, present, and future, telescoped into the community of saints, is very much part of the traditional spirituality of the church. The church has never seriously entered into its spirit. Now it may do so by sharing it with the native people who have a similar concept, the only difference being the term ancestors instead of saints. Black Elk describes it in words of Isaian grandeur:

As I rode in through the rainbow door, there were cheering voices from all over the universe, and I saw the Sir Grandfathers sitting in a row, with their arms held toward me and their hands, palms out; and behind them in the cloud were faces thronging, without number, of the people yet to be.[33]

The ancestors, including both the people who have been and the people yet to be, worshipping together, belong to the dream time, the time beyond all times, the time that is ever-present now, the time in which all are united in spirit. The Sanctus in the eucharistic canon is a fine invocation of the ancestors of the dream time. It is the corporate I AM experience. The native people could help the church comprehend the mystical depth of the community of saints. The church has lost touch with this numinous dimension. The till-we-meet-again epitaphs littering our cemeteries in the west are a sad commentary on the shallow understanding of after-life that an average churchgoer in Europe displays. European anthropologists and "experts" on Indian culture attempt to interpret the idea of ancestors through their coloured glasses and categorize it as ancestor-worship. It is a concept foreign to native people and introduced only by the European, who has relegated his own ancestors to the limbo of the undigested past, unconnected with dream time. Chief Seattle (See-at-hl), addressing the presidential envoy at the Great Tribal Assembly of 1854, spoke about the white man's broken relationship with his own past in these telling phrases:

Your dead cease to love you and the land of their nativity as soon as they pass the portals of the tomb — they wander far away beyond the stars, are soon forgotten and never return. Our dead never forget this beautiful world that gave them being. They still love its winding rivers, its great mountains and its sequestered vales, and they ever yearn in tenderest affection over the lonely-hearted living, and often return to visit, guide and comfort them. . . . To us the ashes of our ancestors are sacred and their final resting place is hallowed ground, while you wander far from the graves of your ancestors and, seemingly, without regret.[34]

Seattle goes on to bespeak the dream time understanding of the ancestors living in the present:

> The noble braves, fond mothers, glad happy-hearted maidens, and even the little children, who lived and rejoiced here for a brief season, and whose very names are now forgotten, still love these sombre solitudes and their deep fastnesses which, at eventide, grow shadowy with the presence of dusky spirits.
>
> And when the last Red Man shall have perished from this earth and his memory among the white men shall have become a myth, these shores will swarm with the invisible dead of my tribe; and when your children's children shall think themselves alone in the fields, the store, the shop, upon the highway, or in the silence of the pathless woods, they will not be alone. In all the earth there is no place dedicated to solitude.
>
> At night, when the streets of your cities and villages will be silent and you think them deserted, they will throng with the returning hosts that once filled and still love this beautiful land.
>
> The white man will never be alone. Let him be just and deal kindly with my people, for the dead are not powerless.

The church has to learn to look at its own creed through the eyes of Seattle to understand and celebrate the community of saints. Then the whole liturgy of the church, including the eucharistic prayer, the Sanctus, the intercessions, and the *anamnesis* as a reliving and a remembering of the Passion of Christ, will take on a new dimension that will earth and root a Christian in the numinous experience of being one Body in Christ with people of all climes and all times. This is the true meaning of the sacred mystery of the ancestors in native spirituality.

Sacred Space

Cyclical time regards every moment as sacred and bound with all other moments in a mystical unity; so also a cyclical awareness of space invests every inch of this created universe with the quality of sacredness. All places become holy. All beings — man, beast and bird — are holy. All things — tree, water, air, and stone — are holy. The body is holy. So is sexuality, sensuality, and the whole gamut of feelings and emotions. The earth is holy. ''Take off your sandals, for the very ground you are standing on is holy.'' Every point in creation is the centre of reality. Jerusalem is not in Palestine. The Holy City is everywhere, in the heart of everyone. Says Black Elk:

> Peace . . . comes within the souls of men when they realize their relationship, their oneness, with the universe and all its powers, and when they realize that at the centre of the universe dwells *Wakan-Tanka*, and that this centre is really everywhere, it is within each of us.[35]

The white Caucasian culture has lost this centre with perilous consequences. In the Hollywood film *Little Big Man*, the ageing chief of the Cheyenne complains to his youthful adopted white grandson, played by Dustin Hoffman, that the major dilemma of the white man is that he has lost the centre of the universe, and hence he is out to destroy the world in which he finds himself a total alien. The Judaeo-Christian man regards the created world as the wholly other, in total alienation from him, unholy and wild, and thus to be subdued.[36] Chief Luther Standing Bear of the Oglala Sioux, observes:

> We did not think of the great open plains, the beautiful rolling hills, and the winding streams with tangled growth as ''wild''. Only to the white man was nature a ''wilderness'', and only to him was the land ''infested'' with ''wild'' animals and ''savage'' people. To us it was tame. Earth was bountiful, and we were surrounded with the blessings of the Great Mystery. Not until the hairy man from the east came with brutal frenzy and heaped injustices upon us and the families we loved was the earth ''wild'' for us. When the very animals of the forest began fleeing from his approach, then it was that for us the Wild West began.[37]

With no centre to anchor him, the Euro-Christian man could not envision the creation as sacred space, as the sacred hoop; and so God's creation was turned into a marketplace of merchandise, to be bought and sold, to be processed and exploited, to be used and discarded. When things were no more regarded as sacred, they lost their value and got a price. When the centre is lost, when the cyclical awareness of space is forfeited, and we are trapped in the assembly line of linear time, then we are stuck with an economics based on price, profit, exploitation, and accumulation. Everything from mountains to animals to people is priced, sold, possessed, and disposed of. Chief Seattle confronts the ambassador of the Great White Chief in Washington, who has come to make a deal to buy native land, with these words:

> Every part of this country is sacred to my people. Every hillside, every valley, every plain and grove has been hallowed by some fond memory or some sad experience of my tribe. Even the rocks, which seem to lie dumb as they swelter in the sun along the silent sea shore in solemn grandeur, thrill with memories of past events connected with the lives of my people.
>
> The very dust under my feet responds more lovingly to our footsteps than to yours, because it is the ashes of our ancestors, and our bare feet are conscious of the sympathetic touch, for the soil is rich with the life of our kindred.

Even as early as 1810 Tecumseh, a Shawnee chief, had bitterly protested to Governor W.H. Harrison about the land sales of 1805-6 in the same spirit of respect for the earth:

> The way, the only way to stop this evil (i.e., land sales) is for the red man to unite in claiming a common and equal right in the land, as it was at first, and should be now — for it was never divided, but belongs to all. No tribe has the right to sell, even to each other, much less to strangers. . . . Sell a country! Why not sell the air, the great sea, as well as the earth? Did not the Great Spirit make them all for the use of his children?[38]

This awareness of the sacredness of the hoop of creation is not just a flash of ''savage'' intuition, nor an expression of animism or primitive communism, as such lofty insights from native people have been patronizingly described by European observers. It is a flowering of sacramental mysticism of which Saint Francis and

Lady Julian of Norwich would have been proud. Unlike European mysticism, however, the mysticism of Black Elk and Seattle is not reserved only for the specially gifted person, but for every common man and woman. For all its loftiness, it is a truly democratic mysticism with a wealth of philosophical reflection. Black Elk contemplates:

> We regard all created beings as sacred and important, for everything has a *wochangi* or influence, which can be given to us, through which we may gain a little more understanding if we are attentive. We should understand well that all things are the works of the Great Spirit. We should know that he is within all things; the trees, the grasses, the rivers, the mountains and all the four-legged animals, and the winged peoples; and even more important we should understand that he is also above all these things and peoples.[39]

Black Elk is careful to make it clear that sacred space is not pantheism (God-in-things), but panentheism (God-in-and-above-all-things). It is a measure of his philosophical astuteness that he points out the transcendent character of the Great Spirit which has so often been misunderstood by western students of native spirituality as the God of shamanistic pantheism. The centre that is present everywhere in sacred space also transcends it. This transcendent reality is an incarnational presence, as much in stone as in man. There is this sense of the web of life and the unity of all creatures in the mysticism of Black Elk. Other creatures, as much as human beings, participate in the spiritual consciousness of sacred space. So Black Elk could say in all seriousness: ''Birds make their nests in circles, for theirs is the same religion as ours.[40]

The Indian Concept of Personhood

The category ''person,'' drawn from the Greek concept of *persona*, is confirmed in its anthropocentrism by the influx of the Judaeo-Christian heresy of the primacy of man. The sub-human species along with inanimate nature are regarded as fodder for man's appetite, on a descending scale of priorities in the economy of the white man's God. Animals have no soul, and man alone is capable of redemption. The western mind is so conditioned to restrict the category "person" to human beings, whereas for native people all beings are persons. They are part of a web of friendship of which man is only one thread. The native concept of personhood is so broad that it embraces even inanimate things. So in their eyes nothing is a thing, every thing is a person. This spirit is captured by Sitting Bull, chief of the Hunkpapa Teton division of the Sioux and medicine man, in his address to his braves at a Powder River council in 1877:

> Behold, my brothers, the spring has come; the earth has received the embraces of the sun and we shall soon see the results of that love! Every seed is awakened and so has all animal life. It is through this mysterious power that we too have our being and we therefore yield to our neighbours, even our animal neighbours, the same right as ourselves, to inhabit this land.[41]

We should not make the mistake of calling native people animists, only because they treated all beings as persons. They do not simplistically perceive everything in the world as invested with life. Hallowell, doing research among the Ojibwa, once asked an Indian: "Are all rocks alive?" To which the Indian replied: "No. But some are." This incident reminds us of a similar conversation we had with a Cree elder at Morley who enlightened us by saying that some trees are more sensitive than men. The category of person extends throughout the material and spiritual world. According to Sam D. Gill, "at the basis of the Ojibwa world-view is the understanding that everything has possibility of being perceived and treated on a person-to-person basis."[42] All things and all beings make up this world. No wonder that the Lakota people of old would conclude all their rituals with the solemn words, *Mitakuye oyasin*, i.e. all my relatives — plants, animals, humans — are one big universal family.

This sacred bond between humans, beasts and the earth is a common thread weaving through the spirituality of the native people. An excerpt from a letter written by a certain Anaquoness, an Ojibwa who fought in World War I, testifies to the fact that this spirit of affinity within the hoop of creation is shared not only by the great orators but also by ordinary native people:

> To us, the forests and the broad hills and the northern lights and the sunsets are all full of life, and we live in tune with them, akin in spirit, as no white man ever could And when we are alone, we talk to the water and the trees and we are not alone. In spite of all their modern inventions, the whites would not be able to live as we Indians live; and when they try to live like us, they succumb for they do not understand what the sun has to say when it sets, and they do not hear the voices of the ancestors in the wind. . . . The white man sees only trees, rocks and water, only the external side of the book of nature, but cannot read the book itself.[43]

The western mind tends to classify and categorize things and people. Even the church has lost the grand vision of God's creation being shot through with the life-giving spirit of the cosmic Christ.[44] European philosophy is forever saddled with the antinomies of spirit and matter, religious and secular, heavenly and earthly. The native person, however, is sensitive to the spiritual underpinning of all categories in creation regardless of status, rank, and quality. Lame Deer reflects:

> Nothing is so small and unimportant but it has a spirit given to it by Wakan Tanka. Tuncan is what you might call a stone god, but he is also part of the Great Spirit. The gods are separate beings, but they are all united in Wakan Tanka. It is hard to understand — something like the Holy Trinity. You can't explain it except by going back, to the "circles within circles" idea, the spirit splitting itself up into stones, trees, tiny insects even, making them all *wakan* by his ever-presence. And in turn all these myriads of things which make up the universe flowing back to their source, united in the one Grandfather Spirit.[45]

Unfortunately, European scholars of native spirituality have made light of such philosophical musings as an expression of primitive magic-mongering. Sociologists of religion, trained in the pragmatic scientific discipline, were only too eager to pillory the supernatural, the magical, the mythical, and the mystical in native spirituality. During the Enlightenment even western Christianity became demythologized and desacralized. Max Weber called this process the disenchantment of the world (*Die Entzauberung der Welt*). A new trend known as the phenomenology of religion came into vogue as the western man increasingly failed to behold the numinous in his environment.

The Groaning of All Creation (Romans 8:19-23)

To the native eye, the material world was suffused with the Holy, and also had an ethical content to it. The welter of matter, which the European was out to colonize, conquer, and exploit, was to the native person a world peopled with stones, trees, birds, and animals who had a personal, sacred, ethical, spiritual, and human quality to their essence. Stones were alive. Trees talked. Birds had feelings. Animals had a conscience. The earth rejoiced and hurt. Here was a world-view deeply mystical, consistently ethical, maturely philosophical, and magically sacramental. It perceived the whole world, and not just man, as involved in an ethical and spiritual struggle. St. Paul echoes this sacramental vision of the universe in need of redemption when he writes about "the groaning creation." The native world-view is characterized by a healthy dialectic between the sacred and the profane; a "personal" link between man and the rest of creation; and a firm rejection of the idea of an extra-terrestrial holiness.

In contrast, western Christianity presented a world-view characterized by a clean divide between the sacred and the profane, salvation and sanctification, the cosmic and the ethical. Obviously western Christianity was blighted by a truncated understanding of sin — sin seen merely as a private individual act; sin to be righted through forgiveness without any provision for restoration on an objective-material level; sin identified largely with sex and sexual aberration; sin in a purely human capacity ignoring its impact on the rest of creation. This was a largely non-sacramental spirituality that betrayed both Hebrew and native spiritualities alike. Absolution from sin meant to the Hebrew a restoration of the conditions in the material world. (Isaiah 40: 1ff)

The fall of man was inextricably connected with the fall of the earth, exemplified by the natural catastrophies of Pharaonic Egypt, and Sodom and Gomorrah. The Book of Deuteronomy illustrates how both man and creation are blessed and cursed in tandem. The Hebrew prophets, like Seattle and Black Elk, knew that what befell man befell also the earth.[46] In the words of J.L. McKenzie, ''nature is integrated into the moral order of Yahweh's government of mankind.''[47]

Sin was not only an act against God, but against creation, and through sin not only man, but the entire creation came to grief. Dr. Adam Cuthand, in an address delivered at the World Future's Conference in Canada in 1980, said:

> Sin, according to the Indian's understanding, is not only sin against our creator, or our fellow men, but includes sin against God's creation. To us, it is a sin to kill a wild animal, to take the so-called trophy and leave the meat to rot. It is a sin to divert rivers, to destroy trees for no reason, to destroy the fowl of the air, and all other created things.

Creation was not just a framework, an arena, for the saving activity of God. Creation was part of the saving activity. The new creation in Christ was very much a continuation of God's creative activity. Creation itself is a saving act of God. Creation is a sacramental image of the Great Spirit. Sin then is not just moral, private, and subjective, but embraces the ecological, the socio-political and cosmic dimensions. This brings us back to Black Elk's paradigm of the tree rooted in the centre of the cosmic hoop. Black Elk, quoted in the famous liturgy prepared by native American women for the Women's World Day of Prayer in 1981, observes:

> All day long, the ''lamenter'' sends a voice to Wakan-Tanka for aid, and walks as described upon the sacred paths which form a cross. This form has much power in it for whenever we return to the centre, we know that it is as if we are return-ing to Wakan-Tanka, who is the centre of everything, and although we may think that we are going away, sooner or later we and all things must return.

Black Elk's vision of the Cross rooted in the centre of the cycle of creation is a supreme corrective to the non-communal, individualistic, non-incarnational, anthropocentric character of sin and redemption of Euro-Christianity. An integration of Black Elk's holistic mysticism will forever purge Euro-Christianity of its twin heresies of private sin and private salvation. As Starkloff explains:

> For the traditional Indian, personal individual morality *is* social morality. There is no boxing-off of two separate categories. Even the celebrated individualism of the plains warriors or hunters was entirely taken for granted as conducive to the tribal well-being. If an individual performed well, the whole community would benefit, and if he was selfish, not only would the tribe suffer but he, too, as virtually an organic part of the body would suffer. As should be evident, the Pauline notion of the Body of Christ is very close to such a doctrine of solidarity.[48]

Sin viewed from the perspective provided by Black Elk and Seattle consists in the breaking-up of the hoop, the loss of the centre, the withering of the tree. Sin is losing power. Sin is privatism, *wasichu*-consciousness, alienation from the community of man and nature. Sin is the rape of Mother Earth. Sin is pricing and holding and trafficking in natural bounties created by the Great Spirit. Sin is as much an ecological as an ethical aberration. Hence, sin can be absolved only on a corporate scale of restoration and sanctification. Sin robs God's creation of its magic, holiness, personhood, fellowship, dignity, and innate self-worth. Joseph Couture writes:

> Original sin . . . would be to consider self as independent, as having absolute freedom. For an Indian, responsibility is compliance with the laws of nature, a compliance which induces transcendence of individual self. . . . To fall out of balance with nature, if within or without, is to do wrong. This fall is into self-consciousness, which causes a sense of shame.[49]

The sacrament of the Vision Quest which we have taken as a symbolic theme of this book begins with an engagement with the reality of corporate sinfulness of humanity aspiring for an equally corporate redemption of humanity along with all creation. The youth enters the sweat lodge called "the womb of Mother Earth," to be reborn. His body would be cleansed by vapours created from the four primal elements: fire, rock, water, and air. Pouring water on the heated rocks, he intones: ''I recall all my evil deeds, and for each misdeed I sprinkle water on these stones.'' In this beautiful liturgy of confession and prayer for unity with creation to the Great Spirit, we find the divide between individual and corporate sin vanishes and the youth for the moment incorporates and represents all fallen creation. A Navaho lament of repentance embodies this cosmic sense of shame:

I am ashamed before the earth;
I am ashamed before the heavens;
I am ashamed before the evening twilight;
I am ashamed before the blue sky;
I am ashamed before the darkness;
I am ashamed before the sun;
I am ashamed before the One
standing within me who speaks to me.

This sweeping awareness of sin runs as a thread through the native Vision Quest. The hope for an equally all-embracing restoration and absolution gives momentum to the native spiritual journey. Absolution means a return to the hoop; to collective ownership of land; to the tribe (and not the nuclear family) as the unit; to the balance between the masculine and the feminine. Absolution is the healing of Mother Earth, the friendship among all of God's creatures — bird, animal, man.

''Your God Is Not Our God''

Established European Christianity has to learn to hear in the oracular prophecies of Black Elk and Seattle, God's truth restated so that we may understand our Christianity a little bit better. Black Elk gave us the vision of the cross set within the cosmic circle. He outlined the map of the cyclical sacred space and symbolically described the defilement of the circle and the space, the withering of the tree, the loss of the centre, and the breaking up of the cycle.

But Black Elk is not indulging in cosmic generalities. In his prophecy he is pointedly referring to the break-up of the hoop of the native world in the wake of the white man's arrival on the scene. Thus, Black Elk's vision of the cross set within the cosmic circle has to be understood with reference to the contemporary political reality of a state of injustice committed against the hoop of the Indian nation by the invading *wasichu*. Black Elk felt himself called to be a prophet to his nation to shore them up against the sin of the expansionist European way of life. The two nations were at war on a spiritual scale. It is as though the God of Black Elk, who guarded the cosmic hoop, was pitted against the God of the *wasichu*, who threatened to wither the tree of life, forfeit the centre, and break up the hoop. We find Black Elk, much like Moses before him, in desperate communion with his God. This God has the same voice as the God of Mount Sinai, jealous and with a bias to the poor and the oppressed: ''I have seen the affliction of my people who are in Egypt, and have heard their cry because of their taskmasters; I know their sufferings, and I have come down to deliver them out of the hand of the Egyptians.''[50]

In Seattle's address to the envoy from Washington we find a fine sense of this tension of the biblical God who takes sides:

> Your God is not our God! Your God loves your people and hates mine! He folds his strong arms lovingly around the white man and leads him as a father leads his infant son, but he has forsaken his red children, if they are really his. . . . The white man's God cannot love his red children or he would protect them. We seem to be orphans who can look nowhere for help.
>
> How then can we become brothers? How can your God become our God and renew our prosperity and awaken in us dreams of returning greatness? Your God seems to us to be partial. He came to the white man. We never saw him, never heard his voice. He gave the white man laws, but had no word for his red children whose teeming millions once filled this vast continent as the stars filled the firmament.

As of old the desert God of the Hebrew slaves was pitted against the God of the mighty pharaoh, so also now Seattle sees his God at war with the God of the powerful white man. The two cannot be the same. How then can one reconcile this radical statement of Seattle's with the following words which have since been thrust into his mouth? ''One thing we know, which the white man may one day discover — our God is the same God. You may think now that you own him as you wish to own our land, but you cannot. He is the God of man, and his compassion is equal for the red man and the white."

"Our God is not your God" and "Our God is the same God" are diametrically opposed statements of faith and cannot logically come from the same source. The former is the authentic version recorded by Dr. Henry Smith for *The Seattle Sunday Star* of 29 October 1887. Seattle's original message was one of confrontation between their respective spiritualities, and of the injustice of his people's suffering. There was very little ecological content in it. It was a powerful political manifesto rejecting spurious forms of reconciliation under the veneer of pious religious slogans.

Unfortunately, this original terse oratory has lately been supplanted by a forgery. In 1970 a film scriptwriter called Ted Perry composed a short film script which included the widely quoted forged version. By his own admission he had no intention of duping the public. The blame for the circulation of this dubious document rests with his clients, the Southern Baptists, a fundamentalist sect in the United States of America notorious for its right-wing leanings and its alliance with the Moral Majority. It is to the credit of Professor William Arrowsmith of John Hopkins University, Baltimore, that this shameless fraud has been exposed. According to him,

> The Baptists made it clear in correspondence that they simply could not imagine what my objection to their falsification of the speech could be. In their minds, so long as one's purpose is pious and one is about God's business, the truth, it seems, is merely a secular or academic concern. They knew very well that the vogue in America of romantic ecology and Indian poetry would ensure their Christian message carrying the day. The sugar-coating is ecology, the pill is Baptist Christianity.[51]

This is not just a ruse to spread Baptist Christianity. It must be made amply clear that this is a sinister strategy to co-opt the oppressed segments of American society, native people included, into a false identity of solidarity with the dominant class by invoking time-honoured Christian slogans. The objective is to blur the polarization between classes and to coax the rebellious into an attitude of false reconciliation with their oppressors without any real change in social structures. It is a common trick practised by reactionary religion to create the illusion of a brotherhood of all people — in spite of basic inequalities — by invoking the fatherhood of God. This is well illustrated by the preamble of the constitution of the Republic of South Africa, which refers to ''Almighty God, who controls the destinies of peoples and nations, who gathered our forebears together from many lands and gave them this their own [land].'' Concerned Black Evangelicals in South Africa, who are critical of right-wing trends in the evangelical tradition, have sharply rejected this presumptious God-talk of the theologians of apartheid in their publication, *Evangelical Witness in South Africa*:

> This ''God'' referred to in this preamble comes across as the god of the oppressor to black people in South Africa. It is a ''God'' of the white people of South Africa. To the township youths who are attacked and killed, this ''God'' is the god of the teargas, bullets, sjamboks, prison cells and death. This type of God to us Christians comes as an antichrist, negating the very basis of our Christian faith.[52]

It was in a similar spirit of critique of the pseudo-Christianity of the white settlers that Seattle declared: ''Our God is not your God.'' He draws the lines between the two conflicting spiritualities in no uncertain terms:

> No. We are two distinct races, and must ever remain so, with separate origins and separate destinies. There is little in common between us. . . . Your religion was written on tablets of stone by the iron finger of an angry God, lest you might forget it. The Red Man could never comprehend nor remember it.
> Our religion is the traditions of our ancestors — the dreams of our old men, given to them in the solemn hours of night by the Great Spirit, and the visions of our Sachems, and is written in the hearts of our people.

Here, we do not have Christianity pitted against paganism. Seattle is only confronting the cold legalistic creed of an angry God worshipped by an expansionist people with the gentle contemplative communitarian spirituality of the heart practised by a people indigenous to the land, and informed by a God of the Spirit, not of might. Seattle is defending a much maligned native spirituality that is truly evocative of the spirit of Christ against the onslaught of a Christian culture that has distorted the very spirit of Christ.

"We May Be Brothers, after All"

Much as Seattle rejects the presumptuous claims of brotherhood made by the established church, he, as a true prophet of the Great Spirit, sees the innate equality of all peoples in the sharing of our common humanity and mortality. It is only when all peoples cultivate enough humility to confess to this our common bond that makes us creatures — human, mortal, sinful, vulnerable, and so in need of grace — that we can comprehend the sacred mystery of God becoming human in Christ Jesus. Seattle calls us all, natives and whites, to this vision and hope of a church where we discover and celebrate our common humanity, which God in his Son shared with us all, through the Great Spirit:

> Men come and go like the waves of the sea. A tear, a dirge and they are gone from our longing eyes forever. It is the order of Nature. Even the white man, whose God walked and talked with him as friend to friend, is not exempt from the common destiny. We may be brothers, after all. We will see.

These words abide.

Bibliography

Ahenakew, Andrew. "Sometimes We Burn . . . Sometimes We Tremble." ACC Video Tape, n.d.

Ahenakew, Edward, edited by Ruth M. Buck. *Voices of the Plains Cree.* Toronto: McClelland and Stewart, 1973.

Ahenakew, Freda and Shirley Fredeen, eds. *Our Language: Our Survival.* Saskatoon: Saskatchewan Indian Languages Institute, 1987.

Barman, Jean, Yvonne Hébert, and Don McCaskill, eds. *Indian Education in Canada.* Vol. 1 *The Legacy.* Vancouver: University of British Columbia Press, Nakoda Institute Occasional Paper no. 2, 1986.

Barman, Jean, Yvonne Hébert, and Don McCaskill, eds. *Indian Education in Canada.* Vol. 2 *The Challenge.* Vancouver: University of British Columbia Press, Nakoda Institute Occasional Paper no. 3, 1987.

Berger, T.R. *Northern Frontier, Northern Homeland.* Ottawa: Ministry of Supply and Services, 1977.

Black Elk with John G. Neihardt. *Black Elk Speaks. The Life Story of a Holy Man of the Oglala Sioux.* London: Abacus, 1972.

Board for Mission and Unity. *Towards a Theology for Inter-Faith Dialogue.* London: CIO Publishing, 1984.

Bowden, Henry Warner. *American Indians and Christian Missions. Studies in Cultural Conflict.* Chicago and London: University of Chicago Press, 1981.

Bowden, Henry W. and James Ronda, eds. *John Eliot's Indian Dialogues. A Study in Cultural Interaction.* Westport: Greenwood Press, 1980. First published in 1671.

Brody, Hugh. *Maps and Dreams: Indians and the British Columbia Frontier.* Harmondsworth: Penguin, 1983.

Brown, Dee. *Bury My Heart at Wounded Knee.* New York: Holt, Rinehart and Winston, 1971.

Brown, Joseph Epes. *The Sacred Pipe.* Norman: University of Oklahoma, 1953.

Brown, Joseph Epes. *A Spiritual Legacy of the American Indian.* New York: Crossroad, 1982.

Campbell, Joseph. *The Masks of God: Primitive Mythology.* Harmondsworth: Penguin, 1975.

Cardinal, Harold. "There Is No Reason for Us to Fear Each Other." *Kerygma*, 18. (1984).

Carrington, Philip. *The Anglican Church in Canada: A History*. Toronto: Collins, 1963.

Citizens Plus. The Nishga People of the Naas River Valley in Northwestern British Columbia. New Aiyansh: The Nishga Tribal Council, 1980 (revised ed. of *Nishga Land Is Not For Sale* , 1976).

Couture, Joseph E. "Indian Spirituality — A Personal Experience." *Kerygma*, 16 (1982).

Crabb, F.H.W. "The Church and the North." In *Rupert's Land: A Cultural Tapestry*. Ontario: published for the Calgary Institute for the Humanities by University Press, Waterloo, 1988.

Craven, Margaret. *I Heard The Owl Call My Name*. Canada: Clarke Irwin, 1967.

Cuthand, Adam. "The Spirituality of Native North Americans." Paper presented at World Futures Conference, Toronto, July 1980.

Cuthand, Adam. "Pastoral Ministry to Native People." Unpublished ms., n.d.

Deloria Jr., Vine. *Custer Died for Your Sins: An Indian Manifesto*. New York: Collier-Macmillan, 1969.

Deloria Jr., Vine. *We Talk, You Listen: New Tribes, New Turf*. New York: Macmillan, 1970.

Deloria Jr., Vine. *God Is Red*. New York: Grosset and Dunlap, 1973.

Drouin O.M.I., E.O. *Lac Ste-Anne, Sakahigan*. Edmonton: Editions De L'Ermitage, 1973.

Duncombe, Patricia. *Within the Circle. Christian Ministry and the American Indian*. Cincinnati: Forward Movement Publications, 1981.

Eliade, Mircea. *Shamanism: Archaic Techniques of Ecstacy*. Princeton: University Press, 1964.

Fireweed. A Feminist Quarterly. Native Women. 22 (1986).

Fontaine, Stan. "The Amerindian Reality: As An Inner Reality." *Kerygma*, 15, 37 (1981).

Frideres, James S. *Native People in Canada: Contemporary Conflicts*. 2nd ed. Scarborough: Prentice-Hall of Canada, 1983.

Getty, Ian A.L. and Antoine S. Lussier. *As Long As The Sun Shines And Water Flows. A Reader in Canadian Native Studies*. Vancouver: University of British Columbia Press, Nakoda Institute Occasional Paper no. 1, 1983.

Gill, Sam D. *Native American Religions: An Introduction*. Belmont: Wadsworth, 1982.

Goodwill, Jean and Norma Sluman, *John Tootoosis: A Biography of a Cree Leader*. Ottawa: Golden Dog Press, 1982.

Gould, S. *Inasmuch. Sketches of the Beginnings of the Church of England in Canada in Relation to the Indians and Eskimo Races*. Toronto: Church Missionary Society, 1917.

Grant, John Webster, ed. *The Churches and the Canadian Experience*. Toronto: Ryerson Press, 1963.

Grant, John Webster. "Indian Missions as European Enclaves." *Studies in Religion*, 7, 3 (1978).

Grant, John Webster. *Moon of Wintertime. Missionaries and the Indians of Canada in Encounter since 1534*. Toronto: University of Toronto Press, 1985.

Hamel, Peter. "Anglicans and Aboriginal People: The Ecojustice Connection." *Jubilee*, 2, 4 (1985).

Hamel, Peter. *Anglicans and Aboriginal Peoples*. Toronto: Anglican Church of Canada, 1986.

Hatfield, Leonard F. *Simon Gibbons. First Eskimo Priest*. Hantsport: Lancelot Press, 1987.

Heeney, William Bertal, ed. *Leaders of the Canadian Church*. Second series. Toronto: Musson, 1920.

Hendry, Charles E. *Beyond Traplines. Does the Church Really Care? Towards an Assessment of the Work of the Anglican Church of Canada with Canada's Native Peoples*. Canada: Miracle Press, 1969.

Hines, John. *Red Indians of the Plains*. London: S.P.C.K., 1915.

Hallowell, A. Irving. "Ojibwa Ontology." In S. Diamond, *Culture in History*. New York: Columbia University, 1960.

Hultkrantz, Ake. *The Religions of the American Indians*. Berkeley, Los Angeles, London: University of California Press, 1979.

Hultkrantz, Ake. *The Study of American Indian Religions*. New York: Crossroad & Scholars Press, 1983.

Jenness, Diamond. *The Indians of Canada*. 7th ed. Toronto and Buffalo: University of Toronto Press, 1977. First published in 1932.

Johnson O.M.I., Jacques. "Kisemanito Centre Training Native Men For The Priesthood." *Kerygma*, 15, 37 (1981).

Johnson O.M.I., Jacques. "Native Spirituality and the Catholic Faith." *Kerygma*, 16 (1982).

Jones, Peter. *Since Columbus: Poverty and Pluralism in the History of the Americas*. London: Heinemann, 1975.

Kennedy, Dan. *Recollections of an Assiniboine Chief*. Toronto: McClelland and Stewart, 1972.

Kinsella, W.P. *Dance Me Outside*. Canada: Oberon Press, 1977.

Kinsella, W.P. *Born Indian*. Canada: Oberon Press, 1981.

Kinsella, W.P. *The Moccasin Telegraph and Other Stories*. London: Arena, 1985.

Koyama, Kosuke. *Waterbuffalo Theology*. London: SCM, 1974.

Lame Deer and Richard Erdoes, *Lame Deer: Sioux Medicine Man*. London: Davis Poynter, 1973.

Lillard, Charles, ed. *In the Wake of the War Canoe. William Henry Collison*. Victoria: Sono Nis Press, 1981.

Lanternari, Vittorio. *The Religions of the Oppressed*. New York: Knopf, 1963.

Luther Starding Bear. *Lard of the Spotted Eagle*. Boston and New York: 1933.

Mackenzie, John A. ''Native Rights and the Church: An Historical and Political Analysis.'' Unpublished lecture at the Vancouver School of Theology Summer School, 1986.

McKenzie, J.L. *A Theology of the Old Testament*. New York: Geoffrey Chapman, 1974.

Mandate special edition, ''A Dialogue with Canada's Native Peoples.'' 16, 4 (1985).

McCullum, Hugh and Karmel Taylor McCullum. *Caledonia. 100 Years Ahead*. Toronto: The Anglican Book Centre, 1979.

Mountain Horse, Mike. *My People, the Bloods*. Calgary: Glenbow-Alberta Institute, 1979.

Muller, Hugo. *Why Don't You? A Look at Attitudes towards Indians*. Moosonee: 1975.

Nabokov, Peter. *Indian Running*. Santa Barbara: Capra Press, 1981.

Nabokov, Peter. ''America as Holy Land: An Indian Understanding.'' *Grapevine*, 13, 10 (May 1982).

Newbigin, Lesslie. *The Open Secret*. London: S.P.C.K., 1979.

Nock, David. ''The failure of the CMS native church policy in southwestern Ontario and Algoma.'' *Studies in Religion*, 9, 3 (1980).

Oliver, Edmund H. *The Winnipeg of the Frontier*. Toronto: United Church Publishing House, 1930.

Opekokew, Delia. *The First Nations: Indian Governments in the Community of Man*. Saskatoon: Federation of Saskatchewan Indian Nations, 1982.

Patterson II, E. Palmer. *The Canadian Indian: A History since 1500*. Ontario: Collier-Macmillan Canada, 1972.

Patterson II. E. Palmer. *Mission on the Nass. The Evangelization of the Nishga (1860-1890)*. Waterloo: Eulachon Press, 1982.

Peelman O.M.I., Achiel. "The Mission of the Church after Vatican II and the Native Peoples of Canada." *Kerygma*, 18 (1984).

Pettipas, Katherine, ed. *The Diary of the Reverend Henry Budd 1870-1875.* Winnipeg: Hignill, 1974.

Pettipas, Katherine. "A History of the Work of the Rev. Henry Budd Conducted under the Auspices of the Church Missionary Society, 1840-1875." Unpublished MA thesis, University of Manitoba, 1972.

Race, Alan. "Truth is Many-Eyed." In *God's Truth*. Eric James, ed. London: SCM, 1988.

Radin, Paul, ed. *Crashing Thunder: The Autobiography of an American Indian.* Lincoln: University of Nebraska Press, 1983.

Red Fox, Chief. *The Memoirs of Chief Red Fox.* London: W.H. Allen, 1971.

Seton, Ernest Thompson. *The Gospel of the Redman. An Indian Bible.* London: Methuen, 1937.

Settee, James. Unpublished Journal. Church Missionary Society Records.

Smith, Donald B. *Sacred Feathers. The Reverend Peter Jones (Kakhewaquonaby) and the Mississauga Indians.* Lincoln and London: University of Nebraska Press, 1987.

Snow, Chief John. *These Mountains Are Our Sacred Places. The Story of the Stoney People.* Toronto and Sarasota: Samuel Stevens, 1977.

Starkloff, C.F. *The People of the Center: American Indian Religion and Christianity.* New York: Seabury Press, 1974.

Starkloff, Carl. "American Indian Religion and Christianity: Confrontation and Dialogue." *Journal of Ecumenical Studies* (Winter 1971).

Starkloff, Carl. "Dialogue with Native Religious Traditions: Toward the Local Church." *Kerygma*, 16 (1982).

Starkloff, Carl. "Religious Renewal in Native North America: The Contemporary Call to Mission." *Missiology: An International Review*, XIII, 1 (Jan. 1985).

Starkloff, Carl. "The Anishnabe Ministry Training Project: Scriptural-Theological Formation." *Kerygma*, 19 (1985).

Steinmetz S.J., Paul B. *Meditations with Native Americans — Lakota Spirituality.* Santa Fe: Bear and Company, 1972.

Steinmetz S.J., Paul B. *Pipe, Bible and Peyote among the Oglala Lakota. A Study in Religious Identity.* Stockholm: Almqvist and Wiksell, 1980.

Steltenkamp S.J., Michael F. *The Sacred Vision. Native American Religion and its Practice Today.* New York: Paulist Press, 1982.

Stock, Eugene. *The History of the Church Missionary Society.* Vol. 1. London: C.M.S., 1899.

Turner III, Frederick W. *The Portable North American Indian Reader.* Harmondsworth: Penguin, 1974.

Underhill, Ruth M. *Red Man's Religion. Beliefs and Practices of the Indians North of Mexico.* Chicago and London: University of Chicago Press, 1965.

Vogel, Virgil J., ed. *This Country Was Ours: A Documentary History of the American Indian.* New York: Harper and Row, 1972.

Walker, James. "The Indian in Canadian Historical Writing, 1971-1981." In Getty and Lussier, 1983.

Walsh, H.H. *The Christian Church in Canada.* Toronto: Ryerson Press, 1956.

Washburn, Wilcomb E. *Red Man's Land, White Man's Law: A Study of the Past and Present Status of the American Indian.* New York: Charles Scribners Sons, 1971.

Waterman, Jennifer. "Dreams and Visions in Native North American Culture." *Kerygma*, 17, 40 (1983).

Endnotes

Chapter 1

1 Charles E. Hendry, *Beyond Traplines* (Canada: Miracle Press, 1969), p. 72.
2 Hendry, p. 71–72.
3 Hendry, p. 80.
4 Lame Deer and Richard Erdoes, *Lame Deer: Sioux Medicine Man* (London: Davis Poynter, 1973), p. 115.
5 Job 33:14–18, *Jerusalem Bible.*
6 Daniel 2:20–23, *Revised Standard Version.*
7 Lame Deer, p. 44.
8 Acts 2:17, *Jerusalem Bible.*

Chapter 2

1 Henry W. Bowden and James Ronda, eds., *John Eliot's Indian Dialogues. A Study in Cultural Interaction* (Westport: Greenwood Press, 1980. First published 1671), p. 63.
2 James Walker, "The Indian in Canadian Historical Writing, 1971–1981," in Ian A.L. Getty and Antoine Lussier, *As Long as the Sun Shines and Water Flows* (Vancouver: University of British Columbia Press, 1983), p. 346.
3 Bowden and Ronda, p. 88.
4 *The Queen, the Empire, and the English-Speaking World, a Diamond Jubilee Issue,* (London: S.P.C.K., 1897), p. 7.
5 Bowden and Ronda, p. 95–6.
6 Walker, pp. 340, 348.
7 John Webster Grant, ed., *The Churches and the Canadian Experience* (Toronto: Ryerson Press, 1963), p. 22.
8 H.H. Walsh, *The Christian Church in Canada* (Toronto: Ryerson Press, 1956), p. 1.
9 William Bertal Heeney, ed., *Leaders of the Canadian Church* (Toronto: Musson, 1920).
10 Lame Deer and Erdoes, pp. 46, 61.
11 Lame Deer and Erdoes, pp. 23, 45.
12 Lame Deer and Erdoes, p. 70.

13 Lame Deer and Erdoes, p. 39.

14 Red Fox *The Memoirs of Chief Red Fox* (London: W.H. Allen, 1971), p. 99.

15 Paul Radin ed., *Crashing Thunder: The Autobiography of an American Indian* (Lincoln: University of Nebraska Press, 1983), p. x.

16 Radin, pp. x–xvi.

17 Marilou Awiakta in *Fireweed*, 22 (1986), p. 110.

18 Frederick W. Turner, *The Portable North American Indian Reader* (Harmondsworth: Penguin, 1974), p. 486.

19 Stan McKay, editorial, *Mandate*, 16 (1985), p. 4.

20 Interview, 18 June 1987.

Chapter 3

1 Peter Nabokov, ''America as Holy Land: An Indian Understanding,'' *Grapevine*, 13 10 (May 1982), p. 2.

 2 Black Elk with John G. Neihardt, *Black Elk Speaks* (London: Abacus, 1972), pp. 194–196.

 3 Edward Ahenakew, *Voices of the Plains Cree* (Toronto: McClelland and Stewart, 1973), pp. 11–15, 75–76.

 4 Ahenakew, pp. 105, 144.

 5 Ahenakew, pp. 104–106.

 6 Ahenakew, p. 69.

 7 *Citizens Plus* (New Aiyansh: The Nisga Tribal Council, 1980), p. 10–11.

 8 Hendry, p. 4.

 9 Hendry, p. 5.

10 Interview, 28 May 1987.

11 *The Promise*, III, December 1986, p. 4.

12 Hendry, pp. 6–7, 16.

13 Interview, 26 May 1987.

14 Ahenakew, pp. 122–124.

15 Interview, 26 May 1987.

16 Interview, 26 May 1987.

17 Hendry, p. 41.

18 John Webster Grant, *Moon of Wintertime* (Toronto: University of Toronto Press, 1985), pp. 134–136, and interview, 28 September 1985.

19 Hendry, p. 21.

20 Jean Barman, Yvonne Hebert, and Don McCaskill, eds., *Indian Education in Canada* (Vancouver: University of British Columbia Press, 1986) and Grant, pp. 176–183.

21 Hendry, p. 63.

22 Jean Goodwill and Norma Sluman, *John Tootoosis: A Biography of a Cree Leader* (Ottawa: Golden Dog Press, 1982), p. 109.

23 Ahenakew, p. 153.

24 Ahenakew, p. 134–4.

25 Ahenakew, p. 127–135, 187.

26 Interview, 23 May 1987.

27 Interview, 28 May 1987.

28 Interview, 25 May 1987.

29 Interview, 20 May 1987.

30 Grant, pp. 261–262.

31 Grant, p. 265.

32 Interview with Archdeacon Ian Mackenzie, 21 June 1987.

33 Barman, Hébert, and McCaskill.

34 *Calgary Herald*, 27 December 1986.

35 Bowden and Ronda, p. 31.

36 Ahenakew, p. 103.

37 Interview, 18 May 1987.

38 Interview, 18 May 1987.

39 Interview, 17 May 1987.

40 *The Promise*, December 1986.

41 Interview, 20 May 1987.

42 Interview, 20 May 1987.

Chapter 4

1 Matthew 9:16–17, *Jerusalem Bible*.

2 Grant, pp. 111, 221.

3 Heeney, p. 69.

4 Heeney, pp. 73–78.

5 Interview, 27 May 1987.

6 Turner, p. 575.

7 Turner, p. 576.

8 Ahenakew, p. 166.

9 Grant, p. vii.

10 Andrew Ahenakew, ''Sometimes We Burn . . . Sometimes We Tremble'' (ACC videotape, n.d.).

11 Ahenakew, p. 183.

12 Interview, 27 May 1987.

13 Interview, 26 June 1987.

14 Interview, 29 May 1987.

15 Carl Starkloff, ''Dialogue with Native Religious Traditions: Toward

the Local Church,'' *Kergyma*, 16 (1982), pp. 187–9.

16 Interview, 22 June 1987.

17 Lame Deer and Erdoes, p. 109.

18 *Toronto Star*, 7 September 1985.

19 Interview with Bishop John Hannen, 22 June 1987.

20 Interview, 16 June 1987.

21 Interview, 25 May 1987.

22 Interview, 25 May 1987.

23 Interview, 18 May 1987.

24 Interview, 17 May 1987.

25 *Kerygma*, 16 (1982), pp. 123–8.

26 Interview, 30 May 1987.

27 *Kerygma*, 18 (1984), p. 55.

28 Interview, 18 June 1987.

29 Interview, 18 June 1987.

Chapter 5

1 Matthew 8:16.

2 James S. Frideres, *Native People in Canada; Contemporary Conflicts*, 2nd ed. (Scarborough: Prentice-Hall of Canada, 1983).

3 Original notes.

4 John Snow, *These Mountains Are Our Sacred Places. The Story of the Stoney People* (Toronto and Sarasota: Samuel Stevens, 1977), p. 144.

5 Turner's notes, 1972.

6 Report, 22 May 1972.

7 *Calgary Herald*, 1 August 1973.

8 Snow, p. 143.

9 Audio-visual tape.

10 Audio-visual tape.

11 E. Palmer Patterson II, *Mission on the Nass: The Evangelization of the Nishga (1860–1890)* (Waterloo: Eulachon Press, 1982), pp. 23–27.

12 Patterson, p. 109.

13 Charles Lillard, ed., *In the Wake of the War Canoe. William Henry Collison* (Victoria: Sono Nis Press, 1981).

14 The McCullums have given a short historical account of the Church Army up to the present, tracing its spread to other native groups, their first conference in 1926, the subsequent decline of the Army, its separation from the established church in many places, and its revival from the 1950s on following the infusion of Anglo-Catholicism into the Diocese. Hugh McCullum and Karmel Taylor McCullum,

Caledonia. 100 Years Ahead (Toronto: The Anglican Book Centre, 1979).

15 Interview, 21 June 1987.

16 Interview, 23 June 1987.

17 Interview, 23 June 1987.

18 Andrew Ahenakew, "Sometimes We Burn . . . Sometimes We Tremble."

19 Jennifer Waterman, "Dreams and Visions in Native North American Culture," *Kerygma*, 17 (1983), 40.

20 Interview, 23 May 1987.

21 Andrew Ahenakew, "Sometimes We Burn . . . Sometimes We Tremble."

Chapter 6

1 Interview, 16 June 1987.

2 Hendry, p. 80.

3 Peter Hamel, "Anglicans and Aboriginal People: The Ecojustice Connection," *Jubilee* 2, no. 4 (1985): pp. 9–13.

4 Hamel, p. 4.

5 Hamel, p. 5.

6 *The United Church Observer*, February 1985.

7 *The United Church Observer*, February 1985.

8 Interview, 18 June 1987.

9 *The Hamilton Spectator*, 2 August 1986.

10 *The United Church Observer*, October 1986.

11 *The United Church Observer*, January 1988.

12 *The United Church Observer*, October 1986.

13 *Consensus Native News*, September 1986.

14 *Calgary Herald*, 27 September 1986.

15 McCullum and McCullum, p. 139.

16 Starkloff, pp. 177–189.

17 C.F. Starkloff, *The People of the Center: American Indian Religion and Christianity* (New York: Seabury Press, 1974).

18 Carl Starkloff, "Religious Renewal in Native North America: The Contemporary call to Mission," *Missiology: An International Review* XIII, 1 (January 1985), pp. 71–81.

19 *The Canadian Churchman*, November 1988.

20 *The Canadian Churchman*, November 1988.

21 Ephesians 4:7, 46.

212

CHAPTER 7

1 Lame Deer and Erdoes, p. 162.
2 Lame Deer and Erdoes, p. 216.
3 Exodus 20:21.
4 Ernest Thompson Seton, *The Gospel of the Redman. An Indian Bible* (London: Methuen, 1937), p. 84.
5 Simone Weil, *Waiting on God* (London: Routledge, 1951), pp. 26–27.
6 John 16:12, 15.
7 Alan Race, "Truth Is Many-Eyed," in Eric James, ed., *God's Truth* (London, SCM, 1988), p. 187.
8 Black Elk and Neihardt, pp. 180, 147.
9 Black Elk and Neihardt, p. xiii.
10 Black Elk and Neihardt, p. 214.
11 Black Elk and Neihardt, p. 217.
12 Black Elk and Neihardt, p. 1.
13 Black Elk and Neihardt, p. 9.
14 Black Elk and Neihardt.
15 Joseph Campbell, *The Masks of God: Primitive Mythology* (Harmondsworth: Penguin, 1985), p. 89.
16 Kosuke Koyama, *Waterbuffalo Theology* (London: SCM, 1974), p. 41.
17 Cited in Paul B. Steinmetz S.J., *Pipe, Bible and Peyote among the Oglala Lakota. A Study in Religious Identity* (Stockholm: Almqvist and Wiksell, 1980), p. 155. The missing lines are in italics.
18 Black Elk and Neihardt, p. 274.
19 Black Elk and Neihardt, p. 235.
20 Black Elk and Neihardt, p. 236.
21 Black Elk and Neihardt, p. 237.
22 Black Elk and Neihardt, p. 247.
23 Cited in Steinmetz, p. 155.
24 Black Elk and Neihardt, p. 38.
25 Black Elk and Neihardt, p. 39.
26 John 8:58, *R.S.V.*
27 Exodus 3:4.
28 John 13:19, *R.S.V.*
29 See John 6:20; 8:24, 28; 18:6.
30 John 17:5, 24.
31 Turner, p. 569.
32 Hebrews 12:22–23. *R.S.V.*
33 Black Elk and Neihardt, p. 44.
34 The speech was recorded by Dr. Henry Smith and appeared in *The*

Seattle Sunday Star, 29 October 1887.

35 Joseph Epes Brown, *The Sacred Pipe* (Norman: University of Oklahoma, 1953), p. 155.

36 Genesis 1:28.

37 Luther Standing Bear; *Lard of the Spotted Eagle* (Boston and New York: 1933).

38 Turner, p. 246.

39 Brown, pp. xx, 59.

40 Black Elk and Neihardt, p. 195.

41 Turner, p. 255.

42 Sam D. Gill, *Native American Religions: An Introduction* (Belmont: Wadsworth, 1982), p. 119.

43 Translated from *Freundschaft mit der Erde* (Vienna: Herder, 1985), p. 17.

44 John 1; Colossians 1; Ephesians 1.

45 Lame Deer and Erdoes, p. 114.

46 Amos 7 and 8; Jeremiah 5:24–5; Hosea 8:7; 9:14; Joel 2:18, 22.

47 J.L. McKenzie, *A Theology of the Old Testament* (New York: Geoffrey Chapman, 1974), p. 199.

48 Starkloff, *The People of the Center*, p. 83.

49 Joseph E. Couture, ''Indian Spirituality — A Personal Experience,'' *Kerygma*, 16 (1982), pp. 86–7.

50 Exodus 3:7–8a, *R.S.V.*

51 *Green Teacher, Friends of the Earth Newsletter*, London, October 1987.

52 *Evangelical Witness in South Africa*, 1986, p. 24.